# DRACULA

D1225406

*By the same author*

SO YOU WANT TO TEACH ENGLISH TO FOREIGNERS
(Abacus Press)

BRITAIN AND SAUDI ARABIA 1925-1939: THE IMPERIAL
OASIS (Frank Cass)

ENGLAND'S QUEST FOR THE WORLD CUP:
A COMPLETE RECORD (Methuen)

# DRACULA
## THE NOVEL & THE LEGEND

### A Study of Bram Stoker's Gothic Masterpiece

### CLIVE LEATHERDALE

THE AQUARIAN PRESS
Wellingborough, Northamptonshire

First published 1985

© CLIVE LEATHERDALE 1985

British Library Cataloguing in Publication Data

Leatherdale, Clive
   Dracula: the novel and legend.
   1. Stoker, Bram. Dracula
   I. Title
   823'.8      RR6037.T617Z/

ISBN 0-85030-383-4

*The Aquarian Press is part of the
Thorsons Publishing Group*

Printed and bound in Great Britain

# CONTENTS

# LIST OF ILLUSTRATIONS

# ACKNOWLEDGEMENTS

D URING the course of the research for, and preparation of, this book a number of people have assisted me in various ways. Bruce Wightman and Bernard Davies, co-founders of the Dracula Society, welcomed me among its ranks, provided numerous stimulating ideas, and made available to me the Society's own archive material. Leslie Shepard of the Bram Stoker Society kindly guided me around Stoker's Dublin, and Richard Dalby also provided useful information.

Dr Paul Dukes, Reader in History, and Dr Bob Lawson-Peebles, Lecturer in English, both at the University of Aberdeen, keenly followed my progress, politely chiselling away at what was not convincing, encouraging what was, and proposing new avenues to explore.

Julia Kruk of the Dracula Society and Pauline Huntington uncomplainingly read and re-read every word I wrote, making suggestions as they went.

The kindly staff at the Rosenbach Museum and Library, Philadelphia, permitted me to consult Bram Stoker's manuscripts in the delightful setting of their reading room. The people of Transylvania fuelled the imagination by being themselves.

Needless to say, my greatest indebtedness is to Bram Stoker himself for providing the sternest challenge to the imagination and the intellect. I hope I have done him justice. If I have not, the responsibility lies solely with me.

CLIVE LEATHERDALE

# INTRODUCTION

IF HE were alive today, Bram Stoker would be an unhappy though undeniably rich man. He would be rich because his novel *Dracula* has never been out of print since it was first published in 1897. There are those who claim it to be the second highest selling book of all time, outstripped only by the Bible.[1] *Dracula* has been translated into numerous languages and the image of 'the Count' is familiar the world over. He is part of the landscape of a universal culture: the black cape, the dripping fangs, the scream of terror. . . .

Bram Stoker would be unhappy, as would any deceased author in his position, because the creation of his pen has been overtaken and habitually trivialized by the creation of the cinema, which has escaped the censure of his furious intervention. A regular answer to the question 'Have you read *Dracula*?' is 'No, but I saw the film.' The consequence of the cinema's prurient debasement of Stoker's novel and complete domination of the public Dracula image is that while 'Dracula' has become a household name, his creator remains a household nobody. One of the world's best-known books was written by one of its least-known authors. As an object of serious critical study the novel has been, until quite recently, almost totally ignored. If the book is like the films, it is asked, what could it hold of serious interest? As one critic has commented: 'Only a few years ago, to write about Dracula meant being taken for an eccentric loafer, and one's main worry was to prove that one's work was legitimate.'[2]

It remains the case that serious examination of supernatural fiction can, and does, frequently sidestep *Dracula*. This wholesale dismissal of the novel borders on the extraordinary. It is akin to discarding Plato from the study of Western philosophy, for *Dracula* is almost *the* Gothic novel *par excellence*, and has given rise to arguably the most potent literary myth of the twentieth century.

A. N. Wilson, in his introduction to the Oxford University Press edition of *Dracula* (1983), decries Stoker as an author, yet still concedes that 'with *Dracula* he composed, indeed, one of the World's Classics'. [3]

An outline of the novel is easily told. A young solicitor, Jonathan Harker, travels to a remote castle in Transylvania to finalize arrangements with a local nobleman, Count Dracula, for the purchase of an east London estate. While Harker is left behind, imprisoned, Dracula journeys to England by sea, landing at Whitby where he encounters his first victim in beautiful, privileged Lucy Westenra. To Dracula's ultimate misfortune, she is well connected. She has three suitors: Arthur Holmwood, Quincey Morris and Dr Seward, the last of whom summons the services of his old master, Professor Van Helsing, in a futile attempt to treat Lucy's malaise. Perchance, her best friend, Mina, is the wife of Jonathan Harker. Abetted by Renfield, one of the inmates at Dr Seward's lunatic asylum, Dracula 'visits' Mina. Shortly afterwards he is nearly cornered in Piccadilly and flees the country for the sanctuary of his castle, to where, in the climax of the novel, he is pursued.

If that were all there is to *Dracula* then, indeed, it would not demand closer attention. But it is not all. First there is the question of 'authenticity' — Stoker's known researches into folklore, the occult and much else. Wilson remarks: 'It would seem likely that he did some — but very little — research for his fantasy'. [4] To read such a statement in a prestigious edition of *Dracula* a decade after the discovery in a Philadelphia repository of three packages of Stoker's surviving manuscripts, detailing over a period of six years many of his researches for his novel-to-be, requires some forbearance. Whatever the extent of *Dracula's* shortcomings, allegations of lack of research on Stoker's part are difficult to substantiate.

Equally worthy of attention is the breadth of vision that *Dracula* attains. It can be read on many levels. Like all 'classics', every fresh reading unearths new insights, new puzzles. With little in the way of previous full-length interpretations to build upon, the present book has many functions to fulfil in seeking to explore *Dracula*. The analysis that follows falls into three sections. First, the ground will be prepared by exploring the notion of 'vampires', and their place in European folklore and literature; surveying the life and works of Bram Stoker; and examining what can be deduced about the origins of *Dracula*. Second, turning to the novel itself, each of Stoker's major characters will be put under the microscope. This is intended to clarify what type of creature Dracula was, as well as outline the purposes and contrasting functions of the novel's male and female cast. Third, we shall embark upon five alternative readings of the novel — allegories that transcend the basic ingredients of vampire, victims, and avengers. *Dracula* can be read as an instrument of sexual repression; it readily yields to Freudian psychoanalysis; it is a testament to the perceived arbitrariness and tangible power of Christ; it pays homage to occult and literary myths in the shape of the Tarot and the Holy Grail; and it opens a window on to the social and political tensions operating in late Victorian Britain. The novel also provides ready-made myths of its own for twentieth-century consumption: *Dracula* has been turned into a manifesto for Marxist economic theory and provides a dark analogue of the Cold War.

At the very least, one aspiration of the present book is to awaken interest in a novel for too long unjustly ignored and contemptuously pushed aside. *Dracula* is not lacking in fertile imagination, complexity of plot or an unsurpassed capacity to send a chill down the spine. In cultural terms it deserves to be treated as a major work of fiction, for *Dracula* possesses that rarest of attributes — an invitation to be read and re-read, each time disclosing fresh glimpses of insight and further layers of meaning and symbolism.

# 1.

# THE VAMPIRE

In all the darkest pages of the malign supernatural there is no more horrible tradition than that of the vampire, a pariah even among demons. Foul are his ravages; gruesome and seemingly barbaric are the ancient and approved methods by which folk must rid themselves of this hideous pest.

Montague Summers,
*The Vampire: His Kith and Kin*, p. ix.

THE modern imagination does not afford excessive respect to the notion of the vampire. Over-exposure to the cult of the horror cinema, and the resultant commercial exploitation of a tried and tested money spinner, has filled our collective consciousness with a sensationalist pastiche of blood, fangs, black cloaks, and sharpened stakes. The word 'vampire' may invite a laugh or a smirk, where in previous centuries it instilled terror.

Few societies in the past did not have their own version of the vampire. Its gradual disappearance from the active superstitions around the world is attributable to many factors. Science has much to answer for, not least for the invention of the electric light, which pierces the shadows of the deepest recesses and denies the shapes of our imaginings their hiding places. For many people, night has lost its mysteries, its secrets, its fears. Were science to have lagged in its headlong rush to annihilate our fantasies, no doubt we should still acknowledge the realm of the vampire, for its intellectual foundations are by no means completely illogical or incoherent. The concept of the vampire is founded upon two precepts: the belief in life after death, and the magical power of blood.

The biological and mystical significance of blood was recognized by the earliest human communities. They knew nothing of viruses or bacteria, or other organisms which can debilitate or kill, but one cause of death was easily ascertained, for it depended on no more than basic observation and could never be refuted. From injuries sustained either by accident or in battle, through the torn flesh seeped a strange, mysterious, bright red fluid. Lose enough of it and you died. No other bodily fluid was endowed with such power.

The sight of blood was the sight of death, and therein lies the basic emotion it evokes — fear. Human strength and health reside within blood. It is the elixir of life; the child's first nourishment in the mother's womb. From awareness that blood was essential to life it was but a short step to the belief that it was, in fact, synonymous with life. The 'soul' of a living creature lay within its veins. Blood was not only life, it was soul — and therefore an object of magic and taboo. Ingeniously, a perverse logic then intervened. If emission of blood weakens and destroys, it surely followed that consumption of that magic ichor could restore, rejuvenate, bring back life. If blood was life, then absorbing blood was absorbing life — and soul.

This 'logical' deduction resulted in widely comparable patterns of human behaviour. Blood came to form the basis of medical care. As their scientific nature was unknown, diseases were presumed to be the consequence of a sinful life and the displeasure of the gods, necessitating the spilling of the sufferer's 'bad' blood, both as cure and repentance. The curative 'bleeding' of patients survives to the twentieth century in societies that would resent the label 'primitive'. Since antiquity, crude blood transfusions from the healthy to the sick have been performed, and an ancient prescribed remedy for leprosy was to bathe in blood. Warriors in battle would drink the warm blood of the slain, not only as a gesture of total domination and possession, but in the belief that the victim's strength and courage would pass into the victor. Blood could also act as a fertilizer and be sprinkled over crops; it was endowed with cosmetic properties and would be generously smeared over the skin; and it would be ceremonially mingled between comrades, even today, in the practice of 'blood brothers'.

Man's preoccupation with this magic substance provides the first prerequisite for belief in vampirism. The second is 'death', as fear-provoking as blood. Its force is irresistible. Death always wins, for no one can fend it off indefinitely. It claims its victims indiscriminately. Throughout history unseen aggressive forces have been held to be responsible not only for violent deaths but also for those who have succumbed in old age and in sleep. Dying could only be the product of a ruthless assailant, seen or unseen, who managed to overpower the unwilling victim.[1]

Moreover, the land of the dead seemed to be a place apart, governed by its own customs and laws of nature, which the living could not penetrate but to which they were inexorably drawn in the course of time. It was a source of apprehension that the world of the dead far outnumbered the world of the living, because should its inhabitants for any reason rise in anger, then the consequences for the living would be dire indeed.

These instinctive fears presuppose a world of the living dead. The concept of nothingness, that death is the total nullification of both spiritual and physical existence, has been throughout most human societies inconceivable. In the wake of death a corpse remains, but what of the spiritual entity, the 'soul' that once inhabited it — where does it go?

The usual explanation was that death was a passage into another world, populated by spirits rather than bodies, but which was otherwise, in the absence of knowledge of alternative forms of existence, not dissimilar to life here on earth — a kingdom in the sky. In other words, death was not 'death' at all, but a new form of 'life'. Dying in this world was a prerequisite and a guarantee of being born in the next.

Not surprisingly, man has always held a morbid preoccupation with the deceased. As the 'dead' were in fact 'alive', inhabiting a spiritual netherworld, elaborate rituals evolved to assist communication between the terrestrial and the celestial. For this purpose blood performed an integral function. As it was indispensable for any form of life, it seemed reasonable that the 'living' spirit world needed it also. Without sources of their own it was up to man to provide it. Blood became the only possible bridge between two disparate universes.

To facilitate this communication, and to guard against the displeasure of the departed, who might seek retribution for wrongs inflicted in life, the practice of blood sacrifices proliferated. This might take the form of mourners beating or lacerating themselves at funerals, or would involve animal or human sacrifices. Whatever form it took, the purposeful spillage of blood fulfilled two functions: it served as a libation for the spirits, providing them with the blood they craved for vitality, youthfulness, and power; and it also propitiated them, removing any temptation to visit harm on the living. By offering the dead what they wanted, it was hoped to forestall the threat of them returning to take it by force.

Of course, it was not only blood that the spirits were thought to covet. Earthly possessions were also in demand for use in the hereafter, instanced by the widespread practice of burying such items as food, armour, jewellery, and household utensils along with the corpse. The dead had physical needs, too — witness the custom of providing a 'woman' for a deceased male. A lifelike female carving, excessively proportioned, would be entombed alongside the corpse to help remove the supposed inhibition imposed by the death trauma.[2] In sum, cosseting the dead by such means would nourish, appease, and distract, all to the calculated advantage of the living.

Already the constituents of vampirism are apparent. The common belief that the dead can sustain life by imbibing the blood of the living is itself an expression of the vampiric process. Donations of blood through the deliberate and controlled medium of sacrifice were both prudent and necessary, whereas the prospect of losing it unwillingly and uncontrollably through perverse activity on the part of the spirit world could induce terror and hysteria. The human imagination was more than equipped to fantasize on this threat and conceive of, and rationalize, all manner of blood-sucking spiritual demons.

The near universally-held belief in these two supposed laws of nature — the rejuvenating power of blood and the presumption of life after death — meant that the product of their combination (the vampire) was equally universal. Legends of the dead returning to drink human blood have been found in nearly every culture where records have survived. Vampires, to borrow a phrase, have appeared almost everywhere that men have bled.[3] Stoker explains this in *Dracula* through his sage, Van Helsing:

> For, let me tell you, he [the vampire] is known everywhere that men have been. In old Greece, in old Rome, he flourish [sic] in Germany all over, in France, in India, even in the Chersonese; and in China ... He have [sic] follow the wake of the berserker Icelander, the devil-begotten Hun, the Slav, the Saxon, the Magyar. [D 18: 285-6]*

Tracing the geography and chronology of vampires is a discomforting undertaking, given the paucity of firm evidence of actual instances and the exaggeration and distortion that is an

* References to *Dracula* will give the chapter number, followed by the page number of the 1979 Penguin edition (reprinted in 1984).

inevitable accompaniment of folklore. Nonetheless, perhaps the most ancient sources of vampire belief stem from the Orient.[4] In Asia, Chinese tales spoke of blood-sucking creatures that were green, covered with mould, and which had a propensity to glow in the dark. The Melanesian *talamaur* was known as the soul of the dead which preyed on the ebbing vitality of the dying. In India vampire lore is largely dissipated by the influence of Brahman- and Buddhist-inspired asceticism and vegetarianism, which, together with the practice of corpse disposal through cremation, effectively removed the foundations of the belief. Notwithstanding, Kali is revered as a blood-sucking mother goddess of disease, war, and death, and Siva is identified with ghoulish (flesh-eating) propensities. The mythical *rakskasas*, moreover, were protean phantoms, changing shape at will; the *hant-pare* would cling leech-like to the open wound of an injured person; while the *vetala* resembled an old hag and would seek the blood of sleeping women — for some reason preferring them drunk or insane.

Possibly the most remarkable, and certainly the most spectacular, of Asian vampires was the Malaysian *penanggalen* which, had he known of its existence, might have furnished Charles Darwin with support for his theory of natural selection. As the only bodily apparatus indispensable to a vampire is a mouth through which to drink and a stomach to house that which was drunk, the *penanggalen* consisted of no more than a head and stomach, complete with dangling entrails. It would soar through the air to pursue its preferred victims: babies or women in labour.

Africa is similarly rich in the diversity of its vampire species. The Ashanti's *asambosam*, for example, likes to suck blood through the thumbs of the sleeping. It is readily identifiable, having in place of feet a pair of books to stand on. More recently the strength of Africa's blood preoccupation was demonstrated in the oath-taking ceremonies of Mau Mau tribesmen in Kenya in the early 1950s. These involved the drinking of sheep's blood — if none of murdered Europeans was available.[5]

Nor are the Americas immune from vampire superstition. In parts of the West Indies the local vampire answers to the name of *loogaroo* (from the French expression for werewolf — *loup garou*) and comes in the guise of an old woman who, in a pact with the devil, sheds her skin and changes into a blob of light in order to draw blood, which is then conveyed to her patron. For their part, the Brazilians refer to a *jaracara*, which resembles a snake and enjoys a penchant for either the blood or the milk of breast-feeding mothers — milk, like blood, being a life-supporting fluid. Wherever vampires stalk, they seem able to appear in animal form: as cats in Japan, pigs in Serbia, snakes elsewhere. Creatures that can fly by night are particularly suspect: butterflies, owls, and bats.

The vampire concept was not confined to the imaginings of far-flung peoples. It is with the European tradition that this study is primarily concerned. The classical civilizations of Europe developed their own, more sophisticated, manifestations of vampiric activity, such as is revealed in Plato's dialogue *Phaedo*.[6] His *Republic*, furthermore, relates an incident of a slain warrior whose body refused to decompose. It returned to life just as it was about to be cast to the funeral flames and proceeded to reveal details of its time spent in the 'other world'.[7] Homer's *Odyssey* recalls how Odysseus offered the blood of slaughtered sheep to ghosts weakened for lack of nourishment.[8] More generally, the literature of ancient Greece and Rome provide encounters with so-called 'lamias', precursors of vampires, ill-defined serpentine spectres emanating from corpses who would divest the living, especially children, of their vitality. By the Middle Ages this particular tradition had acquired distinctly sexual overtones: the succubus, who would seduce young men in their sleep and withdraw their vital fluids at the moment of peak distraction during climax. For the sake of parity there was a male version, the incubus, frequently associated with the devil, who would impregnate suitable female victims, such as witches.

It is at this point that the European vampire of folklore begins to crystallize. The preceding gallery is composed of phantoms that are mutually related as creatures of the spirit world, manifestations of an ethereal existence. Two changes are needed for the successful metamorphosis into the true European vampire: first, the acquisition of corporeal structure; second, the development of sexual predilections, as hinted at in the lamia/succubus tradition. To appreciate these advances in human fantasy it is necessary to return once more to the psychology operating between the living and the dead.

Given that the deceased are inhabiting an unknown spiritual kingdom, the possibility of their return evokes complex psychological responses. More usually they are those of terror. Let the dead remain where they are! On other occasions, especially in the case of severed close emotional ties, the opposite can occur, producing a desperate yearning to be reunited with the dead. Bereaved persons may cherish the thought of their loved ones returning to share their lives, as instanced by Orpheus' frantic endeavours to bring back Eurydice from the Underworld. More morbidly, the desired passage may be in the opposite direction: the living partner may seek reunion in death, for then there can be no more parting sorrow. A loving embrace in death is exclusive possession for eternity.[9]

Inherent in the psychology of grief is the mechanism of projecting emotions on to the deceased. The living do not forget the dead: nor, therefore, can the dead forget the living. Many people do not wish to be forgotten by the dead. They cannot envisage themselves, when the time comes, lying peacefully in their graves: they imagine being impelled to return, whether driven by love, hate, guilt, conscience, the need for revenge, or whatever. The dead, themselves, it is assumed, must surely think likewise. The love ingredient, in particular, is bound up with the European vampire. The separation of lovers, of husbands and wives, of parents and children, is the essence of its manifestation. And from awareness of the love factor springs several consequences: firstly, vampirism frequently entails a sexual aspect; secondly, it is centred around a family unit, for it is relatives and loved ones who are most at risk; and thirdly, it produces the conflicting emotional responses of attraction and repulsion — the yearning for a departed loved one, mixed with the natural terror of contact with the dead. Any initial expression of desire may soon be replaced by loathing, for the vampire does not rejoin the living in life, but draws them back into death. It conforms to a perverse cyclical order: it kills, then recreates; it destroys, then preserves.[10]

The other important modification to the spectral vampires of antiquity is the wrapping of the European variety in real flesh and bone. They are not ghosts but actual corpses on the move. To illustrate this let us skim through the spectrum of man's relationship with the dead. At one end are to be found bizarre but otherwise earthly attachments. These include cannibalistic consumption of human remains (necrophagy), mutilation of corpses (necrosadism), and copulation with a corpse (necrophilia). Likewise the witch is very much alive despite her powers of communication with the spirit world. The vampire's cousin, the werewolf, is similarly human despite his susceptibility to the moon and his capacity, whether through vengeance of the gods, diabolic possession or an undiagnosed mania, to transform into the shape of a wolf, or behave accordingly.[11] In south-east Europe there is held to be a link between lycanthropy (werewolfism) and vampirism, in that a werewolf in life transforms into a vampire on death.

At the other extreme, ghosts, ghouls,[12] phantoms, and the vampiric spirits of Asia, Africa, the Americas, and classical Europe are manifestly dead. They exist as a spiritual presence but do not possess corporeal substance. In European folklore, however, because it was believed that the deceased were resting impatiently in their graves, waiting to walk among the living, a corollary evolved to the effect that dead bodies would not automatically decompose. The dead would obviously need their bodies if they were to rise again. Consequently, the European vampire on the life-death spectrum is usually, and uniquely, described as being situated 'in between'. It is both; it is neither. Physical death, from which no mortal can escape, has taken place, but not the normal accompaniment of death — bodily dissolution. The body dies in the natural sense, but then is resurrected as a risen dead. Demonic spirits reanimate it, and it lives a twilight existence of its own beyond the land of the living but not yet in the land of the dead: living in death. Put another way, it is a kind of amphibious entity with equal access to two opposed worlds.[13] The vampire, then, occupies three-dimensional space, and having a real body, it needs real blood.

The fusion of these characteristics gave rise to the vampire of central and eastern Europe, which is documented from around the fifteenth century onwards. The term itself stems from the Magyar *vampir* and Slavic derivatives: *vapir* in Bulgaria, *upuir* in Russia.[14] The etymology is confused, but seems traceable to 'blood-sucker' or 'blood drunkenness'. Pseudonyms abound, notably 'undead' and *nosferat* (plural: *nosferatu* — plague carriers). There are also local variations. Parts of Romania feared the *strigoi*; the Germans had a species known as *nachzehrer*, which unaccountably kept its left eye open in its grave and clasped the thumb of one hand with the other; the Greek *vrykolakas* referred to both a vampire and a werewolf —the beast having a puffed-up parchment-like skin which reverberated like a drum when struck. The Wallachian *murony* was another vampire-werewolf cross-breed; while the Bulgarians talked of a creature having just one nostril, a boneless frame and fungoid flesh. Whatever the nuances, European communities had little difficulty in accepting the philosophical dimensions of vampires. After all, they had had a proven demonstration of man's capacity to die, to be buried, and to rise again with special powers to visit the living — Christ himself. And had he not promised to resurrect the dead and offer eternal life? Even today the words 'Rest in Peace' which accompany Christian burial contain dark allusions.

Is there a suggestion that the corpse might not rest, but walk?

Central and eastern Europe can rightly claim to be the Pandora's Box of vampirism. This Eurocentric tradition retained the blood/death facets central to all such mythical demons but took on one further aspect, giving the European vampire its distinctive stamp. The Continental model of the undead was conceived and then proliferated under the guidance and doctrine of the Christian Church, and it is from this tradition that Stoker's *Dracula* draws its inspiration.

# 2.
# THE VAMPIRE IN CHRISTIAN EUROPE

It has indeed lately come to Our ears that . . . many persons of both
sexes . . . have abandoned themselves to devils, incubi and succubi.

> Pope Innocent VIII, Papal Bull 1484; Introduction to
> *Malleus Maleficarum.*

It is the height of folly to attempt to deny that such bodies are not
infrequently found in their graves incorrupt, and that by use of them
the Devil, if God permits, devises most horrible complots and
schemes to the hurt and harm of mankind.

> Jacob Sprenger and Heinrich Kramer,
> *Malleus Maleficarum.*

THE source of Christian influence on the vampire superstition in the Middle Ages and post-Renaissance Europe
is impeccable — the Bible itself. Not only does it document
a celebrated instance of a dead body rising from the tomb, but a
persistent theme in both the Old and New Testaments concerns
the power of blood. There exists considerable theological
controversy over the meaning behind these countless references.
In the Old Testament, for example, blood is used as an expression
of violence and death, intimately bound up in the notion of sacrifice,
while there also occur such expressions as 'the blood is the life'.
Then, in the New Testament, St John's Gospel exhorts us to drink
Christ's blood as a means of absolving our sins and becoming closer
to God. Here, the regenerative power of blood could hardly be
more explicit:

> Who so eateth my flesh and drinketh my blood hath eternal life;
> and I will raise him up at the last day. For my flesh is meat indeed,
> and my blood is drink indeed. He that eateth my flesh and drinketh
> my blood dwelleth in me and I in Him. [1]

The Latin Church's celebration of Holy Communion (or the Eucharist) operates on the belief that the taking of bread and wine by the faithful — re-enacting the Last Supper — involves a mystical conversion whereby the bread and wine are not merely *symbolic* of Christ's flesh and blood: they *are* Christ's flesh and blood. Absorbing Christ's uncorrupted blood amounts to a regenerative transfusion. This conversion process has come to be accounted for through the obscure notion of transubstantiation.

The difficulty lay in how far this recommendation to drink blood was to be taken literally. The early Church Fathers had faced the dilemma of needing to stress the primordial link between blood and life inherent in the Eucharist, while simultaneously discouraging too literal an interpretation. In pursuit of the latter objective, they could point to the ample warnings against wanton blood-letting and blood-drinking carried by the Old Testament[2] and later by St Paul.

These aims were largely countermanded in the Middle Ages when trying to convey the essence of transubstantiation, for it seemed to the sceptical to be on a par with ancestor worship and sacrifice. Worse, being asked to consume the *actual* flesh and blood of Christ was surely tantamount to cannibalism. Rather than resort to abstruse theology, the Christian essence was found to be more easily explained to would-be converts in terms with which they were already familiar through pagan superstitions. The Christian grip on medieval Europe was so tenuous that pagan observances were necessarily tolerated at first, then adapted to advantage. Transubstantiation was taught in the language of vampirism. As the devil's objective was to drain the blood of sinners and commandeer their spirits, so the righteous could taste Christ's blood as a means of sharing his Holiness.

The Eucharist was not alone in reinforcing popular beliefs in the mystical properties of blood. The cult of the Virgin Mary provided an excuse for charlatans to prescribe the application of uncorrupted virgin's blood as an antidote for every conceivable malady.[3] Throughout much of medieval Europe maidens were much sought after, not so much for their sexual favours as for their 'innocent' blood.

But it needed more than the multifaceted Christian preoccupation with blood for the spectre of the vampire to come to haunt half a continent. It needed the proselytizing zeal which is the inevitable accompaniment of political and territorial expansion. Between the fifteenth and eighteenth centuries central and eastern Europe was the scene of periodic strife as Christendom took up arms against the encroaching Turks. Within this imperial confrontation there took place a spiritual war as the Western (Roman) Church, the Eastern (Orthodox) Church, and the Ottoman Moslems forged a fluctuating triumvirate battling for the minds of men.

In this context it is not surprising that excesses were committed, spiritual as well as physical. Much could be achieved by putting the fear of the devil into people — literally. Both the Roman and Orthodox Churches preyed on the credulity of the populace, trading on mass ignorance and hysteria as the means of keeping the faithful faithful and threatening eternal damnation for the slightest heresy. Nothing was so ready-made for this purpose as the vampire, taken from its pagan origins and updated with Church embellishments, in order to threaten retribution for errors of prescribed belief. In effect, the two competing pillars of the Christian Establishment took advantage of a closed system: laying down the nature of the vampire menace (and thereby officially sanctioning its existence) and then claiming a self-imposed monopoly on vampire counter-measures.

On the Roman side, threatened from all quarters, within and without, one of the most notorious publications ever to receive the papal seal was prepared in the 1490s. Compiled by two Dominicans, the *Malleus Maleficarum* fulfilled the demand of Pope Innocent VIII for a systematic investigative procedure to look into the activities of witches, incubi and succubi, werewolves and vampires. For two centuries this volume became a principal authority in Rome's battle against satanic influences: although nowadays it is difficult to find formal Catholic acknowledgment even that it exists.

When considering the European vampire it will be helpful to distinguish between its pagan superstitious origins that survived through to the fifteenth century and beyond, and which lay down their own, often conflicting, criteria for the undead, and the distinctively Christian categories of crimes and indiscretions which fused with the pagan base to provide a new genus of vampires: a pagan-Christian alloy. It is more profitable to probe the psychology behind belief in vampires than to trace actual manifestations. Corroboration of their existence is, needless to say, somewhat sketchy. [4] Some facets are spoken of consistently, others are peculiar to small localities. There is therefore little profit in pursuing a systematic approach. Broadly, the area in focus corresponds to what today would be described as laying behind the Iron Curtain.

The pre-medieval heritage, as a rule of thumb, did not distinguish between the innocent and the guilty when recruiting for the undead. People would invariably be cast as vampires through no fault of their own, such as by being stillborn, or drowning, or by meeting their deaths violently. The vampire taint could be hereditary. Victims of unavenged murders were at risk, for they supposedly could not rest in their graves until they had quenched their thirst from the blood of their assailants. Relatives of the victims who did not, or could not, dutifully track down the culprits would likewise be punished for their failure.[5]

Encounters with certain animals could lead to vampirism: for example, eating the flesh of a sheep which had been killed by a wolf (demonstrating the association with werewolf pollution), or allowing a cat or other animal to pass over your grave (here the creature represents a human who expresses hatred for the deceased and demonstrates insufficient respect for the place of burial).[6] For safety's sake it was common practice to keep all animals indoors until after a funeral had taken place. Parental curses could allegedly induce vampirism in the child, and the same fate awaited a pregnant woman who neglected to put salt on her food. Her laxity would seal the baby's future, as would happen if a vampire cast the evil eye on her, unless some antidote were effected.[7]

Interestingly, many omens elsewhere regarded as favourable have their significance inversed in the Balkan states. A seventh son, for example, is held according to Gaelic mythology to possess healing powers. Not so in south-east Europe, where a seventh child was particularly suspect and would grow a little tail to warn of its presence.[8] Similarly, a baby born with a caul (a membrane from the amniotic sac enveloping the head) is held to be lucky in many cultures — outside the Balkans, where there was also a particular fear of the stillborn, illegitimate child of illegitimate parents.

Equally vulnerable to the taint of vampirism were those unfortunate enough to be deformed in certain ways, or the victims of particular nervous disorders. The hare-lipped were automatic candidates for would-be werewolves or vampires, as were those afflicted with a cleft palate, for they would have an involuntary drawing-up of the upper lip. Given the significance of the vampire's teeth, a child actually born with any was an obvious suspect. Persons with unsightly birthmarks, or who were grotesquely deformed from birth, were believed to have the curse upon them.

In regions where brown eyes predominated, those with blue eyes were suspect, and vice versa. Among physical disorders supposed to produce vampirism were epilepsy and chorea (St Vitus's dance), whose seemingly unaccountable and uncontrollable convulsions were put down to demoniacal possession.

By the aforementioned means human societies strove to induce conformity: anybody 'odd' in any way whatsoever was likely to be held responsible for whatever misfortunes befell a remote community. In the hands of the Church a range of new, religious-based offences were adduced as leading to a vampiric afterlife. To the jumbled fears of the peasants were added sharply defined transgressions, each carrying the curse of the undead. These included crimes such as murder, theft, dabbling in black magic, and perjury. But the bulk of the Church's energies were concerned with emphasizing the fate that awaited the excommunicated and the suicide.

Excommunication was the Church's ultimate weapon for those bent on sacrilegious practice: the withdrawal of all spiritual privileges, coupled with lasting damnation beyond the grave. The act of excommunication could not annul the earlier baptism (so that they remained within the Christian fold), but those who were accused were henceforth treated as aliens, exiles, until such times as their misdeeds were absolved. As a matter of course, anyone unbaptized or apostate, and thereby immune to the threat of excommunication, was also scheduled to become a vampire. In view of the great number of excommunications that took place in early modern Europe, the Church felt it advantageous to instil into wrongdoers just what lay in store for anyone denied proper burial rites: the devil could, and would, gain admittance to those who had been deprived of Christ's protection and resurrect them as undead.

Just as recourse was taken to vampire allegories in order to convey to the common people the sacred significance of the Eucharist, so they were also employed as a means of making tangible the nature and implications of excommunication.[9] No great leap in the imagination was required to picture those lying condemned in their graves returning as vampires. Word spread that the corpses of excommunicants inadvertently buried in consecrated ground had been mysteriously thrown up and dumped by the side of their graves. This belief was given concrete encouragement by the Greek Orthodox Church, which began to pronounce excommunication as having physical as well as spiritual ramifications, and which lent itself to one of the signal developments in European vampire lore by proclaiming that excommunicants and other heretics would not decompose in their unhallowed graves.[10] The devil, it was explained, would intervene to preserve excommunicants from dissolution. This had the effect of preventing the release of the soul which had animated the living body, damning it inside the corpse and enabling it to walk as a vampire.[11]

This development, through which the Greek Church in effect awarded to itself power over the body as well as the soul, provided ecclesiastic confirmation of, and explanation for, local superstition. It accounted for the non-dissolution of vampire corpses. But it did more than that. It produced a major clash of interpretation regarding one of the most cherished precepts of the Roman Church. The Latin tradition held that the non-decomposition of a corpse was an exclusive sign of sanctity. For the Greek Church to attribute the suspension of bodily dissolution also to earthly wickedness and diabolic intervention prompted inevitable doctrinal confusion in both Churches. Catholic wisdom would explain vampirism within the doctrine of purgatory: the undead did not inhabit hell, but a place of temporal punishment. The Greek Church resolved its own paradox by the application of cosmetic criteria. The uncorrupted bodies of saints could be recognized by their fragrant odour and purity of complexion, whereas the flesh of the damned would be black, bloated, and mephitic. In the event, the distinction remained largely hypothetical, because when the bodies of known excommunicants were disinterred they were found, invariably, not to be black, bloated, and mephitic, but simply rotted away. This, in turn, warranted the fresh theological explanation that such a corpse was already damned in hell with no possibility of absolution for the soul.

The second major category of religious misdemeanour liable to be repaid by vampirism was the taking of one's own life. In other cultures at other times suicide has been regarded either with indifference or respect. This is not the case in the eyes of the Christian Church, where such action is taken to flout God's arbitration on matters of life and death. As man is not responsible for his own birth he does not possess the right to choose the moment of his death. God is the sole author of life, master over everything (including one's own body), and therefore suicide is a blasphemous act usurping His omnipotence — to the point of denying His existence.

To assist in the campaign against suicides, the spectre of the undead provided an ingenious twist of fate. The Church recruited the public terror of vampires (which it had done much to instil in the first place) by declaring that potential suicides would not attain their objective — oblivion from this world followed by everlasting peace — but, ironically, the torment of everlasting life as a vampire. The penalty for suicide would be immortality.

Over the centuries suicides, irrespective of their association with vampirism, have been subjected to specific provisions, in particular the practice of burying them at crossroads. This served the double precaution of reminding the restless spirit of the sign of the cross which lay above the grave, while confusing the risen suicide in his wanderings. With four paths from which to choose, he would not know which to take. For good measure the suicide could also be staked down in his grave to immobilize him and prevent his soul from travelling abroad; but despite all these precautions sensible travellers would still keep clear of crossroads after nightfall. Aside from wandering suicides they were likely to encounter witches' sabbats and creaking gallows.

Fear of suicides is endemic in British folklore. The Scots held that the corpse of a suicide would not crumble until the time that he or she would have died had nature taken its course. There are also records in England of the graves of suicides being aligned north-south, rather than with the head in the west facing eastwards, as prescribed for proper Christian burial. Not until 1823 did Parliament abrogate the law permitting the transfixing of suspect suicides, and not until 1882 was it possible for the corpse of a suicide to be buried with whatever rites could be arranged. [12]

Aside from the Church's war against excommunicants and suicides, it was inevitable that a great many other hapless people would be accused of vampirism on grounds as spurious and circumstantial as those in pagan cultures. Dates in the Christian calendar came to assume an ominous significance. Babies unwise enough to be born at Christmas were doomed, presumably because their parents had been engaged in base, earthly pleasures at the time of divine conception by the Virgin Mary. In Greece, such infants were referred to as *Callicantzaros*, and to guard against their later transformation it was known for them to have their feet and nails singed. [13] The period known as Epiphany (the twelve days following Christmas) was a period when the forces of evil were widely held to prevail. The Easter child was likewise at risk.

St Andrew's Eve and St George's Eve were dates when the powers of goodness were reputed to be at their lowest. In the case of St

George, not only was he the patron saint of England and protector of other regions, including Bavaria, Venice, and Constantinople, but he was also the divine protector of cattle, horses, and wolves. His guardianship of domestic flocks and herds from the predations of wild beasts and phantoms was at its weakest upon his 'Eve', when the powers of vampires and evil spirits were correspondingly at their peak.

Within the Greek Orthodox tradition Saturday was the most effective day to go vampire-hunting, for the day after the crucifixion of her son was believed to be sacred to the Virgin Mary, who had clung to her faith during her darkest hour. Vampires were allegedly confined to their resting places on that day and were unable to make good their escape if discovered.[14] Witches, too, shunned that particular day and were unable to hold their sabbat. It was widely supposed that people who were born on a Saturday had a special ability to detect ghouls and ghosts, and were immune to the vampire.

Other types of person eligible to become undead through Christian-based superstition were those with red hair (as possessed — it was believed — by Cain and Judas[15]) and the sexually promiscuous. In the case of witches, carnal intercourse with the devil would undoubtedly produce vampire offspring. But most significant and terrifying of all, vampirism was presumed to be contagious. Those who died as a direct result of a vampire attack would themselves transform into the undead: the 'dormant' vampires in life would become the 'active' vampires in death. In other words, they would not 'die' at all: the husk of the body would be taken up to serve the devil, recruited as an energumen. All in all, the total list of qualifications (physical, medical, social, religious, moral, not to mention the purely arbitrary) was sufficiently comprehensive as to threaten to include almost anybody.

But what of the vampire itself? What does it look like; how does it behave; and what powers are at its command? The undead are basically associated with the poorer, more superstitious communities, and their appearance and behaviour naturally tends to reflect their social origins. The notion of tall, handsome aristocrats inhabiting inaccessible, run-down castles is the product of the literary imagination, not traditional folklore. Vampires are more usually depicted as lean, gaunt, hollow-eyed, and with scabs on their arms and legs. Their skin is dry and of extraordinary pallor, save after consumption of blood, when the countenance turns fresh and ruddy and the mouth will be slobbered with blood. The eyes glow red with perdition, and as the life functions have not been arrested the nails will be long and crooked, the hair long, unkempt and matted, but the skin will feel icy to the touch. The lips will be red and blubbery, and may be involuntarily drawn back, in which case they should reveal gleaming white teeth and extended canines — yet another association with the werewolf.[16] Only in repose after 'feasting' is the vampire other than emaciated, for the trunk then swells up in obese repletion. Some locations pursue the animalistic imagery further, speculating that the original dead skin of the vampire slowly peels away to reveal fresh skin and nails underneath.

Their thirst for blood is unquenchable, yet some districts hold that vampires can take normal food and will drink the blood of sheep and cattle in addition to that of humans. The nauseous panting of breath and drooling of saliva is again lycanthropic, as is the downy hair to be found in the centre of the palms. The entire creature reeks of excrement and arrested decay. Yet despite their physical lack of condition vampires are reputed to possess great strength and can run like the wind. Obliged to undertake their nightly journey to and from their graves wearing no more than a burial shroud that is torn, blood-stained and covered with grimy earth, it cannot be wondered at that they present a grisly, and ghostly, spectacle to any who catch sight of one.

Perhaps the most formidable aspect of the vampire's armoury is that of transmutation; the ability to change shape at will into certain creatures, such as the wolf, into phosphorescent specks, or even dissipate into mist, through which the dematerialized essence of the vampire can drain blood from all it envelops. The modern association with the vampire bat lies almost exclusively with literature and the cinema, not with Continental folklore. The vampire bat, so called because it laps blood from a tiny incision made on its warm-blooded victim, is not native to Europe and was only discovered, in South America, in the seventeenth century. The convenient connections with the mythical vampire were not forged before the coming of nineteenth-century vampire literature. As the bat was named after the vampire, and not *vice versa*, the vampire could not add bat-like attributes to its repertoire, save in the imagination of horror writers and artists.

Like others in the devil's army, the undead are nocturnal, loathing the sun but invigorated by the moon. A full moon could revive and even energize the vampire, whereas the sun could, depending on the local belief, either destroy it completely or merely deprive it of its array of supernatural powers between dawn and dusk. A particularly enduring belief is that in daylight the vampire must retain whatever shape it held at the moment of sunrise. The vampires' sensory powers are basically ocular: they possess the visual capacity to induce hypnosis in potential victims, and can see in the dark — with appropriate control over wolves and other creatures of the night.

One feature derived from Christian belief is the devil's inability to conduct commerce with unwilling clients. The undead cannot therefore enter a dwelling unless invited in, consciously or unconsciously, on the occasion of their first visit. This objective is accomplished because the vampire's relatives can be expected to welcome the return of their departed loved one; if not, they can still be hypnotized in order to effect entry. The vampire might also shrewdly arrive during the early hours, when psychological resistance is at its lowest.

The alert villager could determine the identity of any strange visitor by the handy positioning of mirrors. It is a deeply ingrained folk-belief that a person's reflection in a mirror or in a pond (nowadays on a camera film) is that of his/her soul. In the case of vampires, they have no soul (in keeping with all evil spirits) and so fail to cast a reflection. For that reason, upon a household bereavement, mirrors were customarily turned to face the wall, lest the deceased caught a glimpse of his soul and sought to be reunited with it, or else contaminated the reflection of the living. [17]

In the hands of the Church the sexual ingredient in vampirism was amplified, threatening unwanted immortality for the immoral and licentious. Even the physical hallmarks of the vampire — sallow, lean, hairy, smelly — are typical of the Church's conception of the promiscuous. The sexual connection was all the more pertinent in view of the usual target for the vampire attack. Contrary to the literary and cinematic corruptions of the myth, the vampire's motives were neither gratuitous murder nor the recruitment of other vampires, though these may have been secondary effects. Rather, the objective was the more limited one of seeking analeptic nourishment through blood. Nevertheless, the fact that vampire assaults occurred at night, and that the selected victim would frequently be the spouse or lover (another manifestation of ancestor worship) gave the whole procedure a sexual, not to say necrophiliac, undertone. The sexual aspect is further enhanced by the preferred regions of the victim's anatomy. Although some accounts indicate that the vampire can draw blood from any exposed part of the body, a predilection for the neck is most frequently mentioned. The sucking of blood from the external jugular vein, once the victim had been rendered trance-like, invites associations with the sado-sexual activity of the love bite. Psychologists have long been aware of the pain/pleasure ambiguity of the love bite, and that the letting of blood can cause, or relieve, sexual excitation.

Having identified the vampire for what it was, there now arose the matter of precaution. What could be done for the protection of self, family, and homestead? Pagan superstitions in this respect are encyclopaedic. Many pay tribute to man's ingenuity. For example, when burying someone whom it was suspected might return later as an undead, care would be taken to bury him deeper than was usual, so that the corpse would have greater difficulty in reaching the surface. Sensibly, the body could be interred face down, so that on awakening it would unwittingly scrabble downwards into the bowels of the earth. Thorns placed at strategic places, around the coffin or in the home, were helpful in ensnaring any active vampire. By piling stones over a grave it was hoped to obstruct any surfacing demon, and therein possibly lies the origins of cairns and tombstones.[18]

Regional precautions included a Polish method of concocting a bread-like substance from flour mixed with blood taken from the grave of a disposed-of vampire. Future protection was assured if you ate the bread. In Wallachia, rubbing your body with the lard of a pig killed on St Ignatius' day was believed to be efficacious. The popular assumption that the vampire, like the zombie, is somehow lacking in intelligence was illustrated by the noted practice of scattering grain, millet, or any other seeds along the road and around the roof and entrances to the home. The vampire is evidently easily distracted and will apparently, out of curiosity or some other misunderstood motive, stop to count each grain. Preoccupied in this manner it would still be counting at dawn, when it would have to return to its grave.

This last procedure could be carried further by waiting till nightfall and sprinkling seeds on the empty grave. Supposedly, the repleted creature would find self-preservation less imperative than the inner call to count the seeds, whereupon it would be surprised and neutralized by the rising sun. The bloated Greek *vrykolakas*, which had a penchant for squatting on victims to squeeze the life out of them, was prone to an equally nonsensical habit. Visiting its intended victim, it would wait outside the home and call his/her name. The catch was that it could never hail more than once. Consequently, Greek peasants would not answer a surprise knock at their door — unless reassured by its repetition.[19]

For thousands of years certain plants or herbs have been considered potent against malevolent spirits. Pride of place goes to garlic, to which have been ascribed over the centuries various medicinal and insecticidal properties. The most noticeable quality of the garlic plant is its pungent smell, significant in that all demons are supposedly repelled by any strong odour other than their own.[20] Its powerfully bitter smell masks the sickly sweet stench of spilled blood and the noisome after-effects of death. For the purpose in hand, garlic would be applied either to the suspected vampire's grave (keeping it within or preventing its return, as applicable) or to the potential victim's home, by smearing it around window sills and doors, leaving it in flower vases, or garlanding it around the necks of the occupants.

The belief in the powers of garlic, onions, and other strong smelling substances alludes to a primitive homoeopathic protection against demonic threats. Any symbol of purity or holiness was held to have the same effect. Against nocturnal foes the colour 'white' was highly valued, and in some localities people would paint white eyes on a black dog and despatch it to meet an unwelcome night visitor. Water is another pure 'holy' element. Vampires are supposedly unable to cross running water (further evidence of the lunar influence) except at the ebb and flow of the tide. The salt water of the sea therefore provides a compound repellant, for salt is a further sign of natural purity. Deportation of vampires, where appropriate, to tiny islands in the Mediterranean was therefore to be commended, except that growing numbers of vampire colonies would haunt passing sailors with their wailing.

When the Church began to take an official interest in the undead, any symbol, no matter how loosely associated with Christianity, was seized on with frenzied commitment. The authorized, official view was that the most effective general insurance against the undead was to lead a pious life: daily attendance at mass, devout communions, regular recitation of the Rosary, and veneration of Holy Relics.[21] To the peasant communities, these religious observances were more usually supplemented by attributing sacred qualities to various plants and trees. The wild rose has enjoyed mystic associations since antiquity, but in Byzantine Europe it came to be used to repel unholy spirits. Mountain ash, hawthorn, buckthorn, and blackthorn were likewise benignly endowed. There is also derived from primitive magic an association between sharp, erect, blood-letting prickles of thorn and fertility-bestowing phallic symbols.[22] This survives today in several modern languages — in English through the slang term for the male organ. As applied to vampires, it is said that scratches from sacred thorns that draw blood will actually destroy them — presumably a harkback to the image of Christ's crown of thorns.

The Church, moreover, had a store of potent symbolism of its own. The cross, or crucifix, was not only an affront to the Turks. It could likewise ward off the undead, and, like Eucharistic particles and Holy Water, was believed in some regions to be capable of searing its flesh, like acid. If nothing else, if placed on the vampire's tomb such items would immobilize if occupied, sterilize and prevent re-entry if empty. Conscious practices of the above kind would be later outlawed as a profanation of Christ's body, but the custom was retained in Greece of placing a crumb of consecrated bread on the lips of the undead.[23] This was possibly related to the ancient ritual of placing a coin in the mouth of the deceased — the 'Ferry Man's Coin' — designed as passage money, bribery to avoid being landed in hell.

Vampire protection would be employed whenever the need was felt, but inevitably there were occasions when the undead would break through. Whenever a community believed the undead to be in their midst, general safeguards had to give way to stronger measures. As soon as an individual, a family or close neighbours began to complain of sickness which could not be diagnosed, or experienced a sudden death, poor crops, or unexplained disappearance of children or animals, a vampire was likely to be held responsible. In particular, symptoms associated with loss of blood — anaemia, emaciation, langour, tiredness, loss of appetite —if accompanied by inexplicable nightmares and a recent family bereavement, were taken as sure evidence of vampire visitation.

There were so many signs and characteristics of the undead that positive identification often proved troublesome. Fortunately, there was one incontrovertible factor: despite physical death, the vampire's body resists decomposition. Hence, find a corpse that was reluctant to return to ashes, and (presuming it was not earmarked for sainthood) there lay a vampire. In consequence, whenever any of the aforementioned misfortunes began to cause local concern, graves would be opened on the slightest pretext. Under the guidance of the Greek Church, bodies were, in any event, disinterred period-ically as part of a customary procedure to gauge whether dissolution was proceeding at a healthy rate. Once a corpse had proved its innocence by leaving only the bones, these would be cleansed by relatives and reburied with due solemnity. This practice would unknowingly assist in providing a happy ending, because the mere fact of re-exposing a corpse to fresh air would accelerate the decomposition process. Non-Christian China carried the idea one stage further, by refusing to bury potential vampires until they were well on the way to decay.

Vampire detection and disposal demanded the most elaborate ceremonies and rituals. If the marauding presence of the undead was suspected, but no obvious candidate came to mind, it was necessary to determine the vampire's resting place. For this purpose detective work was married to superstition. A virginal young boy would be mounted on an all-black or all-white virginal colt (horses being widely held to be able to detect the presence of evil) and led systematically round an entire burial site. Sooner or later the horse would baulk and refuse to step over a particular grave, irrespective of coaxing or whipping. Popular belief insisted that under such a spot a vampire would be sleeping. There would not, however, be any helpful confirmatory signs such as a fresh pile of earth alongside an exposed lidless coffin to assist detection. As the vampire had the power of dematerialization, it could emerge and re-enter its submerged hideaway by means of small holes, roughly of finger's breadth, passing through the soil above.[24] Such little holes would be assiduously searched for.

As with all other aspects of vampires, the methods recommended for their disposal (you could not 'kill' a vampire: it was already dead) can be divided into the pagan and the Christian. Both traditions concurred that special techniques were required, because methods that would kill mortals would be ineffectual against the undead. Pagan measures retained a strong local individuality. People in parts of Serbia who believed their undead to be invisible, recommended employing a 'dhampire'.[25] The dhampire contradicts the notion held elsewhere of inherited vampirism, for the dhampire is the vampire's son. In effect, he turns Queen's evidence, for he is believed to have inside knowledge of his father's pestilential activities, and in return for a fat fee could be called upon to exorcize him. This feat would be performed by an elaborate ritual which included a public display of nose blowing and wrestling with an invisible opponent (his father), which the dhampire always won. After a suitable lapse of time, emphasizing the strength of his opponent, the exhausted dhampire would announce the destruction of the vampire, and of course nobody could prove otherwise.

Other regions, haunted by visible vampires, were more direct
—and brutal. In Dalmatia the muscles and tendons at the back
of the suspect corpse's leg were severed, rendering walking
impossible. The same result would be achieved in Finland by nailing
the vampire down, or snapping its spine, and other places reported
tying the toes and thumbs together. [26] Bulgarians advocated stealing
up on a bloated vampire and pricking it with a pin to enable its
noisome gases to escape.

Yet it is on the Christian tradition that attention must focus. Here,
the ritualistic element is just as compulsory, After all, a chance
meeting with, and destruction of, any wandering vampire would
otherwise lack credibility — and witnesses to the Church's awesome
power. A priest must be summoned, for only he would have the
requisite knowledge of the nature of Evil and access to the necessary
implements of counter-vampirism which would provide evidence
of God's power over Satan.

Once the lair of the undead has been located and the coffin
opened, the tell-tale signs of vampirism should be present. Following
a nocturnal repast the creature should have a ruddy complexion,
with the mouth and nails clotted with blood. More spectacularly,
it might even be floating on a squelching reservoir of blood, and
if the flesh is punctured with a pin the red liquid should gush forth
as from a burst balloon. Customarily, the eyes will be open, glazed,
staring, and malefic. If the vampire has on occasion gone hungry
(or thirsty) the burial shroud will show signs of having been eaten,
and perhaps also the limbs.

Shortly after dawn is the best time to locate and destroy a
vampire, for it will then be heavy and torpid after its banquet.
Three methods of destruction are prescribed: impalement,
cremation, and decapitation. Impalement with a sharpened stake,
properly known as 'transfixion', should be performed with a single
blow through the heart (or navel). Strange to say, transfixion does
not achieve its effect in the way first imagined. Although there
is a potent symmetry about a blood-fiend being destroyed by
piercing its quintessential vital organ, this is to overlook its stubborn
immunity. The need to impale with one stroke is frequently
emphasized, for if it is repeated the vampire would be resuscitated,
reputedly being able to pull out the stake himself. [27]

The more usual explanation behind transfixion is that the
vampire is thereby immobilized, impaled to the coffin floor. Later
fiction writers and film makers would depart from folklore not
only in having the hero hammer away in a passionate orgy of hate,

but also in showing the vampire 'killed' as a consequence. Another cinematic distortion concerns the vampire's reaction to being staked; blood spurting from every orifice, accompanied by writhing, screaming and foaming at the mouth. These tantrums are not the death-agony of the folklore vampire: they are psychological and contrived.[28] Should the staker keep a steady hand, then the vampire is doomed, but should his concentration falter, or his eyes meet the hypnotic, malevolent stare from within the coffin, then the tables are turned instantly, and the would-be executioner becomes the next victim, and the next undead. It is for this reason that the need to transfix at the first attempt is paramount. Finding the wretched beast is comparatively straightforward compared with the nerves of steel needed to dispose of it.

The Christian connection even found its way into the specifications of the wood to be used as the stake: aspen, maple, ash, oak, whatever the local belief regarding the wood used for the Cross. Proper transfixion would enable the priest to effect irrevocable victory by decapitation or cremation, unless the corpse had been 'dead' for many years, in which case it would crumble into dust. In theory, cremation was the safest procedure, provided that every scrap of flesh and bone was incinerated, and any spiders, lice, worms, or snakes trying to scuttle from the flames (the vampire trying to escape) were tossed back. The ashes would then be scattered to the winds or into a river.

The difficulty with cremating suspect vampires — though if carried out meticulously it was the most efficient means of disposal — was that it ran counter in some places to the approval of the Church. A cremated corpse destroyed the body which Christ had pledged to resurrect at the Day of Judgement. Moreover, cremation seemed to imitate heathen practices and, at least to the Orthodox tradition, consuming with fire a body which had received the last rites and been sprinkled with holy oil smacked of sacrilege.

Decapitation seemed to achieve the same desired effects as cremation, but with fewer drawbacks. The vampire's head would be removed, not with any handy sharp instrument, but by a sexton's spade. The body would then be hacked to pieces, inviting reminders of how, in olden times, certain notorious criminals or political offenders were punished. The value of decapitation would seem to be that it destroys the physical intactness necessary for any creature that wishes to rise again.[29] To be absolutely sure, the heart could be removed, treated with oil or vinegar, and then shredded. Holy Water poured over the now-empty grave should finally spell irrevocable defeat for the vampire.

Other miscellaneous methods to be found in Christian-based accounts include use of a silver bullet (silver being a pure metal), properly blessed by a priest. It was important then to dispose of the vampire away from moonlight, which would otherwise resuscitate it with enhanced malevolence. Perhaps the most ingenious use to which Christian imagery could be put was found in parts of Bulgaria, where the undead would be hunted down with an icon and lured into a huge bottle, which would then be plugged with an equally huge cork decorated with more holy images. The masterminding 'bottler' would be handsomely rewarded, and the whole — bottle and contents — tossed on to a blazing pyre.[30] This particular tale would seem to have its roots in the Oriental belief that evil spirits could be enclosed in glass vessels, and is a classic instance of hybrid pagan-Christian folklore.

Alien as all the foregoing must appear to the modern mind, it is important to try to establish the secular, commonplace occurrences which could give rise to such profound and unquestioning belief in vampires. Inaccurate diagnosis of death was a cardinal factor. Even today, with the brain- versus tissue-death controversy occasioned when a patient is on a life-support system, there is debate as to the precise moment of death. There is no irrefutable test as to when someone is no longer living. Cataleptic trances, for example, which can be induced through both physical and mental disorders, may be accompanied by a rapid slowing of the body metabolism, producing a condition which even to the trained medical eye can seem indistinguishable from death. The limbs may become rigid and the skin cold to the touch. Pronouncements of death, in times and in lands of less developed medical knowledge, were frequently — and tragically — premature. The only incontrovertible proof was, and is, dissolution. In Bram Stoker's time this was openly acknowledged: in 1885 the British Medical Journal confirmed, 'It is true that hardly any one sign of death, short of putrefaction, can be relied upon as infallible.'[31] To the superstitious, logic would dictate that as decomposition was the only sure sign of death, so non-decomposition must be proof of the undead.

This fundamental diagnostic difficulty has, upon a moment's thought, an unpalatable consequence: throughout history many people have unwittingly been buried alive. Some would not have regained consciousness thereafter, but others would — in time succumbing to asphyxia or starvation. A very few would have succeeded in breaking out of their submerged confinement, for burial arrangements were frequently haphazard — makeshift, fragile coffins and shallow graves. The use of communal burial grounds was not commonplace in continental Europe. The dead would be buried almost anywhere: on hills, in caves, in woods, in fields, in proximity to other graves or in isolation, either singly or in family groups.[32] Needless to say, any dishevelled, hysterical, blood-stained, mud-smeared, white-shrouded figure that did somehow escape from its grave would have tried to seek out its relatives, inducing panic in anyone it encountered, and ending up unleashing a vampire mania.

Bodies easily buried could easily be disinterred. And they were — whether in the search for vampires or loot. The age-old custom of taking personal valuables to the grave encouraged a reciprocal profession of grave robbing. Sometimes the theft would be of jewellery, sometimes of the corpse itself — which could fetch a substantial price from no-questions-asked anatomy schools unable to procure adequate supplies from legitimate sources. The infamous Burke and Hare, convicted in Edinburgh in the 1820s, are only the most celebrated British practitioners of the trade in bodies. Naturally enough, the later discovery of a rifled grave, either deprived of its human contents or else showing the corpse in an unnatural pose as the result of violent removal of personal effects, could have only one explanatory cause — the presence of a vampire, for the evidence told of the corpse having moved itself.

The business of decomposition is also relevant in other ways, for its rate is not constant. Soil conditions can vary the speed; dry soils tending to preserve (as, of course, does freezing). The cause of death can act likewise, and a body inadvertently buried alive would take longer to decompose through not being exposed to air once the vital functions had ceased.

Sufferers of particular rare diseases that produce visually alarming symptoms might easily at one time have been condemned as vampires. Albinos possess the requisite pallor and photophobia. A rare disorder known as porphyria, moreover, results in the teeth, hair and nails glowing fluorescently. Sufferers are extremely sensitive to sunlight, and the disease can be hereditary. With iron-deficiency porphyria, the body cannot metabolize iron, and must take it in a readily digestible form — such as drinking blood. For persons with this disorder, the eating of garlic is not recommended, for garlic activates the functions which break down old blood cells, thereby removing the iron that the body needs.[33]

In the case of pernicious anaemia, a serious if rare blood disorder, the body of the sufferer can shrivel up and produce a physical craving for blood. Tuberculosis was more common, and could result in recognizable vampire symptoms: weight loss and fatigue, not to mention coughing and spitting blood in advanced cases. Significantly, the disease has been known to be conveyed by a carrier who is himself immune — an obvious vampire candidate should his identity be disclosed. Cholera dries out the body and produces a physical wasting, and cancer has comparable manifestations — both diseases being suggestive of vampire attack. The later symptoms of rabies, too, can include spasms, convulsions, and difficulty in breathing, together with a manifest terror of water.

Most pertinent of all, however, was the plague, whose epidemics were silent, invisible, and inexplicable — appearing without reason or warning. The Great Plague which decimated London in 1665-6 is now known to have been caused by rats and fleas, but at the time, lacking the necessary medical and scientific knowledge, it was widely attributed to heavenly punishment for earthly sins. In parts of the Continent only a vampire onslaught could account for the massive loss of life brought about by periodic epidemics. For reasons of hygiene, victims were disposed of with unseemly haste. There were not enough doctors and undertakers to cope, with the result that not only were many of the afflicted buried alive, but their graves, too, were amateurish and shallow.

Continental vampire-itis peaked in the 1720s and 1730s. The Ottoman star was on the wane, its troops and administrators pushed inexorably, if intermittently, back through the Balkans. Habsburg Catholics, the ascendant military and religious force, stepped into the vacuum. In the wake of the Turkish retreat conflict continued, ecclesiastical rather than political, this time between Roman Catholicism and Muscovite Orthodoxy. A great wedge of territory — Poland, the Ukraine, western Russia, the Slav and Balkan states — reverberated to the clash between Christian East and West — each side denying that the dead would find eternal peace in the unhallowed soil of the other.[34] The watershed passed through an area of modern Romania known as Transylvania. Originally Greek Orthodox, its peasant communities had been exposed to Turkish Islam and then Catholic proselytization, and were now the terrified and helpless victims of a religious maelstrom. The tentacles of this struggle and its resultant psychosis spread far and wide until large areas of central and eastern Europe were seething under vampire paranoia, as excommunications multiplied and popular superstition was played on and manipulated to serve the goal of true belief.

An indication of the seriousness with which this epidemic was treated, outside the confines of the Church, can be seen in the response of German academia. The intellectual climate had entered the so-called rationalist era of the Enlightenment. Learned treatises appeared one after the other between 1728 and 1734, many of them from the prestigious universities of Leipzig, Jena, and Nuremberg, each trying to account, in theological, psychological, medical, or metaphysical terms, for the sensational vampire stories reaching them from the East. This was still an age when belief in the existence of God was largely unquestioned, and philosophical speculation could not easily avoid that premise. The vampire seemed self-evidently a diabolic creature permitted by God. As everlasting life awaited the pure and holy, it seemed obvious that this longing for eternity would be imitated and parodied by the devil.[35] Much of the debate, in other words, took place against the framework of the devil's challenge to God's earthly order.

Not surprisingly, many of the questions asked were couched in metaphysical terms. Were vampires actual risen corpses, or merely souls not yet freed from earthly bondage? Did the spiritual element of the vampire emanate from its former, living existence, or was it animated by the devil, directing an evil spirit to take possession of the body once the soul of the owner had departed? What unknown forces lay behind the supernatural powers of the undead? If the body of the vampire was spectral, how, and by what means, could it suck the blood of, and engage in coitus with, the living? Similarly, how could an actual, three dimensional body, dead or otherwise, pass from grave to surface, and back again, without disturbing the earth between? In sum, could a corporeal substance possess astral dimensions?

Among the speculative conclusions reached were either that the body of the undead dematerialized before reintegrating outside the grave, or, alternatively, that another body was somehow created by the vampire, independent of the corpse which remained in the grave. Such notions raised profound theological disquiet, for if vampires were indeed endowed by the devil with such talents it implied that Satan enjoyed comparable powers to those of Christ after the Resurrection.

What needs to be appreciated is that popular superstition,

ecclesiastical practice, and the most learned minds of the eighteenth century all fuelled the vampire myth. The spreading psychosis could find no remedy from physicians, so profit-seeking quacks added to the hysteria with their anti-vampire ointments and talismans.[36] East central Europe was no stranger to wars or epidemics, successive waves of Black Death, smallpox, and pestilence having repeatedly savaged the region in the generations prior to the 'vampire' outbreaks. Only later was it generally noticed that the bulk of vampire reports came from that frontier region where Catholic Hungarians and Orthodox Serbs and Wallachs intermingled; where the peasant population was most exposed to the dire consequences of false belief, as described in the warnings of the rival faith.

The multiplying persecution of alleged vampires that ensued was instrumental in turning popular superstition into an actual hysterical epidemic with diagnosable symptoms. Local communities took the law into their own hands, digging up the graves of suspected vampires, until Rome, angered by the 'heresies' preached by the Orthodox schismatics, established an effective legal framework for official vampire trials.[37] These trials did not set out to establish the nature of vampirism or its causes, far less the guilt or innocence of the accused. They restricted themselves to the Catholic precept that, as vampires depended for their existence on the devil, it was God's will that they should be destroyed. God permitted Satan to tempt mankind through evil — in this instance through vampirism — thereby justifying a resolute Christian campaign to eradicate the undead.

That Britain was not party to the vampire craze was due not to a lesser capacity for superstition, but to the effects of the Reformation. Part of the Catholic explanation of vampirism depended, as already mentioned, on the doctrine of purgatory. The Protestant challenge denied the existence of purgatory, and therefore insisted that beings returning from the grave could not be the spirits of the departed. In time, Rome would amend its association between the undead and purgatory, but Protestant clerics, needing an alternative explanation for the vampire phenomenon, subsumed it under the category of 'witchcraft'.[38] Consequently, while central and eastern (Catholic or Orthodox) Europe suffered from vampires, north-western (Protestant) Europe suffered its witches. Britain was virtually bereft of any indigenous vampire lore. When the eighteenth century invasion did take place, it would do so not through folklore but through literature.

Modern Romanian carving of a demon.

# 3.

# THE VAMPIRE
# IN LITERATURE

Her beautifully rounded limbs quivered with the agony of her soul. The glassy, horrible eyes of the figure ran over that angelic form with a hideous satisfaction — horrible profanation. He drags her head to the bed's edge. He forces it back by the long hair still entwined in his grasp. With a plunge he seizes her neck in his fang-like teeth — a gush of blood and a hideous sucking noise follows. The girl has swooned, and the vampire is at his hideous repast!

*Varney the Vampire; or, the Feast of Blood,* vol 1., p. 4.

THE VAMPIRE epidemic and its reverberations which swept across much of the Continent in the second quarter of the eighteenth century was ready-made to excite German academia rather than her writers and artists. The haughty intellectual atmosphere of the Enlightenment viewed vampirism as a phenomenon to be analysed, not romanticized. The plethora of explanatory dissertations streaming from German universities were, in time, translated and worked their way across the English Channel, so that as early as the 1730s the term 'vampire' had made its debut in English writing. For the moment, these startling revelations of walking corpses would find little enthusiastic reception in the higher literary circles of either Britain or Germany while the Age of Reason flourished; but then, as Gothic, followed by the broader Romantic sentiments became fashionable amongst educated society in the later decades of the century, and natural human fascination with the mysteries of love, life, death and the supernatural re-emerged, the vampire became something of a vogue. It would take a century for the transformation to be complete, but the folkloric vampire of central and eastern Europe would eventually metamorphose into the British-built vampire of Romantic literature. Purported fact would live on and derive nourishment as fiction, as a post-Enlightenment literary phenomenon.

Abetted by the earlier labours of their academic countrymen, it was the poets of Germany who first realized the potential of the vampire, and who transported the undead from the Church-dominated plagues of superstition into the respectable channels of verse. Ossenfelder's *The Vampire* (1748), Bürger's *Lenore* (1773) and Goethe's *The Bride of Corinth* (1797) announced the new medium for the vampire tale.[1] *Lenore* was clearly known to Bram Stoker, who would include in *Dracula* (*D* 1:20) its vivid phrase *'Denn die Todten reiten schnell'* (For the dead travel fast). Goethe, in *The Bride of Corinth*, demonstrates his awareness of Greek vampire lore when he fuses the quest for love and blood. A young woman returns from the grave to seek her lover:

> From my grave to wander I am forced,
> Still to seek the God's long sever'd link,
> Still to love the bridegroom I have lost,
> And the lifeblood of his heart to drink.

In Britain, Samuel Taylor Coleridge's *The Rime of the Ancient Mariner* (1797) comes close to the vampire essence with these lines:

> Her lips were red, her looks were free,
> Her locks were yellow as gold:
> Her skin was white as leprosy,
> The Nightmare Life-in-Death was she,
> Who thicks man's blood with cold.

> (Part III, lines 190—4)

But credit for the dramatically unambiguous arrival of the vampire into English verse goes to Robert Southey's high Gothic epic *Thalaba the Destroyer* (1797), which was published complete with explanatory notes for bewildered readers:

> 'Yea, strike her!' cried a voice, whose tones
> Flow'd with such a sudden healing through his soul,
> As when the desert shower
> From death deliver'd him;
> But obedient to that well-known voice,
> His eye was seeking it,
> When Moath, firm of heart,
> Perform'd the bidding: through the vampire corpse
> He thrust his lance; it fell,
> And howling with the wound,
> Its fiendish tenant fled.

A sapphire light fell on them,
And garmented with glory, in their sight
  Oneiza's spirit blood.

                              (Book 8, Stanza II)

The following year Southey's *The Old Woman of Berkeley* ranged
widely over lamias, ghosts, and witches, providing a sound base
for the explosion of the literary vampire that would arrive in the
second decade of the new century. John Stagg's grisly *The Vampyre*
(1810) emphasized the blood and gore aspect of the undead:

The choir then burst the funeral dome
  Where Sigismund was lately laid,
And found him, tho' within the tomb,
  Still warm as life, and undecay'd.
With blood his visage was distain'd,
  Ensanguin'd were his frightful eyes,
Each sign of former life remain'd,
  Save that all motionless he lies.

By this time, the great Romantic poets could discern the potential
of the vampire for their own creative purposes. By 1820 many of
them had experimented in detail with the vampire motif — some
making use of the male vampire as an instrument of domination;
others working with the she-vampire/lamia tradition to project
female seduction. Among the latter category is to be found Sir
Walter Scott's *Rokeby:*

For like the bat of Indian brakes,
Her pinions from the womb she makes,
And soothing thus the dreamer's pains,
She drinks the life-blood from his veins.

Coleridge told of the she-vampire *Christabel;* Shelley preferred to
explore the male version in *The Cenci;* while Keats' prolific output
of vampirish poems — *The Eve of St Agnes, Lamia,* and above
all *La Belle Dame sans Merci* — alternated the sex of the undead.
In *This Living Hand* Keats uses vampiric language to illustrate the
power of love:

This living hand, now warm and capable
Of earnest grasping, would, if it were cold
And in the icy silence of the tomb,
So haunt thy days and chill thy dreaming nights
That thou wouldst wish thine own heart dry of blood
So in my veins red life might stream again,
And thou be conscience-calm'd — see here it is.
I hold it towards you.

Most prominent of all was the influence exerted by Byron, steeped in vampire folklore, whose curse of *The Giaour* spells out all the terror of the vampire — prince of phantoms.

> But first on earth, as Vampyre sent,
> Thy corpse shall from its tomb be rent;
> Then ghastly haunt thy native place,
> And suck the blood of all thy race;
> There from thy daughter, sister, wife,
> At midnight drain the stream of life;
> Yet loathe the banquet, which perforce
> Must feed thy livid living corse,
> Thy victims, ere they yet expire,
> Shall know the demon for their sire . . .
>
> . . . Yet with thine own best blood shall drip
> Thy gnashing tooth, and haggard lip;
> Then stalking to thy sullen grave
> Go — and with Ghouls and Afrits rave,
> Till these in horror shrink away
> From spectre more accursed than they.

What will already be clear from these assembled extracts is that the vampire has radically changed its image — from the pestilential outgrowth of superstition to a vehicle for artistic expression. If the vampire of folklore is notoriously difficult to define — because of its cultural diversity, lack of undisputed corroboration, and the embellishments of Church, rumour, and panic — such an amorphous concept in the hands of poets and writers could only dilute the substance of vampirism still further, as they freely adapted folklore for their own ends. Romantics were not interested in the undead as such. In their hands, vampires ceased to be the 'end', and became the 'means', the catalyst, the medium. The creatures now depicted frequently bore little resemblance to the hideous foamy-mouthed, walking corpses of Slavonic legend. In Romantic literature, generally, vampire imagery is employed not to threaten or frighten, but to illuminate and enlighten.

The Gothic and Romantic, as literary epochs, were well-served by several durable and adaptable myths — among them the Wandering Jew, Don Juan, and the Seeker After Forbidden Knowledge — but the vampire myth could be uniquely harnessed to illustrate one particular aspect of human emotional entanglement: that one partner could mysteriously gain vitality by draining that of the other. Literary vampirism is frequently an expression of energy transfer, psychological as much as intravenous.

The central theme became love, not blood, and the nocturnal visits prompted by earthly rather than spiritual intent. Any vestigial supernatural element may be reduced to no more than a lover returning from death to pursue the source of his unrequited affections. As for the flexibility with which the myth became endowed, this has been well essayed by Twitchell:

> In the works of such artists as Coleridge, Byron, Shelley, Keats, Emily and Charlotte Brontë, Stoker, Wilde, Poe and Lawrence the vampire was variously used to personify the force of maternal attraction/repulsion (Coleridge's Christabel), incest (Byron's Manfred), oppressive paternalism (Shelley's Cenci), adolescent love (Keats' Porphyro), avaricious love (Poe's Morella and Berenice), the struggle for power (E. Brontë's Heathcliff), sexual suppression (C. Brontë's Bertha Rochester), homosexual attraction (Le Fanu's Carmilla), repressed sexuality (Stoker's Dracula), female domination (D. H. Lawrence's Brangwen women), and, most Romantic of all, the artist himself exchanging energy with aspects of his art (Coleridge's Ancient Mariner, Poe's artist in *The Oval Portrait*, Wordsworth's Leech Gatherer, Wilde's Dorian Gray, and the narrator of James's *The Sacred Fount*).[2]

This metaphorical utilization of vampirism to serve social, emotional and erotic purposes meant that the central character would not necessarily be explicitly labelled as a vampire. Further, it would not always be clear whether the person performing the energy transfer *is* actually a vampire, though it is important to appreciate that s/he *acts* as if s/he is. In some cases it was superfluous for the writer to announce the presence of overt vampirism, though the association may be obvious. In other instances greater room for manoeuvre was maintained by the artist distancing himself as far as possible from recognizable features of vampirism — to the point of being unconscious of their very presence.

With the greatest poets of a generation turning their talents to the vampire motif it was only a matter of time before it appeared in English prose. Whereas it is not possible to cite with any precision the date of its entry into poetry (strains of vampire-like activity being depicted long before Southey's explicit reference to 'the vampire'), there is no comparable difficulty in dating its advent into prose. Before the nineteenth century there had been no discernible vampire motif in an English short story or novel, though Matthew Lewis' notorious *The Monk* (1796) does include an episode in which a legendary Bleeding Nun appears in blood-stained habit to drain the blood from the hero with a long, cold kiss. On the Continent, an early obsession with spilled blood was evidenced by the Marquis de Sade's *Justine* (1796), a morbid excursion through blood, sex and excessive violence. *Justine* was, however, devoid of any supernatural presence, unlike Johann Ludwig Tieck's *Wake Not the Dead* (c.1800).

As it turned out, both *Dracula* and that other horror classic, *Frankenstein*, emerged from the same seed. In 1816 Lord Byron was at the peak of his fame and, on account of his personal indiscretions, of his notoriety. Making news for the wrong reasons he left London for Geneva in the company of a young physician and travelling companion, John Polidori, there to meet up with fellow poet Percy Shelley and his young wife-to-be, Mary. A horror-writing contest was decided upon, but it was neither Byron nor Shelley who provided a new direction for English literature. It was Mary who came up with *Frankenstein*, while Polidori developed on a rough outline scribbled by Byron to complete a short twenty-page tale of his own. It was published in 1819 under the title *The Vampyre* and became with hindsight one of the most influential works of the century — albeit unconsciously.

*The Vampyre's* initial impact was almost entirely due to the association with Byron — a coincidence happily encouraged by the publishers — and his lordship was long credited with authorship, despite repeated disavowals. Goethe added to the interest, describing it as Byron's best work,[3] so that it won for itself a readership that spanned western Europe and left Polidori to be pilloried, unjustly, for plagiarism.

Its later impact derived from its seminal position in the development of vampire literature. Not only was *The Vampyre* the first work of its kind in English prose, but its leading character, Lord Ruthven, encapsulated many of the basic ingredients of the literary vampire that would shape the genre to the present day. Ruthven is an aristocrat, world weary, coldly evil, aloof, cunning, and irresistible to innocent women, whom he willingly corrupts. In short, he is the stereotypical, misanthropic, moody, nocturnal libertine — a classic Byronic hero (with whom Polidori had occasion to be personally acquainted) endowed with supernatural trappings. By casting Ruthven as a nobleman, Polidori invests him with greater literary potential: the vampire thereby becomes more mobile, his erotic qualities are enhanced, and he is able to exercise sexual *droit de seigneur* over his victims. Parts of the tale are also situated in Greece (authentic vampire country) to provide added local colour.

The 'blood' aspect of vampirism is played down — Ruthven acting more as a psychological sponge — but the overall impression and originality of the story were sufficient for it to be translated and adapted for the Paris stage within a year of publication. In time, it would appear in comic operas and vaudeville, and invite a host of imitations.[4]

Polidori probably did not think of his tale in vampire terms — to him it was a further variation on the theme of the Gothic villain — but it initiated new possibilities for the fictional vampire. Bram Stoker's *Dracula* would, in time, eventually stand as the apotheosis of the tradition inaugurated by Lord Ruthven, but for the moment the vampire motif would explore new avenues. The lamia-esque appeal of the vampire *femme fatale*, as revealed in the style of *Christabel* and *La Belle Dame sans Merci*, began to break out of its poetic confines on both sides of the Atlantic. Theophile Gautier's little French tale *La Morte Amoreuse* (1836) tells of a priest carnally seduced by a she-vampire, who is ultimately destroyed by holy water. From the United States in the 1830s Edgar Allan Poe wove vampire elements into many of his short stories, without identifying the vampire for what it was. He preferred to explore the ways and means through which lovers — one of whom is usually dead — can suffocate one another outside prescribed conventions concerning vampire behaviour. Poe's stories are full of women dead but alive: Berenice, Morella, Ligeia, Madeleine Usher; and in an innovative twist in 'The Oval Portrait' the artist paints a portrait of his wife, but as the colours are added to the picture they are drained from her. When the portrait is complete and totally lifelike, his wife is dead. The energy exchange has not taken place between people, but between a person and her image.

Several other isolated vampire tales appeared during the mid-nineteenth century which deserve mention: Alexander Dumas' (père) *The Pale Faced Lady*, with its setting in the Carpathian mountains; the anonymously written *The Vampire of Kring*; and contributions by Hoffman, Baudelaire, and Alexis Tolstoy. The year 1847 would turn out to be an eventful one in the history of the literary vampire. The adaptation of Continental superstition was now infiltrating literature of all kinds. Both Charlotte and Emily Brontë took advantage of it. In *Jane Eyre*, Bertha Rochester's promiscuity is presented as so abhorrent that she is described by Charlotte Brontë as reminiscent 'of that foul German spectre — the Vampyre'. As for Heathcliff in Emily's *Wuthering Heights*, his nocturnal wanderings, bloodless hue, refusal to eat, and his ability to drain the vitality of others are suggestive in themselves. But then in the concluding chapter the question is explicitly asked: 'Is he a ghoul or a vampire?' and Brontë includes the following passage: 'I tried to close his eyes: to extinguish, if possible, that frightful, life-like gaze of exultation before any one else beheld it. They would not shut: they seemed to sneer at my attempts: and his parted lips and sharp white teeth sneered too!' (Chapter 34).[5] Brontë does not *say* that Heathcliff is a vampire, but her readers in the 1840s, more so than today, knew enough of the legend to draw their own conclusions.

Mention of *Jane Eyre* and *Wuthering Heights* demonstrates how rarefied and pervasive the original vampire motif had become. Neither sister was writing about, or was especially interested in, vampires *per se*, yet they both reveal themselves to be familiar with its use as a social metaphor. The real significance of 1847, however, lies not with the Brontës but with a contribution from the lower end of the literary spectrum. By this time literacy was increasing and newly-installed steam presses and assembly-line publishing techniques were churning out a succession of 'penny dreadfuls' — blood-thirsty, proletarian pot-boilers, comprising tales of murder, lurid romance, and any other sensationalist happenings that could be laced with sexual innuendo. It was out of these developments that *Varney the Vampire; or, the Feast of Blood* first appeared.

Polidori had told his tale in some twenty pages: the author of *Varney* — James Malcolm Rymer or Thomas Pecket Prest (the authorship is disputed)[6] — needed 868 double-columned pages divided into 220 chapters. Not surprisingly it was reissued in 1853 in penny parts. With *Varney* there is no pretence at literary art; just a rattling story-line told over and over again to be taken on its own terms. Set in the 1730s, the exploits of Sir Francis Varney mark him as the principal literary precursor of Count Dracula. Those ingredients in *Varney* later employed by Bram Stoker include: the maidens' sexual initiation and their mixed reactions of desire and fear; the vampire's roots in central Europe; the quasi-medical-scientific methods of vampire disposal; and the Keystone-Cops-style hunt for the vampire[7] — plus innocent, sleep-walking victims, and the villain dressed in a black cloak, able to climb down castle walls, who arrives in Britain aboard a shipwrecked vessel during a tempest.

After *Varney* there seemed no other avenues for the fictional vampire to explore; the genre seemed exhausted, both as a literary metaphor and as a scaremonger in its own right. But there remains to be considered one further mainstream vampire work pre-dating *Dracula*, whose author, like Stoker, was an Irishman. Among the five tales comprising *In a Glass Darkly* (1872), by Joseph Sheridan Le Fanu, appeared the novelette *Carmilla* — credited by many aficionados as the finest vampire tale ever written. Despite its advanced date, *Carmilla* is soundly Gothic, down to evening mists, full moons, black stagecoaches and central European locations.

Unlike *Varney*, *Carmilla* is a tasteful, sensuous work; yet what gives it its distinctive flavour is not so much the fact of Carmilla being a she-vampire, but that she is a lesbian. The monopoly of the feminine perspective for both vampire and victim serves to heighten the sexual quality of the vampire act, which is described in greater erotic detail than in any previous example of the genre. Moreover, the vampire is here no longer a supernatural fiend or disguised Gothic villain, but a complex, self-motivated personality. The female vampire would become a popular acquisition for film makers, who would link Carmilla with the real-life Hungarian mass-murderess Elizabeth Bathory (see Chapter Five) to create a further sub-cult of the vampire species.

The dying years of the nineteenth century witnessed a curious Indian summer for the Gothic novel. Stevenson's *Dr Jekyll and Mr Hyde* (1886) and Oscar Wilde's *Picture of Dorian Gray* (1891) are — along with *Dracula* — perhaps the most memorable examples of this unexpected burst of symbolic energy;[8] but the vampire motif once again began to sprout and bloom in unexplored directions. H. G. Wells' *The Flowering of the Strange Orchid* dealt with vampire plants; Conan Doyle's *The Parasite* delved into psychic sponges; and Jules Verne's *Carpathian Castle* presented evil scientists posing as vampires.[9] Guy de Maupassant's little cameo, *The Horla*, vividly tells of the anguish and symptoms of a vampire assault from the perspective of the victim and the madness it induces.

*Dracula* would be the next, and last, great vampire work, so it will be useful to enumerate the various changes that had taken place over the course of a century from the vampire of folklore to the totally different creature presented by the vampire of literature. The one is something to be believed in and feared: the other an artificial construct to illuminate and to entertain. In literature, the social background of the undead is commonly transformed from the peasantry to the nobility, and they are able to travel beyond their native community to plague great cities where they can hide in total anonymity. Whereas the folkloric vampire tends to restrict its activities, at least initially, within its immediate family and friends, and is not strictly bound to visit the opposite sex, the literary vampire frequently has no family and can attack whom it pleases where it pleases. Victims would often be from outside the vampire's own ethnic group, and (with the notable exception of Carmilla) will usually be drawn from the opposite sex.

With regard to its age, the vampire of superstition will not have been long dead, yet will be zombie-like, thick-headed and stupid — the opposite of his fictional counterpart, who, though he may have been dead for centuries, will have used his time profitably to become learned, intelligent, and adroit. The sexual element is latent in folklore; exaggerated in fiction, and embellished by perversions and the corruption of innocents. The religious ingredient is usually indispensable in literature, the arrival of the priest/hero being integral to the plot. In addition there may be a sense of pity for the vampire — not encountered in folklore — a feeling that he is as much a victim as victimizer, in keeping with the tradition of Faust and the Wandering Jew. The vampire of folklore, as earlier outlined, may have acquired its condition for any one of countless reasons. The origins of its literary cousins will either be left undisclosed, or else will result from some form of pact with the devil. Finally, the vampire of literature possesses remarkable staying powers and regenerative abilities (like the villain in modern crime thrillers, the vampire must not be caught and destroyed too easily), and the means for his/her destruction will normally comply with the more sensational methods prescribed by folklore — the gorier the better from the reader's point of view. [10]

The wealth of folklore and literary antecedents was thoroughly assimilated by Bram Stoker. *Dracula* fuses the tradition of the Byronic hero/Gothic villain with that of the *femme fatale*, and overlays the whole with a rich veneer of folklore. Stoker ignores the popular device of siting his tale in a remote land in a bygone age, and brings his all-powerful Count to contemporary England — to the crowded streets of London in the 1890s. The late Victorian upsurge in tales of the supernatural assisted him to construct a character far more evil than Carmilla and far more substantial than Varney, for as Wolf has said: 'There is nothing in Varney, nothing at all, that is capable of sounding anything like the chords of dark understanding that reverberate in page after page of Stoker's *Dracula*.'[11] With that reminder, it is time to take a closer look at Bram Stoker — the man who wrote *Dracula*.

# 4.

# THE LIFE AND WORKS OF BRAM STOKER

In my babyhood I used, I understand to be, often at the point of death. Certainly till I was about seven years old I never knew what it was to stand upright ... This early weakness, however, passed away in time and I grew into a strong boy and in time enlarged into the biggest member of my family ... I was physically immensely strong.

Bram Stoker, writing of himself in
*Personal Reminiscences of Henry Irving*, vol. 1, pp. 31-2.

C LOSE acquaintance with Bram Stoker is regrettably not possible. His immortal creation lives on but the author remains elusive. Even with the arrival of a number of biographies, nothing but the basics of Stoker's life have been revealed. It is known what he did, but not who he was. The principal source on Stoker is a two-volume biography he wrote about the actor Henry Irving, with whom he spent nearly thirty years of his life, but in which Stoker indulges in plenty of personal reminiscences of himself.[1] Most of his personal papers have failed to survive, so that this major work provides the mainstay of his own biographers — Harry Ludlam and Daniel Farson (Stoker's nephew)[2] — though neither could do more than offer tantalizing glimpses into the personality who created arguably the most extraordinary, and certainly the most enduring, figure of nineteenth-century fiction. Finally, to supplement these biographies and unwitting autobiography there exist the voluminous writings of Bram Stoker, although caution should be exercised when attributing characteristics of an author's fiction to the author himself.

Bram Stoker was born on 8 November 1847 at 15 The Crescent, Clontarf, just north of Dublin. Ireland was then still an integral part of Britain, though nationalist sentiment was on the rise, as evidenced by the activities of such organizations as the 'Young Ireland' group. His father was Abraham, a tall, kindly man, devoid of strident ambition, being content to fend for his growing family through a humdrum existence as a civil servant in Dublin Castle. Abraham was forty-eight years old when Bram was born — the third of seven children all born in the space of ten years: William, Matilda, Abraham junior (Bram), Tom, Richard, Margaret, and George.

Bram's mother, Charlotte, eighteen years younger than her

Bram Stoker (Dracula Society).

husband, was a handsome, strong minded woman who, if she could see no ambition in her husband, was determined to invest it in her sons. Three — William, Richard, and George — would enter the medical profession, and William would become an eminent surgeon and be knighted in 1895. As for her daughters, Charlotte 'did not care tuppence.'[3] So far as the responsibilities of rearing a large family permitted, Charlotte was an ardent social reformer and visitor to the workhouses, and, perhaps surprisingly in view of her attitude to her daughters, was active in promoting women's rights. She was also Irish to the core, reared on Gaelic mythology and folk tales.

For the infant Abraham, named after his father and reputedly the closest to him of his sons, the first years of life were taken up with no more than simple survival. He was bed-ridden for his first seven years. The cause or nature of this disorder has never been established, nor even hinted at with any confidence. In view of the complete recovery that Bram made, and the athletic feats which were to follow, it is plausible that the malady had its cause in his mind rather than his body.

Through spending his early years bed-ridden, Bram had time to hear more than his share of Irish myths and legends from his mother. Incapable as he was of physical activity, he was also encouraged to turn to books from an early age, availing himself of his father's well-stocked collection. When fully recovered he attended a private school run by a Reverend Woods, and by the age of sixteen he was already a compulsive scribbler. He was admitted to Trinity College, Dublin, where the once retiring introvert was introduced to the cut and thrust of university life. He blossomed into an effective debater and holder of the most prestigious student offices, not to mention the sporting honours that came his way. The one-time infant invalid was capped at football and became marathon walking champion.

His personality at university developed into that which was recognizable in him in adulthood. 'Hearty' and 'stalwart' is how Farson describes him, very much a man's man, and chivalrous towards women.[4] He took an active part in the literary and dramatic activities of Trinity and was not deterred by controversy — taking up cudgels on behalf of the then highly controversial American poet, Walt Whitman, and writing long, passionately supportive letters to him across the Atlantic.

Now a burly six footer and the bearer of a lush, reddish beard, Stoker graduated with honours in science (pure mathematics). His outgoing and genial personality did not at first overcome the need for job security, and Bram followed his father into the civil service as a junior clerk in Dublin Castle. This was hardly a suitable outlet for Bram's prodigious energy or his ambitions, and he ensured that any spare time was productively filled. To alleviate his parents' mounting financial difficulties he indulged in private tuition. He continued his studies, eventually gaining a Master of Arts and achieving the office of Auditor of the Historical Society—the equivalent of President of the Union at Oxford and Cambridge. Such high office, together with acquired social graces, gave Stoker access to the cultural élite of Dublin society. Among his acquaintances were Sir William and Lady Wilde (parents of Oscar). They were both authorities on Irish folklore, and Sir William was a noted Egyptologist.[5] Bram's visits to him would help sow the seeds of one of his later novels, *The Jewel of Seven Stars*.

Bram inherited from his father a deep interest in the theatre, and lack of regular theatrical coverage in the Dublin press resulted in 1871 with his taking on the responsibilities of unpaid drama critic of the *Evening Mail*. He also found time to develop his short-story writing. The efforts of an unknown author in finding a publisher were as confidence-sapping then as now, but the breakthrough came in 1872 when *The London Society* published 'The Crystal Cup', a dream fantasy climaxing with the evil king 'pallid with the hue of Death'.[6]

Urging himself to new challenges, Stoker used his Dublin connections to become a newspaper editor (again unpaid and part-time). Dublin's new evening paper, *The Irish Echo*, could not, however, build up a sufficient circulation, not even with a change of name to *The Halfpenny Press*, and after four months he resigned the editorship.[7] Yet failure in one venture was countered by another writing success. Le Fanu's sophisticated vampire tale *Carmilla* appeared in the Dublin University Magazine. It was met with critical acclaim and made a deep impression on Stoker. More short stories followed, one of which heralded a significant departure from the light fantasy of his first. The four-part serialization of 'The Chain of Destiny', appearing in *The Shamrock* in 1875, was pure horror, mixed in with romance, nightmares and curses, and introducing the 'phantom of the fiend'.[8]

In the meantime, Bram's father had retired, and under financial pressure had taken his wife and daughters to the Continent, where the cost of living was easier to bear. Abraham senior continued to fret about his son's restlessness, counselling against his moving to London to try his hand at full-time authorship, as well as disparaging Bram's idea of applying for the post of Dublin city treasurer on the grounds that 'none but an advanced Liberal or a Roman Catholic would be elected'.[9]

This remark hints at the political and religious tensions operating in nineteenth-century Ireland — the suggestion being that the Stoker family were neither advanced Liberal nor Roman Catholic. It is known that they were Protestants, living in a land of Catholics. Trinity College was still at that time a Protestant university. The Stokers' political affiliations, however, are less clear. It is true that the Dublin Castle elect to which father and son aspired were steadfastly Tory,[10] but if Bram was at one time a Tory he became a Liberal later in life (becoming a member of the National Liberal Club). He was a political animal: his inaugural address as Auditor of the Trinity Historical Society had been on 'the necessity for political honesty' and a plea for a forerunner of the United Nations.[11] His memoirs of Henry Irving, written many years later, are peppered with his own political views, among them his support for Gladstone's attempts to introduce Home Rule — the failure of which would eventually split the Liberal Party. Stoker described himself as a 'philosophical Home-Ruler',[12] yet one who was opposed to the extra-Parliamentary activities being addressed by certain Irish agitators.

Stoker senior died in 1876 in Naples, with the knowledge that his son's security had not yet been tossed to the wind; but within months Bram would experience a chance encounter that would transform his life. It was in his Trinity days that Bram, a regular theatre-goer to Dublin's only sizeable auditorium, the Theatre Royal, first set eyes upon a rising actor destined to become the Olivier of his day. In this respect it was fortunate that Dublin could attract the major touring players. The young actor was Henry Irving, playing Captain Absolute in *The Rivals*. Stoker was then nineteen, Irving ten years older. The star-struck student was enraptured by the burgeoning talent before him.

Now, ten years later, on a further trip to Dublin, Irving played the lead role in *Hamlet*. Stoker was overwhelmed and conveyed his feelings to the Dublin public through his theatre column. This time it was the actor's turn to be impressed, inviting the critic backstage. During the course of several meetings that followed, a bond, personal and professional, was forged between the two men. Stoker was among a select group privy to a private recitation of Thomas Hood's *The Dream of Eugene Aram*, at the conclusion of which Irving slumped from the emotional effort, leaving Stoker to gape entranced by the actor's virtuosity: 'Here was incarnate power, incarnate passion ... Irving's genius floated in blazing truimph.' As for his own reaction, Stoker described this in a striking piece of autobiography:

I burst out into something like a violent fit of hysterics. Let me say, not in my own vindication, but to bring new tribute to Irving's splendid power, that I was no hysterical subject. I was no green youth; no weak individual, yielding to a superior emotional force. I was as men go a strong man, strong in many ways. [13]

Describing their mutual admiration, Stoker wrote: 'Soul had looked into soul. From that hour began a friendship as profound, as close, as lasting, as can be between two men.' They continued to meet regularly over the next two years; Stoker enjoying Irving's unique talents, the actor benefiting from Stoker's astute criticism. It seemed that Stoker's life was advancing in all directions. He had been promoted at work to become an Inspector of Petty Sessions, removing him from the monotony of his desk-bound existence and enabling him to tour the Dublin courts. The clerical muddles his visits unearthed prompted him to turn his hand to non-fiction, and he commenced work on a weighty tome which was finally published in 1879. It was Stoker's first full-length book, and bore the unlikely and unromantic title *The Duties of Clerks of Petty Sessions in Ireland*. 'Dry as dust' Stoker would later call it, [14] but it became a standard reference work in its field.

As if these labours were not keeping him busy enough, Stoker had also found time to woo his future wife. Nineteen-year-old Dublin beauty Florence Balcombe was already sufficiently eligible and mature to be able to number Oscar Wilde among her ex-suitors. [15] She and Bram planned to marry in 1879 but the date was brought forward at short notice. Henry Irving had taken over his own theatre company — the London Lyceum — but was dissatisfied with the incumbent management. He had already appointed a new stage manager, Harry Loveday, and in December 1878 approached Stoker to look after the business side of the new venture. Bram needed no second invitation to resign his lengthy stint in the civil service, forfeit his pension, move to London with his new wife, and plunge in at the deep end as Acting Manager of the Lyceum Theatre.

Abraham senior would not have approved his son's decision, and Charlotte was notably displeased. The acting 'profession' was widely throught of in those days as being socially disadvantageous.

When Bram had earlier written of his attachment to a certain actress, his father had replied that he did not think that actors and actresses 'are altogether desirable acquaintances to those not connected with their own profession (if I may call it) . . . Under all the circumstances I believe such acquaintanceship is better avoided.' Now, upon sacrificing all his security to throw in his lot with Irving, Charlotte scolded her son for becoming a 'minstrel to a strolling player'.[16]

Stoker's reputation, not to say his prosperity, was thereafter inextricably linked to the fortunes of Henry Irving. The actor would always be a controversial figure of the stage. Aside from his autocratic and egotistical temperament, the very principle of an actor simultaneously being a theatre manager rankled the critics (among them Bernard Shaw), who would complain of Irving ensuring that the talents of the Lyceum's supporting cast were transparently inferior to his own.[17]

For the moment, the newly-weds set up home in fashionable Cheyne Walk in Chelsea, and within a year Florence gave birth to Noel, their only son. The immediately succeeding years were probably the most absorbing and enjoyable of Stoker's life as, without any prior business experience, he threw himself into his new challenge. Such were his responsibilities — controlling a full-time staff well in excess of a hundred, grappling with the accounts of a new and precarious enterprise, and protecting Irving from those eager to exploit any association with him — that all thoughts of fiction writing were temporarily eclipsed.

Proximity to Henry Irving meant for Stoker acquaintance with the rich and famous. The 1880s-90s saw London's theatreland become the hub of high society, with the Lyceum the most glittering of places for the capital's well-to-do. Stoker became something of a celebrity snob: he could count among his neighbours the artist James McNeil Whistler and the novelist George Eliot. He would, by the end of his life, be introduced to no less than four American Presidents, as well as merit an entry in his own right in *Who's Who*.

Stoker had only been in London a couple of years when, through his widening network of contacts, the publishing firm of Sampson Low expressed interest in a collection of 'weirdies' — stories that Stoker had written over the years and which were gathering dust instead of royalties. As he still had no time for writing, this unexpected outlet for some of his past efforts brought the power of his literary imagination to general notice. *Under the Sunset*, as the anthology was called when published in 1881, was a far cry from the *The Duties of Clerks.*

Bram Stoker was not the first writer to perceive a market for children's stories. Lewis Carroll's Alice adventures, together with his *The Hunting of the Snark,* had appeared between 1865 and 1876, but Stoker's tales were altogether more bizarre and frightening for the younger reader. Liberally scattered with lurid illustrations from William Fitzgerald and W. V. Cockburn, the book was a sequence of allegories about a mysterious land far, far away — a land 'under the sunset'.

Although each of the constituent tales is self-contained, they all concern themselves with repeated motifs: familial love; the division of the world into Good and Evil; the horrendous punishments meted out to those who sin; the inevitable triumph of Good; and the mysterious boundary between life and death. The oppressive moralizing that pervades them all was a feature common to many nineteenth-century fairy tales, and even the barbarous cruelty that Stoker gratuitously describes was not out of keeping with the mainstream of the genre. It is frequently forgotten how gruesome are the actual conclusions of a number of popular fairy tales: Cinderella's stepsisters being rendered blind and crippled; and Snow White's stepmother being forced to dance to her death in red-hot slippers.[18]

Nonetheless, the overall package was a triumph of imagination, and at that level was well received by the critics. 'Charming', said *Punch.*[19] 'Delicate and forceful allegories', agreed the *Daily Telegraph,* while others noted the book's 'dreamy beauty of style' and its 'remarkable purity and grace'. The *Spectator* noted: '*Under the Sunset* may be tried with the grown-up world with perfect success. To its intellectual and critical perception, the literal charm of the stories . . . will commend themselves highly.'[20] On another level, however, that of suitability for infants, there were far sterner reservations:

> The judicious mother may prefer to omit some of the . . . dismal doings which might banish sleep from the children's pillows . . . A terribly grim picture . . . might haunt any little one's imagination for many a night; while the words . . . are . . . decidedly 'creepy'.
>
> We can quite believe that this sort of picture may have a kind of fascination for young readers, but we very much doubt whether it is well to subject them to it, and could therefore wish that these lurid passages had been expunged from a book which in many respects is very pleasing.[21]

At the very least, Bram Stoker's fiction writing talent had now been publicly appreciated, and only lack of time and opportunity prevented any sequel as he revelled in the world of theatre management and mixed with society's élite.

In September 1882, an incident occurred which revealed two sides to Stoker's character. Whilst travelling down the Thames on a steamboat, a would-be suicide jumped overboard. Stoker leapt after him, and despite struggling against a strong tide and against the man's wish to die, managed to haul him back on board. Efforts at resuscitation failed, whereupon Stoker took the apparent corpse back to his Chelsea home and laid it out in the dining room, in front of a horrified Florence, until such time as a doctor could come and finally pronounce death. [22] For his extraordinary bravery Stoker was praised at the inquest and later awarded the Bronze Medal of the Royal Humane Society: but his morbid displaying of a corpse in his home put an extra strain on his four-year marriage. His nocturnal existence — much of his work at the Lyceum was done in the early hours following the final curtain fall — and his natural preference for male company, meant that his wife and son saw little of him.

The evidence is hazy, but there is more than a suggestion of marital estrangement after the first happy months. Certainly the couple were to be separated for long stretches, as when Irving decided to take his entire company on a six-month tour of North America — crossing the Atlantic complete with scenery and equipment, an unprecedented undertaking in theatre history. In addition to the major American cities of the east coast, performances were given as far inland as Chicago, St Louis and Cincinnati, as well as in Toronto, Canada. Irving was a famous name in America even before he arrived, and the tour was such a success that it would be repeated at regular intervals for the next twenty years. A second tour left England in September 1884, just five months after returning from the first, and this time it would result in another Bram Stoker publication.

The United States made a considerable impression on Irving's acting manager, who was painfully aware of British ignorance of everything American. There existed at the time no balanced instructive source of general information for a British public contemptuously prejudiced against her ex-colony. Stoker set to work, and on his return to Britain delivered a lecture in December 1885 to the London Institution entitled 'A Glimpse of America', which was published the following year.

Stoker extolled almost everything to do with the United States, whether it be her constitution, her education system, her fire-fighting service, her workmen, good manners, hospitality, practical spirit, sense of humour, or tolerance. He admired American fire-fighters, and held them up as exhibiting that 'calm coolness that marks the brave'.[23] Against this, his confessed admiration for America's apparent lack of class consciousness must be treated lightly, for it is abundantly clear from his reminiscences and his later fiction that Stoker was highly class conscious. To all intents he was a model, upright Victorian gentleman, imbued with all the prejudices of his station — a station granted by God. One example of his social prejudices is discernible on the occasion of one of Irving's Dublin visits. The two men came across an organized street fight. Stoker later wrote: 'We saw the gathering crowd and joined them. They did not know either of us, but they saw we were gentlemen, strangers to themselves, and with the universal courtesy of their race put us in the front . . .' Elsewhere his language bordered on the extreme: 'An individual who is not in any way distinguishable from his fellows is but a poor creature after all and is not held of much account by anybody.'[24] He reserved his most ferocious tirade for America's tramps and criminal elements: 'The criminal classes are the same the world over, only they would molest a woman . . . tramps and other excretions of civilisation . . . a percentage of incurable drones . . . they form a dangerous element.'[25] Towards the end of his life Stoker proposed his own solution to the American tramp problem: it was to 'brand' them, preferably about the ears, so that they could be readily identified, sent to a labour colony, and taught the virtues of hard work to which he had ascribed all his life.[26]

Even with her occasional blemishes, America was still a land of which Stoker was proud, and he concludes his glimpse in positive fashion. It was a 'joy that England's first born child has arrived at so noble a stature . . . We have not, all the world through, so strong an ally, so close a friend . . . America has got over her childhood. Our history is their history, they are bound to us, and we to them.'[27] Praise for Stoker's little book would come from many, including the explorer Henry Morton Stanley, who carried it on one of his African expeditions and later confessed that it contained more information about America than any other book.[28]

*A Glimpse of America* illustrated much more than simply Stoker's admiration for that country and his contempt for society's misfits and outcasts. It also underlined his obsessive view of women, which was one of the prime shapers of his character. He praised the American 'high regard with which women are held . . . and the deferential and protective spirit afforded to them'[29] — such as inviting them to jump queues. On a later occasion, when a fire broke out on stage and one of the audience bolted for the exits, he was seized by the throat and hurled to the floor by Stoker, who then demanded he return to his seat, adding: 'It is cowards like you who cause death to helpless women.'[30]

A more detailed look at Stoker's attitude towards women will be postponed for later consideration, though the following remark made of actress Ellen Terry (whose beauty is commented upon in *Dracula* [*D* 13:213]), is typical: 'Doubtless she has her faults. She is a woman; and perfection must not be expected even in the finishing work of creation.'[31] To Stoker, women were hopelessly dependent upon the valour of strong men. Following a storm at sea he wrote: 'In such cases the only real comfort a poor woman can have is to hold on to a man. I happen to be a big one, and therefore of extra desirability in such cases of stress.'[32] Evidently any woman who was not a cowering wreck was not truly a woman.

In the company of his own sex Stoker was quick to appreciate strength of character. For instance, during his early trips to America he fulfilled a Trinity ambition and was introduced to the ageing poet Walt Whitman. His observation of that poignant moment is striking: 'I found him [Whitman] all that I had ever dreamed of, or wished for in him: large-minded, broad-viewed, tolerant to the last degree, incarnate sympathy, understanding with an insight that seemed more than human . . . A man amongst men.'[33] His reminiscences of Irving are likewise saturated with hero-worship, nowhere permitting his subject to be criticized, let alone ridiculed. Stoker viewed his employer with a mixture of worship and fear: it is not stretching the point to say that he was, at heart, married to Irving, not Florence.

This idealized, almost boyish, guileless appreciation of strong men can be detected all through his memoirs. So can his preoccupation with describing striking facial features, especially the mouth and teeth. Of Lord Tennyson, who became a close acquaintance (and who would receive a signed copy of *Dracula*), he noted: 'Tennyson had at times that lifting of the upper lip which shows the canine tooth.' And Sir Richard Burton, the intrepid Oriental explorer/scholar, he described in the following remarkable language: 'The man riveted my attention. He was dark, and forceful, and masterful, and ruthless. I have never seen so iron a countenance

... Burton's face seemed to lengthen when he laughed; the upper lip rising instinctively and showing the right canine tooth ... As he spoke the upper lip rose and his canine tooth showed its full length like the gleam of a dagger.'[34] Evidently Stoker would experience no difficulty when he later came to describe vampires.

By 1888 — having completed ten years with Irving and undertaken three tours of the United States — Stoker began to feel the need to widen his personal horizons. He already had a strong legal background, derived both from his time in Dublin Castle and from handling the legal matters of the Lyceum. Now he found the necessary hours to study for the Bar, being called to the Inner Temple in 1890. He also made time to write his first romantic novel. Set in Ireland and full of Irish brogue and customs, *The Snake's Pass* (1890) concerned a wealthy young Englishman who finds himself caught up in the bogs while on a quest for lost gold. As with Stoker's previous writings, *The Snake's Pass* was highly applauded by the critics, even winning praise from Tennyson and Gladstone[35] — the latter a frequent Lyceum visitor. As if to confirm Stoker's arrival as a major Irish novelist, an episode from the book called 'The Gombeen Man' (an Irish Money Lender) would later win a place in a collection of classic works from Irish authors and poets.[36]

Enjoying the flush of recognition, Stoker was already making notes for a massive novel on a vampire theme, but these notes were progressing slowly and did not impede the output of other works. The direction that much of his future fiction would take was affected by his discovery, while holidaying alone in 1893, of Cruden Bay, situated between Aberdeen and Peterhead on the Buchan coastline of north-east Scotland. Cruden Bay is a picturesque inlet surrounded by towering cliffs upon which stands Slains Castle, inhabited since the thirteenth century by the Earls of Erroll.[37] Stretching across the mouth of the bay lies the Skares reef, one of the most savage and merciless destroyers of ships to be found anywhere on the British coastline. The visual effect of the area on Stoker must have been profound, for he would return every summer, occupying rooms at the Kilmarnock Arms Hotel until eventually taking a small summer cottage in the hamlet of Whinnyfold on the southern lip of the bay.

Immediately after his first visit to Cruden, Stoker — now in his late forties — departed on another six-month Lyceum tour of America, but his pen was already beginning to turn out a succession of novels and short stories, many of them staged in, or inspired by, Cruden Bay. One such story was 'The Man from Shorrox's'

(1894), a light-hearted, droll tale about a sales traveller asked to
share a bed in an inn with a corpse. 'Crooken Sands' (1894), set
in a thinly disguised Cruden Bay, tells of a London merchant on
holiday who kits himself out in full highland regalia and casts eyes
upon his own image being sucked down under quicksand. Two
other short stories dating from the same period were even more
horrific. 'The Burial of the Rats', set among the garbage heaps
of a Paris suburb, and 'The Squaw', a euphemistically-named iron
torture chamber which claims its victim through the wiles of a black
cat, clearly showed the direction in which Stoker's literary talents
would most profit.

The short novel *The Watter's Mou* (1894-5) (Buchan dialect for
'The Water's Mouth'), centred around a deep, narrow gorge running
into the North Sea just to the north of Cruden Bay, serene on
occasions, tempestuous on others. This romance features two lovers,
Maggie and Sailor Willy, who found themselves involved in
smuggling and shipwrecks; but it brought a rare experience to Stoker
at that time, earning indifferent reviews on account of its excessive
melodrama and 'stagey' writing.[38] But no sooner was it published
than its successor appeared. *The Shoulder of Shasta* (1895) was
another torrid romance, written in the wake of the Lyceum's
performances in California during the 1893-4 tour. It concerned
the love of a frail young city girl for Grizzly Dick, a husky mountain
man living on Shasta, an extinct volcano in northern California.
This time the critics were merciless: *The Athenaeum*, for instance,
castigated the book for its lack of maturity, its haste, poor humour,
weakness of plot, and lack of characterization.[39] Nothing Stoker
had previously written had been so maligned. An author of
acknowledged potential was now in danger of ridicule.

Whether or not Stoker took any notice is not known, and in
any case it was too late, because he was deep into the writing of
*Dracula*, which was published by Constable in June 1897. The novel
was sufficiently broad in panorama to please (or displease) a wide
cross-section of the 1890s reading public, which was still receptive
to works on the occult, adventure, detection, and high romance.
Many critics have concurred that had *Dracula* been written at the
beginning, not the end, of the nineteenth century its impact would
have been far greater. It was less likely to succeed in an intellectual
climate of scientific rationalism and scepticism. Moreover, *Dracula*
was not set, as with mainstream Gothic romance, in a far-off land
in a far-off time: it was here and now — a vampire stalking the
streets of late-Victorian London.

Critical response was mixed. The *Daily Mail* compared it favourably with Mrs Radcliffe's *The Mysteries of Udolpho*, Mary Shelley's *Frankenstein*, Emily Brontë's *Wuthering Heights*, and Poe's *The Fall of the House of Usher*. The *Pall Mall Gazette* thought it 'excellent', and *The Lady* admitted that the book was so fascinating that it was impossible to put it down.[40] Other reviewers were more equivocal. *The Bookman* conceded that:

A summary of the book would shock and disgust, but we must own that, though here and there in the course of the tale we hurried over things with repulsion, we read nearly the whole with rapt attention. It is something of a triumph for the writer that neither the improbability, nor the unnecessary number of hideous incidents recounted of the man-vampire are long foremost in the reader's mind, but that the interest of the danger, of the complications, of the pursuit of the villain, of human skill and courage pitted against inhuman wrong and superhuman strength, rises always to the top.[41]

*Punch*, too, saw flaws as well as virtues:

It is a pity that Mr. BRAM STOKER was not content to employ such supernatural anti-vampire receipts as his wildest imagination might have invented without rashly venturing on a domain where angels fear to tread. But for this, [the reviewer] could have unreservedly recommended so ingenious a romance to all who enjoy the very weirdest of weird tales.[42]

Other reviewers could find few redeeming features. *The Athenaeum* once again emerged with all guns blazing. *Dracula* it assessed as being highly sensational but the novel was 'wanting in the constructive art as well as in the higher literary sense. It reads at times like a mere series of grotesquely incredible events . . . he merely commands an array of crude statements of incredible actions.' Even the summary was grudgingly given: 'his object, assuming it to be ghastliness, is fairly well fulfilled.'[43]

The most glowing response of all came from Stoker's mother: 'It is splendid, a thousand miles beyond anything you have written before, and I feel certain will place you very high in the writers of the day . . . No book since Mrs Shelley's "Frankenstein" or indeed any other at all has come near yours in originality, or terror — Poe is nowhere. I have read much but I have never met a book like it at all. In its terrible excitement it should make a widespread reputation and much money for you.'[44] In the event, it did neither.

Stoker's final book to be written in this intense phase reverted to the slush sentimentalism to which he was regrettably prone; a tear-jerker full of romance, honour, and the unquestioning acceptance of fragile womanhood. *Miss Betty* (1898) — dedicated to his wife, Florence — is today deservedly forgotten. He wrote no other books during the following few years, and for this gap account should be taken of a series of setbacks for Henry Irving's theatre company. Stoker's *Dracula*, which marked the crowning achievement of its author's fiction, coincided with the beginning of the Lyceum's slide. In 1895, as the novel was taking final shape, both Stoker's family and employer had been honoured. His elder, surgeon brother, William, was knighted, and so too was Henry Irving — the first actor to be so decorated. This honour brought tribute to the entire acting profession, establishing the precedent that would later enable Laurence Olivier to be made a peer.

Ironically, troubles then escalated for Henry Irving. At the end of 1896 he slipped down some stairs, injured his leg, and was compelled to close the theatre for a number of weeks. In February 1898 worse disaster struck when the Lyceum storehouse was consumed by fire, destroying two thousand items of scenery and stage props. The entire repertory paraphernalia of the company was lost. Total damage was estimated at £60,000, but insurance cover had been reduced to only one tenth that figure. Coming on top of a recent drop in audience figures and the emergence of flourishing rival theatre companies, the fire reduced the Lyceum's finances to disarray. Before the year was out Irving succumbed to pneumonia and pleurisy, and the management of the Lyceum was sold, much against Stoker's advice, to a syndicate (which would later collapse). By this time even Stoker's own trusted position was becoming precarious. Irving hired the services of a press agent, without consulting Stoker, and a close working relationship of twenty years standing was superseded by a perceptible rift between actor and manager. [45]

There are many indications that Stoker jealously guarded against intrusion into his close relationship with Irving. As for his deeper responsibility for the fortunes of the Lyceum, other biographers of the actor are either dismissive or contemptuous of Stoker. In a two-volume biography of Irving, the press agent in question, Austin Brereton, scarcely mentions Stoker by name; and the actor's grandson, Laurence, offered the following damning personal assessment. Stoker was:

> inflated with literary and athletic pretensions [and] worshipped Irving with all the sentimental idolatry of which an Irishman is

capable, revelling in the patronage which, as Irving's manager, was at his disposal, and in the opportunities which this position gave him to rub shoulders with the great ... This weakness and his emotional impetuosity handicapped him in dealing with Irving's business affairs in a forthright and sensible manner ... Stoker, well-intentioned, vain, impulsive and inclined to blarneying flattery was perhaps the only man who could have held his position as Irving's manager for so many years; from him Irving got the service he deserved, but at a cost which was no less fatal because it was not immediately apparent.[46]

From 1900 Stoker had to contend not only with an ailing Lyceum, but also with the loss of his fiction's greatest enthusiast, when his mother died in Dublin. As his stories once more began to roll, it was again to Cruden Bay that he turned for inspiration. *The Mystery of the Sea* (1902) features Gaelic runes, ancient manuscripts in cryptic writing, hidden treasures, secret agents, castles with hidden passageways, shipwrecks on the Cruden skares, and even a futuristic naval gun battle. As always, there would be the predictable romantic element; blushing heroines and the importance of male valour.

By the time *Mystery* was published the Lyceum syndicate had folded and Irving had become an actor without a theatre, having to turn to provincial tours and spells in other London auditoriums. Stoker sought relief from these pressures with his next novel. *The Jewel of Seven Stars* (1903) was indebted to those discussions on Egyptology with Sir William Wilde held way back in Stoker's Dublin days. As with *Dracula*, in *The Jewel* Stoker brought a foreign-based tale to England, constructing it around mummies, witchcraft, and an Egyptian queen intending to resurrect herself five thousand years after her death. Later editions would contain a less traumatic climax, at the publisher's request.[47]

The grand old Lyceum reopened as a music hall, and as if to bow to the changing cultural patterns of British life, Irving, now in his late sixties, decided to embark upon a two-year grand tour of retirement, taking in Britain and North America. The scheduled farewell was never completed: Irving collapsed and died at Bradford in October 1905, and his remains were laid to rest in Westminster Abbey. Bram Stoker, approaching his fifty-eighth birthday, was now without a regular source of income for the first time in his adult life. Without the spark provided by Irving, he was also rudderless. He made an attempt to look after the business interests of an American opera singer, but the venture collapsed, as did a proposed lecture tour. His pen would now provide his sole revenue for the rest of his days. The earlier torrent of books had partly coincided with the discovery of Cruden Bay: his final rush of publications would be prompted by sheer survival.

*The Man* (1905) was actually written before Irving's death, though after his decision to retire, and, in the light of the higher things promised in *The Jewel*, was an unwelcome return to naïve romance. There followed his two volumes of *Personal Reminiscences of Henry Irving* (1906), consisting of a catalogue of impressions and incidents dating from the time Stoker met the actor until the latter's death. It is not a biography as such, for there was no attempt at a calm, detached appraisal of his subject, just unabashed adulation.

Bram Stoker was still sufficiently involved in high society to be invited to the wedding of Winston Churchill in 1906, but his failing health (he had a stroke following Irving's death, suffered from Bright's disease, and was losing his sight), coupled with financial insecurity, made his final years less than happy ones. Of the novels to come, *Lady Athlyne* and the theatrical tales in *Snowbound* (both 1908) were rushed, hack works that could not raise his fallen literary reputation. He then turned his hand to a final work of non-fiction. In *Famous Imposters* (1910), Stoker rambled through the great impersonators, hoaxers, and swindlers of history. In it he demonstrated his familiarity with the great myths of romantic literature: he includes a chapter on the Wandering Jew, together with others on the practitioners of magic, witchcraft, and clairvoyancy.

For an author inextricably associated with literary terror, it should be remembered that only four of his final tally of eighteen books were novels on the supernatural: to *Dracula* and *The Jewel of Seven Stars* were added in his last years *The Lady of the Shroud* (1909) and *The Lair of the White Worm* (1911). *The Lady of the Shroud* dealt with an apparent she-vampire who turned out to be playing at deception. It is perhaps most intriguing for its conclusion, which contains a prophetic air battle, written just months after the Wright brothers had made their inaugural flight. *The Lair of the White Worm* would be Stoker's last and most disturbing novel, based on the ancient British legend that giant serpents/worms once dominated the landscape. He resurrected one such worm, gave it human, feminine form, and housed it in a slimy, subterranean cave.

The White Worm was riddled with hallucinatory and sexual imagery, and was clearly the work of a sick man. Nonetheless, it still gave insights into its author's extraordinary imagination, and for that, if nothing else, the book was charitably received by reviewers. But Stoker, the one-time athletics champion, was now bed-ridden as in his infancy. He died on 20 April 1912 at 26 St George's Square, London, at the age of sixty-four, when *Dracula* was in its ninth edition. He was cremated at Golders Green, north London. It was somehow typical of the man that his death, as his life, should be overshadowed. Just five days previously the *Titanic* had sunk. In the shocked and numbed aftermath no one could be expected to pay much attention to the deceased theatre manager and part-time author, particularly as he chose to die on the opening day of the American enquiry into the disaster. Only one obituary appeared, but it was where Stoker would have wanted it — in *The Times*. In those days Stoker was still principally associated with Irving, though *The Times* conceded that 'he was the master of a particularly lurid and creepy kind of fiction'.[48]

One more volume of Stoker fiction remained to be published, posthumously. He had died while sifting through piles of his earlier short stories in the hope of assembling a suitable anthology. This task was completed by his widow, and the compendium was released in 1914. It was named after one particular tale: a short, self-contained incident entitled 'Dracula's Guest'. As for Stoker, himself, he would be consigned to historical oblivion. Even though his creation, *Dracula*, is familiar throughout the world, it is still difficult to find any general encyclopaedia with an entry under 'Bram Stoker'.

Bram Stoker — civil servant, drama critic, theatre manager, barrister, author — was inescapably a man of his time, a Victorian gentleman for whom good manners, proper decorum, and a chivalric attitude towards women were prime forces in character development. Even so, those of his writings which touch on questions of morality reveal a certain prickliness and brittleness. He may have been the owner of a strong physique, but he does not come over as a strong character, and there are numerous indications of how his life was shaped or modified by those stronger than he: his mother, Henry Irving, and the countless celebrities of whom he wrote like an awe-struck adolescent. If subjectivity be permitted, then examination of his eyes in the few surviving photographs of him suggest a vulnerability, a far-off frightened look. This adds to the complexity of the man, known to be bluff and hearty in male company, and who obviously did not lack physical courage.

With so little surviving incontrovertible evidence pertaining to his life, it is perhaps inevitable that half-truths, rumour, and gossip should circulate to fill the gaps. The most controversial new 'information' to emerge was put forward in Farson's biography. Stoker's death certificate reads 'Locomotor Ataxy 6 months Granular Contracted Kidney. Exhaustion'.[49] Farson equates this unequivocally with tertiary syphilis. Such a revelation of course, if correct, could transform the whole moral perspective of Stoker's life. It is said that he and Florence did not enjoy a close marriage, that she became frigid after the birth of their son, and that he had to seek satisfaction elsewhere. Farson does not blanch over Stoker's reputation as a womanizer.[50] Certainly, if that was the case, he would have found no shortage of opportunity. Work for the Lyceum took him to all the fleshpots of Europe and America, and even in Victorian Britain there would have been the equivalent of the modern 'groupie': young impressionable girls offering Stoker physical favours in return for access to their stage idol.

This is not to say that he took advantage of them. This kind of speculation is dependent on the validity of Farson's assertion, which is, in fact, far from proven. The brief words on the death certificate, while consistent with syphilis, do not rule out any alternative cause of death — although the seeming vagueness and ambiguity of the wording was typical of that used to refer to certain sexually transmitted diseases (syphilis was then virtually an unmentionable term, particularly for someone from the respectable middle classes, for its use was bound to bring shame and dishonour upon the family of the afflicted).

Leaving aside Bram Stoker the man, there is also the question of assessing Bram Stoker the author. No one would claim that he was a 'great' writer. He was an author of extremes, veering from sentimental romances which make the modern reader squirm, to exploration of supernatural themes which were always on a higher plane. It should not be overlooked that Stoker was a part-time writer — save in his last years when he was already terminally ill — who crammed in his books in whatever spare minutes he could find. He was never given the luxury of time in which to eradicate the haste so often apparent in his works. However, a writer ought not to be judged by style alone. In Stoker's case, his principal literary attribute was a quite exceptional imagination, and in *Dracula* this vision was harnessed to immense power of presentation.

How does one assess an athlete who never rises above the second rate, but then quite unexpectedly shatters the world record, only to succumb to mediocrity again? Such is the difficulty in assessing

Bram Stoker, a hack writer who in one solitary work wrote as if inspired. It is now time to examine how *Dracula* came to be written.

# 5.

# THE ORIGINS OF *DRACULA*

Having some time at my disposal when in London, I had visited the British Museum, and made search among the books and maps in the library regarding Transylvania; it had struck me that some foreknowledge of the country could hardly fail to have some importance in dealing with a noble of that country. I find that the district he named is in the extreme east of the country, just on the borders of three states, Transylvania, Moldavia, and Bukovina, in the midst of the Carpathian mountains; one of the wildest and least known portions of Europe.

Jonathan Harker's Journal, *Dracula* 1:9-10.

I N VIEW of the paucity of detailed information that exists concerning Bram Stoker's life, a satisfactory account of how and why *Dracula* came to be written is still lacking. Some of the more speculative literary and psychological influences on the author will be postponed for discussion in later chapters: here we will be concerned with surveying the more direct contributory factors — his background, acquaintances, and known researches.

Of course, Stoker had the entire Gaelic tradition of folklore to call upon, for Ireland is one of the most superstition-ridden lands in Europe. Its geographical position on the western extremity of the continent has given it a unique heritage. Because Ireland escaped conquest by the Romans, the classical imprint so evident in the mythology found elsewhere in Europe is absent; yet, like the ripple effect on a pond, those Continental myths that did filter through to Ireland continued to circulate long after their disappearance from their points of origin. These European influences both merged with, and existed independently of, the indigenous Irish folk tradition, and the consequent richness and diversity of modern Gaelic superstition has acted as inspiration to many Irish authors.

In Stoker's case, he had availed himself of the fund of folk tales collected by Sir William and Lady Wilde, both of whom published major anthologies on Irish folklore.[1] Above all, his mother had provided an early and possibly determining stimulus to Stoker's fiction, and her graphic written description of the 1832 Sligo cholera epidemic[2] (highlighting cases of premature burial and the deadly suspicion of strangers) had directly inspired one of his fairy tales. 'The Invisible Giant', from *Under the Sunset*, told of a young girl who sees in the sky beyond the city 'a vast shadowy Form, with its arms raised. It was shrouded in a great misty robe that covered it, fading away into air so that she could only see the face and the grim, spectral hands . . . the face was as that of a strong man, pitiless, yet without malice; and . . . the eyes were blind.'[3] A second tale from the collection can likewise be seen to anticipate *Dracula*. 'The Castle of the King' relates a young poet's quest to find his beloved, who has apparently died in a strange castle. This quest is obstructed by various horrors, until the hero finally arrives at the castle — huge, dead, and shrouded in mist.[4]

Although from a Protestant family himself, Stoker's homeland was, of course, overwhelmingly Catholic; and it is a feature of Catholic lands across Europe that they are more likely to sustain belief in vampires than are Protestant regions. The vampire is almost as entrenched in the folklore of Ireland as it is in that of the Continent, though divested of most of its usual macabre manifestations. The Dearg-due (the red bloodsucker) of ancient Ireland was reputed to use her beauty to tempt passing men and then suck their blood. Similarly, the Leanhaun Shee (the fairy mistress) was supposedly an eye-catching fairy whose charms were irresistible to men. Energy would be drawn from the ensnared male until he eventually wasted away, or else procured an alternative victim to take his place.[5] In general, Irish fairies were presumed to be bloodless, and their abduction of humans was assumed to be designed to remedy that deficiency.[6]

It is possible to discern other, non-vampire, elements from Irish folk superstition in *Dracula*. The devil, for instance, to whom the Count is related, is traditionally in Irish lore depicted in human guise — as opposed to the grotesque animalistic representations found elsewhere in Europe, or the spirit form familiar to the East. The devil in Irish tradition is also able to adopt feminine form and assume the role of temptress, but despite his awesome powers he can nevertheless be outwitted.[7]

Children would often be stolen by the Irish spirit world, with 'changelings' (deformed or senile fairies) left disguised in their place.

Changelings, as with vampires, are said to be vulnerable to fire or water. Any children who had not been baptized ran an increased risk of abduction by the spirit world.

Certain Irish fairies are gregarious. Others are solitary beings, for instance the leprechaun and the cluricane — the latter feared for its cunning and reputed ability to escape if discovered by becoming invisible. The Dullahan is variously conceived of as a headless ghost at the reins of a Death Coach which appears at midnight, or, alternatively, a black coach drawn by headless horses; but whichever guise it takes, the Dullahan portends death.[8]

The bitter-sweet, tingling music of seduction with which Stoker arms his vampire ladies might have been suggested by the 'banshee', the indecipherable yet distinctly female wailing which signals an impending death. Stoker's vampires are also capable of transformation into phosphorescent specks, like the other Irish omens of death, the Water Sheeries — the souls of those who have been refused permission to enter either Heaven or Hell. They frequent churchyards, can appear if they choose as dancing flames, and can be repelled with a crucifix.[9] Evil spirits are thought to be capable of being confined in, or passing through, narrow interstices, and certain plants or herbs — notably the rowan (mountain ash) — are widely held to offer protection to the bearer against the fairy world.

One specific instance of Irish lore discernible in *Dracula* concerns the climax to the novel. The Count is destroyed on 6 November. In Ireland the feast of St Martin is celebrated on the 11th of that month, and it is the custom for blood to be shed either on St Martin's Eve or earlier — during the nine-day interval following Hallowe'en. If St Martin fails to receive his blood sacrifice in that timespan the neglectful family can expect ill luck in the year ahead.[10] Dracula's destruction, occurring when it does, thereby fulfils the hunters' obligation to St Martin.

As well as his Irish heritage, Stoker was well versed in Gothic/Romantic literature. Among the myths which can be recognized in the character of Dracula are those of Faust and the Wandering Jew — who insulted Christ while making his way to Calvary and who was condemned to wander the earth until Christ's second coming. Stoker's compatriot, Charles Maturin, had utilized this myth in *Melmoth the Wanderer* (1820). Melmoth was condemned to everlasting life for signing a pact with the devil which had granted him eternal youth. Dracula, however, not only *could* not die, he *would* not die. In this, he resembles Faust, and overall

*Dracula* provides a curious blend of these two myths, together with those of the Flying Dutchman and the Demon Lover.[11]

The literary precursors of *Dracula* have already been discussed, but it can be seen that Stoker was also aware of, and drew upon, the works of contemporary writers. Stevenson's *Dr Jekyll and Mr Hyde* (1886) reworked the Doppelgänger motif with considerable dexterity, and Stoker would also utilize the 'split personality' theme. Stevenson, like Stoker, wrapped his weird tale in late Victorian Britain, and wove detective work throughout the narrative. Again, it is notable that Dr Jekyll did not want to be evil — he could not help himself — a feature observable in Count Dracula.

Five years later Stoker's fellow Dubliner and former suitor of Florence, Oscar Wilde, wrote *The Picture of Dorian Gray* (1891), in which Dorian, like Jekyll, leads a double life — one respectable, the other soaked in sin. The core of *Dorian Gray* is the search for immortality: the hero does not age, instead his portrait is left to bear the deterioration resulting from his sinful existence — a theme mirrored in Dracula's progression towards youthfulness. Dorian becomes entranced by the notion of blood sacrifice: he preys on the energies of the innocent, and ultimately stabs the artist in the neck and the painting through the heart in order to gain release from his torment.[12] Critics have read into *Dorian* just about every favourite Victorian myth — including Faust, Mephistopheles, and Narcissus — and a biographer of Wilde has observed that *Dorian* is 'from one of the sources of the Dracula myth'.[13]

Yet it is necessary to return to an earlier work for the most profound literary influence upon *Dracula*. One of the nineteenth century's most popular novels, Wilkie Collins' *The Woman in White* (1860), can be seen imprinted on *Dracula* at two levels. The most obvious is the similar epistolary style. Collins had noticed how, during a court trial, each witness contributed a separate piece of information in a succession of evidence. Each testimony might vary considerably yet still be directed towards a common cause. Most important of all, interest was maintained in the public by this constant switching of point of focus.[14] Collins adapted this court-room experience to his novel. The omnipresent first or third person narrator was dispensed with, and substituted by a multiplicity of perspective. Stoker made use of the same device in *Dracula*, relating the tale through a compendium of diary entries, letters, ship's logs, newspaper reports, and spoken testimony recorded on to a phonograph. This technique permitted greater authenticity: an isolated individual's account of vampires might be dismissed as hallucinatory; but not the accounts of the entire cast, proffered independently.

Collins' influence, however, goes beyond that of narrative structure: there are also strong similarities in the story-line and the *dramatis personae*. [15] The principal villain of each work is a Count — Fosco in one, Dracula in the other. Both are endowed with personal magnetism and telepathic powers, rendering their victims' reactions ambivalent; both share an affinity with the animal world; and both are introduced to the reader solely through the impressions given by the mainstream characters. Furthermore, both novels see a young hero embarking on a wild adventure, climaxed by a child becoming heir apparent to the collected piles of written evidence. As for particular scenes, 'graveyards, insane asylums, dreary mansions, old chapels, zoological gardens, spectral trysts and moonlight nocturnes' feature in both novels [16] — while Stoker adapts to his own purposes Collins' scene in which children are attracted to a beautiful lady in a cemetery.

Relevant works of non-fiction also came to Stoker's notice. In 1890 there appeared Sir George Frazer's *The Golden Bough*, an encyclopaedic excursion through the taboos and superstitions of man, including a detailed account of the vampire myth. The real world, too, could not escape reports of vampire attack. In the autumn of 1888, in panic-stricken London, the following passage appeared in the *East London Advertiser:*

> It is so impossible to account, on any ordinary hypothesis, for these revolting acts of blood that the mind turns as it were instinctively to some theory of occult force, and the myths of the Dark Ages arise before the imagination. Ghouls, vampires, blood suckers . . . take form and seize control of the excited fancy. [17]

This extract demonstrates the facility with which any unexplained blood-shedding could be put down to vampire visitation. The source of these 'vampire' attacks in Victorian London? — the activities of Jack the Ripper!

There were also personal contacts for Stoker to draw on. His long-time friend Hall Caine — to whom *Dracula* is dedicated ('To my dear friend Hommy Beg', Caine's Manx nickname) — was one of Stoker's most potent sources of supernatural stimulation. Caine, a renowned novelist, was steeped in the folklore of his Isle of Man homeland, and he, Irving, and Stoker would while away many a night in earnest discussion of other-worldly topics. It has even been claimed that Stoker was a member of the occult Hermetic Order of The Golden Dawn, whose ranks included W. B. Yeats. In fact, there is no evidence for this whatsoever, [18] though Stoker was an acquaintance of J. W. Brodie-Innes, who invited him on at least one occasion to a gathering of the 'Sette of Odd Volumes' (a bibliographical society) which discussed occult ideas. [19]

Richard Burton was also doubtless influential. He and Stoker exchanged tales of myths and legends during their infrequent meetings between 1878 and 1886. [20] It was during their last recorded meeting (when Stoker had noted his visitor's sharp canine teeth) that the conversation turned to the *Arabian Nights*, which had just been published and which featured its own vampire character. Stoker would mention the *Arabian Nights* in *Dracula* (D 3:42), but it would seem probable that Burton's greatest legacy for Stoker was an anthology of Indian vampire stories — *Vikram and the Vampire* — which he had translated, and which delved into the ancient origins of the undead.

One other of Stoker's known acquaintances is worthy of mention. Among his London neighbours was the celebrated poet and artist Dante Gabriel Rosetti. Rosetti's wife, Elizabeth Siddal, had died in 1862 from an overdose of laudanum and had been buried in Highgate cemetery, with a volume of poems that her husband had written to her carefully wrapped in her long golden tresses. Seven years later he wanted them back, and friends exhumed the body by firelight one autumn evening in 1869. The corpse was almost perfectly preserved, and the golden red hair almost filled the coffin. [21] It is known that Stoker was deeply impressed by this episode: he would adapt it for one of his short stories, 'The Secret of the Growing Gold', and certain cemetery scenes in *Dracula* would be modelled upon it.

As for more direct incentives for Stoker to write *Dracula*, a number of commentators have relayed, parrot fashion, Ludlam's suggestion (itself offered tongue-in-cheek) that in 1895 Stoker had a bad dream following 'a too generous helping of dressed crab at supper'. [22] As an explanation of *Dracula*'s origins this will hardly suffice, not merely because it was an apocryphal remark, but, more damagingly, because Stoker had already been at work on the novel for at least five years before the dream was supposed to have occurred.

Other commentators have put forward the names of Stoker's mother and his cold, 'lifeless' wife as possible dominating figures who found their way into the omnipotent character of the Count.

More plausible is Stoker's relationship with the theatre and with Henry Irving. It must not be overlooked that on the subject of dramatic art Stoker was a professional: an astute critic and confidante to the biggest theatrical name of his generation. It can surely be no accident that *Dracula* would eventually achieve success on stage as well as in print. In fact, its very first stage production took place on 18 May 1897 at the Lyceum, within days of publication — a hasty adaptation designed solely to protect the copyright. It is said that Irving was unimpressed: 'Dreadful' was his supposed retort. [23]

Lyceum audiences had come to expect spine-chilling excitement and bloody melodramas: along with productions of Shakespeare, they were Irving's stock-in-trade. He never fought shy of striking fear into his audiences, and performed all the demonic roles of the supernatural in one form or another. *The Bells* and *Vanderdecken* (based on *The Flying Dutchman*) were standard Lyceum plays. *Faust*, too, was performed on numerous occasions between 1885 and 1894, and Irving's powerful rendering of Mephistopheles left a deep impression on his acting manager. It was after researching the background to *Faust* with Irving in Nuremberg that Stoker was moved to write one of his most powerful short horror stories, 'The Squaw'.

It is with *Macbeth*, however, that it is necessary to pause. Stoker acknowledged that this was the play which intrigued him most, and that he held profound differences of opinion with his employer over some of its finer points. [24] Irving had performed the leading part many times prior to his meeting Stoker, but in the weeks preceding the 1888 Lyceum production a great many hours had been spent debating the nuances of the central character.

Even a casual glance is sufficient to notice some of the ways in which *Dracula*'s plot can be seen to resemble *Macbeth*'s. Both are centred around a lonely, desolate castle, to which an unsuspecting stranger is lured and then 'visited' in his sleep. Both works have as their focus the personification of Evil — not earthly, but supernatural Evil — for Macbeth and Dracula each receive a kind of immortality as a result of their pacts with supernatural forces. This Evil is portrayed as more fascinating and more potent than the powers of Good arrayed against it, for Macbeth's ultimate downfall, like Dracula's, cannot totally be accounted for by the ingenuity of his enemies. It is, in both cases, their own schemes that sow the seeds of their destruction. The contest between Good compared to Evil is shown to be an unequal one — the gap emphasized by the representatives of the former being unable to trust one another, undermining their strength by concealing their thoughts. Furthermore, the Evil which both works distil is in a very real sense dependent on the victims' complicity — the would-be target must accept the touch of evil/vampirism willingly.

Dracula, like Macbeth, was once a fearless warrior, grown to manhood through the spilled blood of his enemy's armies; a heroic figure for whom the fall from military power to perpetrator of evil is a major mystery. Both are, as it were, the first victims of the disease which eventually spreads before them, before they are driven remorselessly back to the castle from whence they came to have their throats sheered. The 'contagion' in both works is combated by a team of adversaries skilled in medical science. Similarly, what motivates both principal characters is not a thirst for blood (either literally or metaphorically) but single-minded power and ambition. Nonetheless, the two works feature blood as a central motif, and contain three weird and evil women in a symbolic form. The three witches that open *Macbeth* are reincarnated as vampires near the beginning of *Dracula*.

Two other comparisons deserve mentioning: first, the respective conclusions when the arch-fiend is destroyed. With the death of Macbeth the cry is 'The time is free'; following Dracula's eventual demise the response is 'The curse has passed away' (*D* 27:448).[25] Second, the historical elements of both are abstract rather than factual. The Scotland of *Macbeth* exists in the mind rather than as any geographical entity. The same could be said of Stoker's Transylvania.

In the light of such cross-comparisons it is possible that, presented with the basic *Macbeth* plot, Stoker wove the vampire theme around it with the intention of creating his own novel/play, envisaging Irving, with his saturnine appearance and harsh, metallic, hissing voice, in the title role. The set of coincidences is extended when, in 1893, Stoker paid his first visit to Cruden Bay. His holidays were never intended solely for relaxation: they were working holidays, where he would either catch up with his own writing, or else put in a little field research for future Lyceum productions. It has been suggested that his walking tours of the Buchan coastline were undertaken to explore some of the atmospheric aspects of *Macbeth*,[26] and certainly the towering — and at that time inhabited — Slains Castle, perched high on the edge of the jagged cliffs which keep the North Sea at bay, presents one of the most evocative Gothic sites in Britain.

Slains Castle, Cruden Bay, taken when the castle was
still inhabited. It is now in ruins.

This particular part of Scotland, furthermore, was a rich
repository of pagan beliefs: the local population, with whom Stoker
chatted a great deal, were among the most superstitious in Britain
— as is clear from some of his later fiction set explicitly in Cruden
Bay. The inlet is situated near the most easterly point in Scotland,
facing out towards the rising sun, and its environs were once known
for sun worship and fertility rites — with many remnants of stone
circles still to be seen. Despite opposition from the Church of
Scotland (the Kirk) it was in Stoker's day still the custom, for

example, to leave part of the land uncultivated so that wild oats could be used by the spirit world. These spirits were presumed to visit the living at certain times of the year, so it became customary to light hallows fires to deter them, or alternatively to appease them by food offerings, such as goats' milk or bannocks. It is still known for a piece of mistletoe or rowan to be hung above an ailing child in the hope that any unwanted 'visitors' will leave and search for another source of sustenance.[27]

Many of the funeral customs of the people of Buchan reflected their fear of the undead, like locking up cats and hens immediately prior to a funeral, in case they were evil spirits in disguise. To prevent the deceased catching a glimpse of his/her old home, which might later be recognized, roundabout routes would be taken by the mourners to the graveyard. As insurance, some portion of the funeral feast would be set aside as a peace offering, to assist the departed soul on its way to the next world. Pennies would be placed over the eyes of the deceased; salt placed in a container on the chest; mirrors would be covered, and onions laid on window sills. All these, and other local tales, would be avidly noted by Stoker. Coincidence or not, following his discovery of Cruden Bay a persistent theme of his fiction would be the returning of the dead to haunt the living.

On the question of when *Dracula* came to be conceived, it is now possible to answer with greater confidence than was previously possible. For many years it had been assumed by Stoker's critics that, because *Dracula* was released amid a batch of his published fiction between 1894 and 1898, it had been as hastily assembled and written as some of his other, notoriously hack, productions. It is still popularly believed that he began writing *Dracula* while holidaying at Cruden Bay in August 1895, completing it within a year in the odd moments he found free from Lyceum commitments — which allowed another year for it to appear in published form in June 1897. Connoisseurs of the novel, in contrast, have long felt that Stoker's meticulous regard for detail in *Dracula* is inconsistent with the notion of a 'rush job', yet only with the serendipitous discovery in the 1970s of Stoker's working notes for the novel in a Philadelphia museum[28] have their suspicions been vindicated.

These notes, written in his own hand or typed, and some dated, not only reveal that *Dracula* was conceived at least as early as 1890, but also that Stoker was remarkably thorough in his research. The year 1890 is significant because it marked the publication of his first full-length novel, *The Snake's Pass*. Its favourable reception possibly encouraged Stoker to begin preparing his *magnum opus* there and then, time and opportunity permitting. Far from being a casual yarn, spun from the top of his head and recounted with only minimal preparation, *Dracula* would take a further seven years before it appeared in book form.

The Philadelphia notes are dated between 1890 and 1896. They were written on anything available, including Lyceum notepaper and even a piece of Philadelphia hotel stationery. It is, regrettably, still not clear exactly when the novel took its final form, for the earliest papers include neither the precise vampire theme, nor the name of 'Dracula'. Even so, the earliest dated note — 8 March 1890 — reveals that the initial chapters had taken recognizable shape, in epistolary form, and a week later, on 14 March, the plot is laid down, complete with four sub-books (titled 'To London', 'Tragedy', 'Discovery', and 'Punishment'), each comprised of seven, later nine, chapters. This quaternary breakdown is suggestive of four acts of a play, and the fact that the finished novel would contain most of the narrative in two multi-roomed dwellings (one in Transylvania, the other in London), as if inviting a future stage adaptation, suggests that Stoker was alive from the start to *Dracula*'s theatrical prospects. Moreover, the chapter divisions frequently serve no obvious scene-separating function. Many chapter endings appear quite arbitrary and operate more as curtain calls, providing a pause at regular intervals.

With regard to relevant locations in Britain, almost every place that Dracula stalked, Stoker had preceded him notebook in hand. He had toured Whitby, for example (scene of the Count's dramatic shipwreck), as early as August 1890, and notes taken then would appear almost verbatim in the finished novel. The tombstone inscriptions in the novel are authentic. He had also noticed the name 'Swales' on a Whitby grave and lent it to one of his Whitby characters, giving him a dialect meticulously in keeping with a glossary of local terminology.[29] He had chatted to the locals, listened to the tales of naval tragedies from old sailors, and consulted logbooks and meteorological records. Several actual shipwrecks were noted, including that of the Russian schooner *Dimetry* on 24 October 1885, which had crashed through Whitby harbour. In *Dracula*, Stoker's Russian ship would act likewise and be called the *Demeter*. Other first-hand field researches included a trip to Regent's Park Zoo, where Stoker observed the behaviour of certain animals, and to various other parts of London which would feature

Photograph of old *Whitby: Dock End* by Frank Meadow Sutcliffe
(the Sutcliffe Gallery, Whitby).

in the book. His notes outline a theory of dreams, [30] while from his surgeon brother William, Stoker learned the symptoms and treatment of specific head injuries, which he would later employ for Dracula's attack on Renfield. One of the latest additions to the notes was a newspaper feature entitled 'Vampires in New England' from a copy of *The New York World*, dated 2 February 1896.

Having established the bare bones of his tale, Stoker now needed a location. It needed to be a truly dreadful place, a fitting haunt for a monstrous Count. His early inclination seems to have been to borrow Le Fanu's siting for *Carmilla* — namely Styria (now in eastern Austria) — but at some early stage he revised this location in favour of Transylvania further to the east (the northern and western part of modern Romania). His notes indicate his familiarity with the writings of Emily de Laszowska Gerard, whose article 'Transylvanian Superstitions', [31] which sketched out the local beliefs on vampires and devilry, he carefully summarized. Gerard had also, in 1888, published a book on her expanded researches called *The Land Beyond the Forest* — the literal meaning of Transylvania — much material from which would find its way into the opening chapters of *Dracula*. As Stoker says through his mouthpiece, Jonathan Harker: 'I read that every known superstition in the world is gathered into the horseshoe of the Carpathians' (*D* 1:10), and it was there that Bram Stoker eventually opted to base his vampire Count. Further research was undertaken at the British Museum to supplement the many works listed in his notes as having been consulted. [32]

It is apparent from reading the novel that Stoker clearly used a calendar when compiling the plot. The journals and newspaper extracts all come from a particular year, but as he refers to dates, not days, there has been much speculation as to which it was. It has now been established beyond doubt to be 1893, for his notes contain the novel's timescale reproduced in a diary. [33] This evidence lends weight to the suggestion that Cruden Bay occupies a special place in the inspiration behind *Dracula;* for it was first visited by Stoker in 1893.

So much for the time and place in which *Dracula* was set. There remains the origins of the name 'Dracula', for in his early notes Stoker refers instead to a Count 'Wampyr'. Popular wisdom apportions credit for this switch to a Hungarian professor. Stoker's *Reminiscences* record that on 30 April 1890 he was introduced to Professor Arminius Vambery, a distinguished historian and Orientalist from the University of Budapest, who had just returned from an expedition to central Asia following in the steps of Marco Polo.[34] A further meeting took place two years later in Dublin.

The suspicion that Vambery played some part in Stoker's still-crystallizing ideas stems from little more than the author's habit of taking real-life acquaintances and transplanting them, with little if any change of name, into his novels. In *Dracula*, when Van Helsing seeks a detailed picture of the demonic Count, he requests assistance from 'my friend Arminius, of Buda-Pesth University' (*D* 18:287-8; 23:359). This has led to the unwarranted presumption that fact mirrored fiction: that the *real* Arminius Vambery supplied information on the *real* Dracula. Such a presumption is dangerous because Stoker's use of nomenclature was, on occasions, inconsequential. Another of the cast of *Dracula*, for example, borrowed the name of a Lyceum painter and decorator,[35] without there being any suggestion of a more profound association. What seems more curious about Vambery, *vis à vis* Stoker's researches, is that in most of the encyclopaedias Stoker would have consulted, the entries 'Vambery' and 'vampire' are juxtaposed.[36] Unfortunately, nothing is known of the content of Stoker's and Vambery's conversations or later correspondence, and if Vambery ever wrote on the subject of vampires, or a so-called Dracula, no record has survived. What is, finally, the most persuasive argument against the primacy of the Vambery connection is that all the important information in the novel on Dracula or vampires in general, and which is attributed in *Dracula* to Arminius, can be found in the books and articles listed in Stoker's notes.[37] These notes do not mention Arminius Vambery. In other words he may or may not have featured in Stoker's enquiries, but either way it would appear that *Dracula* could have taken its final form without him.

Stoker's working notes provide evidence of his first known acquaintance with Dracula. It transpires that during his vacation at the Yorkshire port of Whitby in August 1890 Stoker did not content himself with local researches. In Whitby library he came across an *Account of the Principalities of Wallachia and Moldavia,* written in 1820 by William Wilkinson, one-time British consul at Bucharest. On pages 18 and 19 Stoker was introduced to the activities of a fifteenth-century Wallachian Voivode (Prince) — Dracula.

With this discovery, and the researches that followed, the necessary ingredients of the novel were established. In a note dated 29 February 1892, not only does the name 'Dracula' appear as an original entry, but basic locations of the finished novel are mapped out: Whitby in England, and Bistritz and the Borgo Pass in Transylvania.

Modern Romania comprises three provinces: Transylvania and, to the east and south, Moldavia and Wallachia respectively. The historical links between these three regions are not recent — they date back to Roman times, from which Romania derives its name. In medieval Europe these three states existed as semi-independent principalities, being squeezed between the Holy Roman Empire, which extended over central Europe to the west, and the encroaching tentacles of the Ottoman Turks to the south. The Orthodox heritage of the Romanian peoples was therefore simultaneously under threat from Catholicism and Islam. In such times it was difficult for any ruler of a threatened principality to survive, let alone carve a name for himself in history; but 'Dracula' was such a man.

He was born around 1430-1 in the Transylvanian town of Sighisoara, but it was in the neighbouring, southern territory of Wallachia that he, succeeding his father, would eventually make his reputation. Around the time of Dracula's birth his father was bestowed by Sigismund, the Holy Roman Emperor, with a title that would pledge him to devote his life to the service of combating the Czech Hussites and the Turks.[38] He was granted the throne of Wallachia *in absentia* and invested with the 'Order of the Dragon'; a semi-military, semi-monastic designation which, crucially, was to be hereditary. The Romanian word for 'Dragon' happens to be 'Dracul' (pronounced Dra-cool) and the Order's escutcheon showed a cross beneath which hung a dragon. The first holder of the office became popularly known as Vlad Dracul (Vlad the Dragon).[39]

Vlad Dracul presumably enjoyed something of a reputation: one source credits him with being a descendant in the direct male line of Ghengis Khan.[40] He managed, in 1436, to seize the Wallachian throne, but his precarious balancing feat between his patrons and the Turks could not endure. In 1447, together with his eldest son Mircea, Vlad Dracul was put to death at Christian hands, whereupon the Wallachian throne passed to rival claimants.

The second son, Vlad junior, was in no position to contest the matter. For some years he, and his younger brother Radu, had been 'guests' of the Ottoman hierarchy.[41] It was while being imprisoned in various parts of Anatolia that the teenage Vlad came to learn at first hand the weight of Turkish methods, discipline, and barbarity — the psychological weapon of terror put to full use. The Turks, when confident that he had been cleansed of his father's duplicity and was fully indoctrinated with Ottoman virtues, saw

Vlad Tepes — the Impaler. Portrait in the collection of
Ferdinand II at Castle Ambras, Innsbruck (Dracula Society).

in young Vlad a suitably pliant ruler of Wallachia, and with their
approval he snatched power for a few brief weeks at the end of
1448. However, he was soon overthrown and forced to seek refuge
in both Turkish and Christian lands before he found new sponsors.

In 1453 Constantinople fell to the Turks, the remnants of the
Eastern Christian Empire disintegrated, and all surviving Christian
Europe shuddered at the prospect of an infidel empire sweeping

everything before it. Wallachia, hitherto subservient to Ottoman hegemony only to the extent of paying tribute, was now in the front line. Whereas it had been the Turks who first assisted Vlad to assume control over Wallachia, it was now the turn of his powerful Hungarian neighbours to patronize him. Beginning in 1456, he ruled his principality with an iron hand and in so doing acquired the sobriquet 'Dracula' — literally, son of the Dragon[42] — the name by which he became known to his western contemporaries.

Yet such was the verve with which he set about centralizing his power, so that news of his gruesome exploits careered across Europe, that he soon earned himself a more colourful, and accurate, nickname: Vlad Tepes (pronounced Tsepesh) — the Impaler. Torture and execution by impalement were hardly novel: such methods could be traced back to antiquity and were practised by the Turks themselves. It was the sheer scale and sophistication of Tepes' operations that caused a sensation. In its most 'artistic' form the stake would be rounded, greased, and introduced into the fundament with the weight of the body bearing down upon it. Death could take hours, or, preferably (from his point of view), days. For variety, stakes could penetrate other parts of the body.[43] The methods would vary according to the age, rank, sex, or

'Vlad Tepes' Feast': painting by T. Aman (Dracula Society).

nationality of the victim, and to fulfil aesthetic criteria the stakes would be arranged vertically in concentric circles or other pleasing patterns, with the noblest victims perched highest of all. Woodcuts of the time depict Tepes seated at a table in the open, feasting alone amid rows of impaled and mutilated bodies.

In the absence of the centralized authority which Tepes now set about establishing, the Romanian principalities were racked by factional interests. His power remained strictly notional until he could deal with two deeply entrenched and privileged minority groups. The boyars (landed noblemen) effectively lived as they pleased, immune to the demands of their princes, and happy to foster the claims of any aspiring ruler sympathetic to their privileges. Tepes' rival claimants found sanctuary among boyar communities, so he dealt with their treason in forthright manner — by impaling them in their thousands. The economic infrastructure of the Romanian lands was largely controlled by traders and merchants of Saxon descent, whose own monopolistic privileges dated back to when the region was being effectively colonized from German sources in the twelfth and thirteenth centuries.[44] Tepes sequestrated foreign merchants' trading rights and instituted protectionist measures designed to safeguard native Wallachian commerce. He then redistributed their properties to his acolytes in an attempt to forge new economic alignments beneficial to himself and his consolidation of power.

Tepes was no less compromising when he turned his attention to the Turks. In 1459 he felt sufficiently secure at home to refuse traditional payments of tribute, thus endearing himself to the Christian powers. Two years later, spurred on by the demands of Pope Pius II for a fresh military campaign, he earned himself a place in the annals of Christian crusading by marching an army south across the Danube. He temporarily liberated those territories recently conquered, and impaled those Turks unfortunate enough not to escape or be killed outright in battle.

By embarking on this crusade Tepes was not declaring his devotion to Christ. He was a gifted military strategist, and was doubtless aware of the need to secure his southern gateway to Wallachia, across the exposed plains of the Danube.[45] Ingrained hatred of the Turks for past sufferings probably accounted for any personal motivation. Yet his situation was precarious without material assistance from other Western, Christian, leaders. None was forthcoming. Probably they feared the Turkish backlash. In the event, Tepes, upon his retreat, found himself imprisoned by Matthias Corvinus, King of Hungary, who had earlier received bags which contained several thousand pieces of Turkish anatomy as evidence of Tepes' effectiveness. Corvinus probably acted as he did out of fear of Tepes' increasing autonomy: he was becoming too much his own man, showing too little deference to his Hungarian neighbours and patrons. The irate boyar class had also pressured Corvinus to act against their hated overseer; the lowland peasants had been alienated by Tepes' scorched earth policy of poisoning wells and burning settlements to inconvenience the Turks; and he was rumoured to have adopted Islam, scandalously, in an attempt to save his own skin.

Imprisonment in Hungary spelled the end of Vlad Tepes' spectacular activities. Between 1456 and 1462 he had carved himself a niche in Europe's hall of fame. After twelve years' forced residence in Hungary he was released by Corvinus, who was now anxious to display his magnanimity, renew the struggle with the Turks, and make use of the talented warrior in his custody. According to some sources, Tepes renounced his Orthodox faith and embraced Catholicism as his passport to freedom.[46] By the end of 1476 he once again reigned supreme in Wallachia but lost his life in combat with the Turks a few weeks later. What happened to his body is a matter of speculation. Some say his head was detached and presented to the Sultan in Constantinople.[47] Legend has it that his corpse, with or without his head, is buried in an island monastery at Snagov, outside Bucharest. Whatever the case, his legacy was to have personally authorized during his lifetime the deaths of some one hundred thousand people[48] — the equivalent of one fifth of the population of his native Wallachia at that time.

All rulers invite controversy: it is all a matter of perspective. Yet few can have been the subject of such conflicting evaluations as Vlad Tepes. He became a Renaissance European legend in his own lifetime. Largely inspired by boyar intrigues to discredit him, accounts of his misdeeds — both real and exaggerated — were disseminated throughout Europe. Saxons, Hungarians, Turks, and Russians all had cause to despise him. Word of mouth, embellished in the passing, soon portrayed him as one of the great demented psychopaths of history. Wandering minstrels put his atrocities to song, and technological advances in German-speaking parts of Europe spread the message further. Hand-written reports were gradually supplanted by news sheets tumbling off the newly-invented printing presses. The new medium had found a celebrity and by the end of the century he was providing some of the favourite

Bran Castle, Romania. This fortress is of the type
the historical Dracula would have occupied. Stoker
located his fictional castle near the Borgo Pass.

reading matter of the continent, vying for space with Columbus' discovery of America. One source maintains that for a while incunabula devoted to Dracula's activities were outselling the Bible.[49] By 1558 news of Dracula's excesses even reached Britain, when Sebastian Munster's *Cosmographia* was translated into English.

It would have been these German-based versions of events which gripped Stoker's attention through the books and articles he consulted, possibly supplemented by the Hungarian perspective of Arminius Vambery. There was, however, another slant: that of the heroic exploits of a fearless Christian crusader. Unfortunately for his self-image, Tepes could not so easily be defended by the peoples of Wallachia, had they so chosen, because facilities for printing lagged behind those of the West. Not until a century after his death were counter-versions of his motives available from his homeland.[50] In the interim it was left to chroniclers in lands untouched by his atrocities to present him in a less brutal light and to rationalize his deeds as anticipating the thoughts of Machiavelli, for whom almost any act was justifiable in the name of *raison d'état*. Even Machiavelli admitted it was better to be feared than loved.

As the centre of gravity in European affairs moved steadily westwards, Vlad Tepes became a forgotten man. He would be resuscitated by two quite disparate developments. The first was Bram Stoker's novel, which sent researchers scurrying after its source: the second was the formation of the Romanian Socialist Republic in the 1940s, faced with the task of searching for national heroes who could help bind modern Romania to its past. Vlad Tepes had all the credentials. He is not known inside Romania as 'Dracula', but as 'Tepes' — after his favourite form of execution. His memory has been rehabilitated. In Romanian eyes he is guilty of no more than *realpolitik*. He is the equivalent of England's Robin Hood, someone who took from the rich in order to give to the poor; a freedom fighter and curber of foreign privileges; a man who virtually single-handedly eliminated theft and other crime; and whose excesses are viewed as consonant with the general cruelty of the age in which he lived.[51] He is seen as a founding father of the Romanian nation-state; a hero of the Orthodox Church — a kind of Caesar and Pope all in one.

But the previously mentioned, condemnatory assessment of Vlad Tepes was the one with which Stoker was familiar, and as such the Impaler was ideally suited to be resurrected and transformed into a fictional vampire. Besides, the finished novel would possess added authenticity through being woven round an actual, historical character. What would also have intrigued Stoker was an ambiguity surrounding the name 'Dracul'. As is made clear in the Wilkinson article which Stoker consulted at Whitby, Dracul did not only refer to a dragon: 'Dracul in Wallachian language means Devil.'[52] It is, however, unlikely that a founder of monasteries and close consort of religious leaders (for whatever ulterior motives) would have been referred to in this derogatory fashion, let alone sign himself 'devil'. The 'dragon' alternative is the more plausible. Moreover, although 'devils' are not linguistically confused with 'vampires' in that part of the world, there is still a tradition in German-Romanian frontier regions of depicting vampires as dragon-monster-serpents.[53] But the interlocking imagery of devil and dragon in Christian mythology, and the frequent overlapping of the etymologies of 'vampire' and 'devil' in various languages, may have provided Stoker with an ingenious concept: Vlad the vampire.

The linkage between Vlad Dracula and Count Dracula is not a matter of conjecture: it is made explicit in the novel.[54] When Van Helsing decides to take others into his confidence he explains:

> He [Count Dracula] must, indeed, have been that Voivode Dracula who won his name against the Turks . . . If it be so, then was he no common man; for in that time, and for centuries after, he was spoken of as the cleverest and the most cunning, as well as the bravest of the sons of the 'land beyond the forest'. (*D* 8:287-8)

Earlier in the book the Count outlines his own background and the convoluted history of Transylvania from the time of Attila the Hun (*D* 3:40-2). Furthermore, Stoker's physical description of his Count bears a strong resemblance to surviving woodcuts of the Impaler — copies of which would have been available in the British Museum — though the Count's physical characteristics are also those typically given to Gothic literature's villains.

Critics of the novel have seized on what they see as inaccuracies in Stoker's historical and ethnological sketches as indicative of his slovenly use of source material. They point out that his history is distorted at best, erroneous at worst, exemplified by the fundamental error of basing Dracula in Transylvania when his actual power base was in neighbouring Wallachia. As a result of this discrepancy a whole Dracula-industry has flourished, bedevilled by cross-purposes. True, Stoker *does* begin and end the novel in Transylvania; the path of the climactic chase to eastern Europe *does* take the characters through named places in

Transylvania; and Castle Dracula — mythical though it may be — *is* sited in that province, near the Borgo Pass. The problem arises because the Romanian authorities, anxious both to capitalize on the tourist potential to be exploited from *Count* Dracula and to disassociate him from their own hero, *Vlad* Dracula, have gone to great lengths to direct Western tourists to the castles of Vlad Tepes — which happen to lie in Wallachia, well away from less accessible Transylvania, where perchance there are fewer suitably impressive castles to show off.

Yet, in a sense, discussion of Stoker's historical licence is immaterial. He was, after all, a novelist, not a historian. It was not his concern to portray an accurate picture of medieval eastern Europe; besides, the sources available to him concerning Tepes were fewer and less reliable than those of today. Rather, he was concerned to gather only enough insights into the place and period for him to be able to impart something of their flavour to the Victorian reader, even down to local recipes.

It remains to be considered why Stoker alighted on Vlad Tepes as the historical figure to resurrect in fictional form as his demon Count, for whatever his many crimes and inhumanities, nowhere was Vlad the Impaler accused of being a vampire. Spilling blood was more his style, not drinking it. Yet there were many other tacit associations between Tepes and vampirism. His chosen method of execution — impalement — happened to be the same as that recommended for vampires; Tepes was eventually decapitated in the manner of accused vampires; and his alleged resting place in Snagov was itself opened up and pillaged[55] — suggestive that he had risen up. Stoker may even have learned of the legend that Tepes never really died, but was waiting to rise up and protect his homeland if threatened: he was, in other words, lying in wait — 'undead'. Again, according to Catholic sources, he had renounced the Orthodox faith in which he was baptized — a technical offence in Orthodox eyes that would indict others, who followed suit, of vampirism. Excessively evil persons were also reputed to turn into vampires, and Tepes' general obsession with human blood was in itself suggestive enough to Stoker.

On the other hand, there are certain features of the fictional Count that are far removed from the known characteristics and circumstances of the Impaler. Principally, they stem from Stoker's puzzling decision to label his vampire a 'Count', when Vlad Tepes had been a 'Prince'. This is not simply a matter of semantics. The title 'Count' is alien to the Romanian social hierarchy but is native to Hungary. Tepes' principality, Wallachia, is properly Romanian, whereas Transylvania was at that time a Hungarian province. Moreover, although later occupied by the Turks, Transylvania was once again administered by Hungary, within the Austro-Hungarian Empire, when Stoker came to write *Dracula* (Transylvania only became a part of modern Romania following the First World War). Count Dracula, in other words, was Hungarian, not Romanian, and refers to himself as a 'Szekely' (*D* 3:41) — of Hungarian descent.

This Hungarian emphasis is appropriate not only in view of Stoker's reliance on Western (namely Saxon and Hungarian) sources concerning the Impaler, but also because Hungarian folklore is more fertile than that of Romania in the expression of vampire superstition. Indeed, Montague Summers asserts that 'Hungary [has] the reputation of being that particular region of the world which is most terribly infested by the Vampire and where he is seen at his ugliest and worst.'[56] In consequence, it is evident that Stoker's relocation of Dracula northwards from Wallachia to Transylvania was intentional, and not the product of careless attention to detail.

One further historical figure should be mentioned in this connection. Stoker's general focus on Hungary was enhanced by his reading in Sabine Baring-Gould's *The Book of Were-Wolves* of the exploits of Elizabeth Bathory, born 130 years after the Impaler. Apart from the fact of her being a woman, Bathory supplied the pieces absent in Tepes. She was Hungarian; she was a *Countess*; her crest also featured a dragon; and, unlike the Impaler, she actually drank blood — she was a living vampire. *The Guinness Book of Records* accredits the 'Blood Countess' as the most prolific murderess in history, with at least 610 confirmed victims. They were invariably young maidens — virgins — tortured and killed in ingenious ways in order to supply the Countess with a liberal supply of fresh blood, which she believed possessed rejuvenating properties. Application of fresh blood made her look and feel younger; a coincidence eagerly borrowed by Stoker in the case of Dracula. When finally convicted of her abominations early in 1611 Bathory was walled up in her castle at Csejthe. She died in 1614, the most notorious and best authenticated practitioner of vampirism on record.[57]

So powerful were the twin influences of Le Fanu's fictional *Carmilla* and the real-life Elizabeth Bathory, that they were probably jointly responsible for Stoker's initial intention to base his novel in what is now Austria. One of the expunged chapters of

*Dracula* (popularly known as 'Dracula's Guest') goes so far as to feature a vampire Countess from Gratz. Fortunately for the sake of *Dracula's* originality, Stoker eventually distances himself from the more obvious Carmilla/Bathory connections, though they remain potent sources of influence and inspiration.

Curiously, it can be noted that for all Stoker's debt to Vlad Dracula it was not his original intention to title his novel in the Impaler's honour. The manuscript which Stoker submitted to the publishers bore the intended title 'The Un-Dead'.[58] Much of the novel's later success can be put down to Stoker's, or his publisher's, inspired last minute switch to bring the name 'Dracula' to the fore.

# 6.

# FROM VLAD DRACULA
# TO COUNT DRACULA

[Dracula's] face was a strong — a very strong — aquiline, with high bridge of the thin nose and peculiarly arched nostrils; with lofty domed forehead, and hair growing scantily round the temples, but profusely elsewhere. His eyebrows were very massive, almost meeting over the nose, and with bushy hair that seemed to curl in its own profusion. The mouth, so far as I could see it under the heavy moustache, was fixed and rather cruel looking, with peculiarly sharp white teeth; these protruded over the lips, whose remarkable ruddiness showed astonishing vitality in a man of his years. For the rest, his ears were pale and at the tops extremely pointed; the chin was broad and strong, and the cheeks firm though thin. The general effect was one of extraordinary pallor.

Jonathan Harker's Journal,
*Dracula* 2:28.

**B**EFORE attention is turned to some of the deeper themes of Stoker's most famous novel, it will be helpful to look more closely at the characters he created and the purposes they fulfil — beginning with Count Dracula himself. Stoker spared no effort to present his demonic vampire as dramatically as possible. Other, mortal, figures he leaves under-sketched, relying on the reader's imagination to fill in the flesh on the bones he provides, but Dracula is painted with enormous attention to detail. After the first four chapters he is 'offstage' for most of the rest of the novel,[1] yet not for a moment is the reader allowed to forget the Count's awesome presence.

Visually, aside from his facial features (described above), Dracula is clean shaven save for a long white moustache, and dressed without a single speck of colour about him anywhere. He is a tall old man. He could not have been uncommonly tall, however, for Dracula makes off wearing Harker's clothes — which presumably fit satisfactorily — and Harker, himself, when later described by others invites no comments as to his size. Moreover, the accepted notion of Dracula's ever-present black cloak would seem to be an obsession of the cinema. Only once is such a garment mentioned (*D* 3:47) and the more usual description 'clad in black from head to foot' (*D* 2:25) would hardly be appropriate had the Count's dress been confined to just one conspicuous garment.

Compare Harker's description of the Count with the only known written description of Vlad the Impaler:

> He was not very tall but very stocky and strong with a cold and terrible appearance, a strong and aquiline nose, swollen nostrils, a thin and reddish face, in which the very long eye lashes framed large wide-open green eyes; the bushy black eye brows made them appear threatening. His face and chin were shaven, but for a moustache. The swollen temples increased the bulk of his head. A bull's neck connected his head [to the body] from which black curly locks hung on his wide shouldered person. [2]

Consider, too, a description of Henry Irving: 'a tall, spare man . . . a peculiarly striking face, long grey hair thrown carelessly back behind the ears, clean shaven features remarkable for their delicate refinement, united with the suggestion of virile force [and] rather aquiline nose.' [3]

As a fictional character, Count Dracula is an alloy: he combines in his persona certain qualities taken from his real-life namesake; from Elizabeth Bathory; the tradition of the literary vampire descended from Lord Ruthven and Sir Francis Varney; the great myths of Romantic literature from which Stoker liberally borrowed; the wealth of Continental folklore to plant the novel firmly back in its roots; as well as an original flourish by Stoker to turn his Count into a master magician — as we shall see.

Being a literary vampire, Dracula conforms to the requirement of belonging to the ranks of nobility. He boasts of having a distinguished lineage, possessing in his veins the blood of Attila the Hun. In some respects, Dracula's behaviour is what one might expect of the conventional literary aristocrat. He exudes charm of manner; he is contemptuous of the common man; and he speaks several languages — German excellently, and more impressive English than the Dutch professor, Van Helsing. At intervals, Stoker puts in little touches which increase Dracula's sense of refinement. The Count is seen wearing white kid gloves and a straw hat, and he leaves around a brush for his clothes and a brush and comb for his hair. But on many other levels he does not act like a nobleman at all. He lacks the typical aristocrat's high standard of living and conspicuous over-indulgence. He does not eat or drink to excess, nor does he pursue women (as normally understood). His lifestyle does not revolve around fashionable clothes, the theatre, or hunting; he does not hold receptions or build stately homes. He actually chooses to live in a Gothic ruin. Not even his violent pastimes are undertaken purely for pleasure.[4] Perhaps most unusual of all, for a thriving aristocrat, is the complete absence of servants. Dracula is not averse to performing all the necessary menial tasks — driving the calèche, preparing meals, and even making beds — to prevent Harker, his guest, from deducing that he employs no domestic staff.

By way of character, Dracula is more than just a vague presence of malice. Stoker endows him with a recognizably human (if intensely evil) personality. He has a mannerism of tugging his moustache during animated discourses on his family history — the only topic touched on in the book capable of making him pleasantly excitable (D 3:40). He does, however, exhibit a full range of other emotions, all of them used negatively: hate, passion, anger, disdain, baffled malignity, vanity. His mental gifts are largely borrowed from those of his namesake. The Count, like the Voivode before him, has a mighty brain, is fearless, remorseless, a shrewd leader and cunning soldier — not averse to executing a strategic retreat in the face of disadvantageous odds, as the handbooks on guerrilla warfare dictate. Stoker plays down the tyrannical aspects of Dracula's pre-vampire life, for when speaking of his own past the Count naturally does not see himself as a merciless psychopath, but as a stern, principled statesman. And Van Helsing concedes: 'he was in life a most wonderful man. Soldier, statesman, and alchemist . . .' (D 23:359). In this, of course, Dracula resembles Mephistopheles in Goethe's *Faust*, whose portrayal by Irving left such a deep impression on Stoker. Overall, legal-minded Harker is so impressed by his host's great foresight and intellectual prowess that he utters the book's most memorable understatement: Dracula, if he chose, 'would have made a formidable solicitor' (D 3:44).

This intelligence and urbanity, while allowing Dracula to be firmly located within the tradition of the literary vampire, only partly accounts for his all-pervading menace. He also exemplifies those characteristics notable in the vampire of folklore. In particular, Stoker is keen to highlight the animalistic quality of his master-vampire, taking full advantage of the folkloric connection between vampires and werewolves. Besides having pointed ears and protruding canine teeth, Dracula possesses coarse, broad hands with squat fingers — as werewolves are frequently described as having. His palms, too, are hairy and the nails cut to a sharp point. His eyes glow red. The unalleviated stench which clings to his places of rest, and which produces a feeling of nausea to those in proximity to him, is the stench of excrement, of all the ills of mortality, of death, of arrested decay — augmented, when his thirst has been slaked, by the sickly-sweet, acrid smell of blood. Even his persona is animalistic: anti-rational, childlike, instinctive. His vitality is shown as feral, and his cunning is that of an animal that resorts

Painting by Bruce Wightman of Dracula as described by Stoker in the novel (Dracula Society).

to swift physical action to counter any errors of judgement.

Dracula enjoys an exaggerated gymnastic animal repertoire. He can climb face-foremost down a castle wall, gripping the vertical surface with toes and fingers — though of course he does not fear death should he fall, being immune to the natural laws of mortality. These wall-descending activities are described as 'lizard-like' (*D* 3:47). Later, Dracula's agility is expressed as 'panther-like'; he has a 'snarl' on his face; and shows 'lion-like disdain' (*D* 23:364). His general empathy with the animal world is demonstrated by his control over the lower forms of life: rats, bats, and wolves.

In many other of his attributes and propensities Dracula is a classical example of the vampire spoken of in European folklore. Being undead, his flesh is icy to the touch; he casts no reflection in the mirror, and when standing in front of flames does not obstruct a view of them. He is unable to impose his presence on a victim at the time of first contact, unless the target shows complicity in some form. This is evident in Harker's stepping over the threshold at Castle Dracula (*D* 2:26), and in the Count's later visits to Lucy and Renfield (*D* 21:332). Dracula possesses enormous physical strength and speed of movement; his eyes can induce hypnotic effects; and with selective victims he is capable of psychic transfer.

Dracula can direct the elements around him, such as creating a puff of wind. He can see in the dark and vaporize himself at will. He is able to change into a dog, wolf, or bat; he can dematerialize to be transported as mist; and he can take shape from phosphorescent specks riding on moonbeams — which can themselves weaken powers of resistance. He is restricted by the presence of running water, being unable to cross it except at the slack or flood of the tide, unless with manual assistance. He sleeps and wakes with the precision of clockwork — dawn and dusk being calculated to the second. While sleeping, Dracula appears to be dead, eyes open with no pulse or respiratory motion. All the while he is 'conscious' of activity around him, although searching hands cannot 'wake' him (*D* 4:67).

Crucially, although Dracula can be repelled by garlic and other pagan safeguards, he is essentially a vampire of the Christian mould. In other words he is a representative/client/manifestation of the devil (in London he aptly assumes the alias 'Count *de Ville*' [*D* 20:326]) and must therefore be shown to be vulnerable to Christian icons and imagery. The crucifix — arch-symbol of the Christian faith — makes him recoil and cower, and the application of a Holy

Wafer can sterilize his place of rest.[5]

But Stoker was not content to restrict his vampire-king within the parameters prescribed by folklore. Dracula would have to be special, both in his attributes and in his manner of becoming a vampire. In particular, there are several qualities about Dracula which differentiate him from more common varieties of his ilk. The first concerns Stoker's insistence that Dracula can sleep only in consecrated earth: 'in soil barren of holy memories [he] cannot rest' (D 18:288). This requirement would seem to possess neither folkloric nor historic antecedent.[6] According to the superstition of Orthodox lands, the undead, if excommunicated, were reputedly *unable* to rest in hallowed soil. Stoker probably intends Dracula's sacrilege to heighten the reader's sense of outrage and blasphemy: it also makes the Count's lairs harder to locate, 'sleeping' deceitfully as he is among God's true dead. And, of course, Vlad Tepes himself was buried in consecrated earth.

Another example of Dracula's uniqueness as a vampire is his immunity to the rays of the sun. The vampire of superstition is the quintessential apparition of night; it being assumed that sunlight could pass through, or harm, sensitive tissue. Dracula, however, cannot be destroyed by direct sunlight as film versions would have us believe. That would make him too vulnerable. Once he is strong and vigorous from the consumption of fresh blood, he is permitted in the book to wander the streets of London quite naturally. The only handicap is that his vampire powers become neutralized during the hours of daylight, when he reverts, to all intents, to being a mere mortal. He must therefore take care that at the moment of sunrise he is in the place and form that he wishes to be for the coming day. Otherwise he must await the precise moment of noon or sunset to effect the desired transference (D 22:347-8).

Most important of all, Stoker could not allow his arch-fiend to have become a vampire originally by any of the numerous qualifying procedures, for they all imply falling victim in some manner. Count Dracula can be a victim of nobody and nothing. As he has become a vampire it must be because he *wanted* to be one. He was neither bitten whilst alive by another undead, nor was he sentenced to a vampiric punishment for any of the appropriate transgressions. In his human life, Count Dracula was an alchemist and magician. He had studied the secrets of the black arts and other aspects of devilry through being a student at the Scholomance (D 18:288; 23:360) — a mythical academy situated high in the Carpathian Mountains overlooking the town of Sibiu (known in Saxon as Hermannstadt).[7] The patron of the academy is the devil himself, who instructs on the dark secrets of nature: he provides an understanding of thunder and lightning, the language of animals, and magical spells. Those who studied the causes of natural phenomena were assumed to be capable of mastering them. Legend has it that the Scholomance would admit students ten at a time. Upon acquisition of the devilish insight nine would return to their everyday lives, leaving the tenth to be taken up by the devil as group payment. He would be mounted on an *ismejeu* — dragon (another merging of the devil/dragon association with Dracula) — and recruited as the devil's aide-de-camp.[8] Needless to say, Dracula was the tenth student, whose arcane wisdom is demonstrated by Stoker early in the novel when the Count inspects mysterious blue flames appearing in the forest which, according to folklore, conceal treasure and gold.

Stoker was not content to leave Dracula's transition from man to vampire to the reader's imagination. At the instant of the Count's 'death' such were the resources of his brain that, together with the magical powers gleaned from the Scholomance, his mental faculties survived physical death (*D* 23:360). But not intact. He paid the price of having much of his memory faculty destroyed, and has to engage in the re-learning process almost in the manner of an infant. Van Helsing, the guru of Dracula's adversaries, is an exponent of the scientific method of 'experimentation'. He appreciates the Count's emerging mental powers because he, Van Helsing, also employs scientific method, reaching out to acquire knowledge slowly but surely, one step at a time. Van Helsing's fear is not only that Dracula has acquired immortality through forging a special, yet undisclosed, relationship with the devil, but also that he has centuries ahead of him to develop his intellect and his evil. In fact, Dracula undergoes a dramatic shift in power during the course of the novel. At the outset he appears as a rather cautious, insular old man, not yet sure of the powers at his command. He is in the position, despite his longevity, of a fledgling bird about to leave his nest and fly for the first time. He has not yet employed the full range of his vampire powers which are about to be unleashed.

To reinforce Dracula's grasp of black magic, Stoker invests the Count's native Transylvania with suitably mysterious rocks and waters. It is a land

> full of strangeness of the geologic and chemical world. There are
> deep caverns and fissures that reach none know whither. There have

been volcanoes, some of whose openings still send out waters of strange properties, and gases that kill or make to [sic] vivify. Doubtless there is something magnetic or electric in some of these combinations of occult forces which work for physical life in strange way [sic] (D 24:380).[9]

These gases are discovered at first hand by Van Helsing when he sniffs sulphurous fumes inside the chapel of Castle Dracula (D 27:438). Stoker's Transylvania, in other words, is not only a land beyond the forest, it is also a land beyond scientific understanding — a netherworld — where the known laws of nature are suspended. It is a fitting haunt for an agent for diabolism.

Awareness of Dracula's vampire origins leads to the next, vital, question — his motives. He is no zombie-like automaton driven solely by an unthinking lust for blood, as folklore tends to represent its vampires. The relationship between Dracula and blood is much more subtle. For one thing, its consumption can actually change his appearance. His countenance undergoes a rapid transformation according to the frequency of his blood intake. Absorption of blood enables him to change from an old man, into a younger, stronger man with dark, not white, hair. In as short a space as three days between 'meals' his hair would revert to showing white streaks (D 11:167).

Dracula is not desperate to drink every drop of blood that comes his way. He does not patrol nightly in search of liquid nourishment in order to keep alive. Rather, his is the addiction of the junkie or the alcoholic. Dracula will not die if no blood is available, any more than will the alcoholic if deprived of spirits. It is more accurate to say that in both cases only a single substance can supply that extra vigour, that pepped-up fuel. It is not that Dracula *likes* drinking blood: he *needs* blood. He does not need it for life, which he is blessed/cursed with anyway, but for power. It functions as a stimulant.

The only exception to this function is when his taking of blood performs a tactical purpose. Dracula's blood-banks are always female.[10] His szgany (gypsy) henchmen, for example, who do his earthly bidding, do not go in fear of his teeth. Renfield, similarly, becomes a servant of Dracula, not his blood supply. Still more illuminating is Dracula's ultimately trivial interest in Jonathan Harker, who is his passport to Britain and his English language tutor, not his provider of nourishment. When Harker cuts himself shaving, Dracula only momentarily loses control of himself, suggesting that the sight of blood induces in him a love-hate ambivalence, again not dissimilar to the reactions stimulated in the alcoholic by the prospect of liquor.

Dracula's strategic, as opposed to his biological, interest in blood is to take it for the purposes of ensnaring female victims who, in turn, will ensnare their menfolk. Here, Stoker acknowledges the folkloric requirement that vampires always seek out their nearest and dearest: 'the holiest love was the recruiting sergeant for their ghastly ranks' (D 22:354). Dracula is well aware of how he can turn this to his advantage: 'Your girls that you all love are mine already; and through them you and others shall yet be mine — my creatures, to do my bidding and to be my jackals when I want to feed' (D 23:365).

In no instance does he destroy the lives of his victims for pleasure, but always in order to make use of them. As it is not a threat to his continued existence that prompts his quest for blood, the search must stem from a deeper psychological drive. Dracula tells an unsuspecting Harker of his ambitions: 'I long to go through the crowded streets of your mighty London, to be in the midst of the whirl and rush of humanity, to share its life, its change, its death, and all that makes it what it is' (D 2:31).

This confession is revealing. In the Europe of the 1890s Dracula has become historically obsolete.[11] Transylvania is depicted as a peasant land in decline, unfitting as the continued habitat for a proud descendant of Attila. Admittedly it is Dracula's own nocturnal activities over the centuries which are partly responsible for the lack of vitality and stimulation of his native land, for its depleted population are now uniformly superstitious and able to flout his authority by immunizing themselves with garlic and crosses. He feels cheated and deprived, and his hunting has been restricted to defenceless children. Moveover, there are no longer any invading Turks left for him to wage war against. But by coming to London, the hub of Western industrialism, thereby switching his arena and his methods of operation, he sees new opportunities to exploit as a means of self-advancement.

His objective is thus to establish a contemporary vampire empire in Britain, the fulfilment of which would be unwittingly assisted by British laws and customs. The rational West will not suspect him: it is contemptuous of Eastern superstitions and will leave him free; its democratic customs will enable him to flourish undetected; and its legal principle of presumption of innocence will work to his devious advantage. Gaols cannot hold vampires. British society will unconsciously provide both his sheath and his armour, and 'the doubting of wise men would be his greatest strength' (D 24:382).

Notwithstanding, Dracula's motives also contain a more personal element. When narrowly escaping ambush in London he reveals his driving grievance: 'My revenge has just begun! I spread it over centuries, and time is on my side' (D 23:365). Revenge? Revenge for what? Stoker seems to be harking back to the life of Vlad Tepes, who was undoubtedly partly driven by revenge when he became ruler of Wallachia: seeking to avenge the deaths of his father and brother, and his own adolescent incarceration at the hands of the Turks. But if Count Dracula could not take revenge against the Turks, the superpower of his time, he could at least direct it against the modern superpower. Britain must pay the penalty for the crimes of the Turks. Further, Britain has come to symbolize the ingratitude and treachery of Christian Europe, which betrayed Dracula while he was fighting the Turks in their interests (D 21:343).

Yet even this desire for revenge is somehow not totally persuasive: it seems both incomplete and superficial. Although he is not technically immortal, since he can be destroyed, Dracula is, like the Wandering Jew, doomed to wander the earth for eternity unless his Achilles Heel (or heart) be pierced. The Count is bored. It is sport he is after: a challenge. He is toying with his adversaries, taunting them, almost defying them to pit their puny wits against him. Despite this range of motives and grievances, it is not Stoker's aim to elicit sympathy for Dracula, or reveal him a victim as much as a victimizer. Stoker portrays him as incarnate evil, without any redeeming features, someone deserving not the least vestige of sympathy.

Stoker's intention was, presumably, that the reader breathes a sigh of relief when Dracula meets his eventual doom. Or was it? Clearly his pursuers think they have destroyed Dracula, and continue to think so several years afterwards. But have they? This is how Mina describes that climactic moment:

> As I looked, the eyes [of Dracula] saw the sinking sun, and the look of hate in them turned to triumph. But, on the instant, came the sweep and the flash of Jonathan's great knife. I shrieked as I saw it sheer through the throat; whilst at the same moment Mr Morris' bowie knife plunged in the heart . . . the whole body crumbled into dust and passed from our sight . . . in that moment of dissolution there was in the face a look of peace such as I never could have imagined might have rested there (D 27:447).

This might seem conclusive enough, until it is remembered that earlier Van Helsing had given precise instructions on how to be rid of the vampire. Folklore, too, insists on almost ritualistic observation of prescribed rites. These are not followed in the case of Dracula, who is despatched as if he were human, with cold steel. No wooden stake is used; the head is not detached from the body; and there is no corpse left to be properly treated or devoured by flames. Initially it seems that Dracula's look of 'triumph' is premature, but could it be the attackers' sense of satisfaction that is misplaced? Stoker had already informed his readers that vampires have the power of dematerialization and can transform themselves into specks of dust. Conceivably, then, the Count has dematerialized just in time, and realizing his narrow escape prefers to maintain a low profile, until such time as Stoker might have chosen to resurrect him in a sequel.

# 7.

# 'THANK GOD FOR GOOD BRAVE MEN'*

[Stoker] has in the first place the deficiency commonly found among writers who concern themselves almost exclusively with occult themes, of having either no interest in human personality, or no ability to analyse it. Despite the fact that he uses with unsurpassed skill the technique most suited to revelation of character [namely diary entries and the like], the people in the story are totally unconvincing, with the partial exception of the demon himself, whose personality is of course inhuman.

Glen St John Barclay,
*Anatomy of Horror: Masters of Occult Fiction*, p. 44

IT IS a commonplace criticism of Gothic romances in general that they lack vividness of characterization, that their heroes and heroines are uniformly stereotyped and one-dimensional, and that this failing stems from the principal preoccupation of the genre—the threat of the supernatural. Other-worldly beings inevitably take precedence over this-worldly ones. *Dracula* has not escaped from this line of attack; indeed, it has received particular vituperation from certain critics. Even those otherwise well-disposed towards the novel have flayed Stoker's inability or unwillingness to give greater substance and credibility to the mortals lined up against the Count.

While the novel might have been improved had Stoker paid as much attention to his living beings as to his vampire, it can be contended that the book survives this blemish. It is not the case that Stoker lacked the *ability* to make his characters credible. One of the reasons for *Dracula's* established place as a horror classic is the masterly way the author paints his central creation. So

*Dracula* 23:370.

omnipotent is Count Dracula, and so all-encompassing is his evil, that it is necessary for the cast of mortals to pale alongside him. When Dracula sneers at his adversaries, 'You think to baffle me, you — with your pale faces all in a row, like sheep in a butcher's' (D 23:365), he is speaking for Stoker. Compared to the Count they *are* like sheep — pitiful, lacking depth, vision, and character. They must be that way. Had Stoker laboured to present them with greater vigour, the essential imbalance of the contest between Good and Evil would have shifted, and Dracula's omnipotence diluted. None of them are a match for him. Compared to a creature like Dracula, they are mere putty in his hands. Only collectively do they possess any strength, and that realization is central to the novel. This is how one scholar summarizes the typical antagonist of the literary monster: he 'will always be, by contrast, a representative of the present, a distillation of complacent nineteenth-century mediocrity: nationalistic, stupid, superstitious, philistine, impotent, self-satisfied.'[1] All this can be applied to the adversaries of Dracula.

Because Stoker's characters are so flimsy, readers must make of them what they can. The resulting interpretations are by no means mutually consistent. One aspect to be borne in mind in the personality surveys that follow is Stoker's objective in choosing particular names for his characters. Sometimes it appears he gave no thought to the matter, conjuring up names at whim; but on other occasions it will become clear that his names were carefully pre-selected for ulterior purposes.[2] Only when Stoker's characters have been analysed and their functions ascertained will it be possible to dissect the novel in terms of its multi-faceted symbolism.

## Jonathan Harker

It is fitting that a discussion of the cast of *Dracula* begins with Jonathan Harker. It is he who is responsible for bringing the Count to London at the beginning, who suffers irredeemable guilt for so doing, and who appropriately severs the villain's throat at the conclusion to rid the world of his menace. A search for the source of the name 'Harker' does not take long. Arminius Vambery was not the only personal acquaintance whose name was given to posterity through Stoker's fiction. Harker acquired his name from one Joseph Harker, who had occasional assignments as scenic designer and painter for the Lyceum.[3] But this has not prevented further ingenious speculation. 'Hark', it has been suggested, refers to a danger signal,[4] or an injunction to heed and listen.[5]

Jonathan Harker, like Bram Stoker, is a man of the law: to be exact, he is a recently qualified solicitor in his early twenties, practising in Exeter. Whether he is Exeter born and bred is not clear. Most likely he is not. Stoker is notoriously fastidious about accent and dialect, but Harker's does not draw comment. When the Count requests lessons in English conversation, so that he will not stand out as a foreigner in London, he does not seem concerned that he might be absorbing a strong west-country lilt that would defeat his purpose.

Like Stoker, too, Harker is a Protestant. He possesses a clever, strong, youthful face, and a quiet, frank, business-like manner. He has the virtues of discretion associated with his profession. His hair at the outset is dark brown, but Stoker has the aim of pivoting Harker and Dracula around their common 'wife' — Mina — and as Dracula appears younger and more vital as the plot unfolds, Harker, once his wife has been 'visited', is drained in reverse. He becomes haggard, his spirits are sapped, and his once dark hair turns snowy white virtually overnight as his energy is transferred, via his wife, to the Count.

This visible deterioration has contributed to wildly conflicting views as to what kind of person Harker is. To some, Harker is simply not much of a man, and appears in much of the book in a passive or supine state.[6] He is something of a half-witted creep, a goody-goody; someone who puts duty before all else. He is a provincial philistine, is no connoisseur of food and drink, and is a creature of monotonous habit — insisting that he winds his watch before going to bed and folds his clothes in a certain way. He harbours a naïve and simplistic belief in the value of the English legal system with a criminal's right of protection under the law. Even his wife describes him as 'sweet and simple', though in a way that is meant to be flattering, and he has evidently never had to face any real responsibility in his life, prior to his Transylvanian ordeal. His very existence in the novel is almost apologetic: a 'sufficient substitute' to act for his employer who was too ill to undertake the trip himself (D 2:27). Throughout, Harker knows his humble place, particularly when in the company of the other, socially superior, Dracula-hunters. Morally, he is something of a prude — objecting to the tight-fitting clothes of Transylvanian women — and is intellectually curious only in the bigoted way of an insular Englishman who wants his preconceptions confirmed and is completely nonplussed otherwise.

But there is another, more positive, side to Harker. He is no Little Englander, even though this is his first trip abroad, and seems fascinated by foreign places and customs. The mere fact of his travelling to a virtually unknown land which is in the grip of superstitious mania testifies to his adventurous spirit. He can converse in German and his diary reveals him as both observant and alert. In the Castle he eventually ascertains the nature of his plight through his own mental and physical resources: he cannot take advantage of the guiding light provided by Van Helsing. Harker demonstrates both surprising initiative and immense personal courage in trying, while a prisoner, to outwit the Count. Evidently he works better under strain. Moreover, he has a healthy contempt for snobbery and is adept at playing 'prigs' at their own game if the occasion demands (*D* 20:317).

What is most remarkable in Harker is the way in which this unassuming, normally placid, solicitor, who gives no impression of ever having lifted a finger in anger in his life, is able to resort to extreme physical violence when aroused. Not only is he prepared to take a shovel to the sleeping Count's face, but at the climax the outraged husband wields a great Kukri knife to sweep past a ring of Dracula's armed gypsy bodyguard. Awestruck, they step aside to permit Harker to slice the throat of their master. When motivated, Jonathan Harker is no mouse. But, overall, his most enduring achievement, and the one by which he is best assessed, is that he is one of the few fictional characters to have lived among, and been imprisoned by, vampires, yet who by his own guile and courage survived to tell the tale.

More than one of the male characters in *Dracula* can be seen to be in certain respects a projection of Stoker himself — though Harker is the most obvious candidate. Not only is he, like Stoker at a comparable age, a provincial Protestant man of the law, but Harker reveals to the reader how both he and Stoker came by their knowledge of Transylvanian history and customs — through the British Museum. Furthermore, Harker's sexual fantasies are undoubtedly an extension of Stoker's: a question to which we shall return.

Harker also features prominently in one of the major riddles of *Dracula*. Among the selection of short stories published after Stoker's death was 'Dracula's Guest', after which the anthology was named. The tale speaks of an unnamed young man journeying to visit Count Dracula who meets with perilous adventures in Munich en route. In view of the fact that the adventures which befall Dracula's guest occur on Walpurgis Nacht — 1 May, following which the novel *Dracula* opens — it is evident that the two tales are related in some way. It is widely believed that 'Dracula's Guest' (as published in 1914) is the excised opening chapter of *Dracula*.

In fact, the relationship between 'Dracula's Guest' and *Dracula* cannot be that straightforward. Stoker's papers dated 29 February 1892 reveal that the Munich events — which were scheduled to span two chapters — were themselves to be preceded by an opening chapter presenting a flurry of legal correspondence relating to property sales. It appears, then, that the entire introductory section of the novel, comprising three chapters, was at some stage (or stages) discarded. Further confirmation of this can be found in the page-numbers of Stoker's now-discovered manuscript of *Dracula*; where page-number '3' overrides a deleted typewritten page-number '103'.

Stoker's original timetable for the novel shows he intended three separate incidents to befall Jonathan Harker in Munich. Taken in sequence these are, firstly, an adventure in a snowstorm with a wolf; secondly, a visit to the theatre to see a production of *The Flying Dutchman* (presumably as an aperitif for the real-life immortal he was about to meet); and thirdly, a spooky encounter in a 'Dead House', wherein Harker confronts an image of what later transpires to have been the Count.

A deleted reference to the 'Dead House' actually appears near the beginning of Stoker's *Dracula* manuscript. But as neither the Dead House nor the Flying Dutchman episodes feature in the 1914 version of 'Dracula's Guest', it fails in its supposed function as the prelude to *Dracula*.

'Dracula's Guest' concerns itself solely with the first of Harker's three Munich experiences; when he shelters from a snowstorm in an eery, forbidding tomb, catches sight of a beautiful woman within, and is 'rescued' by a wolf. Stoker's constant switching of timetable further confuses matters. Originally it was to be the Dead House incident which took place on Walpurgis Nacht, not that involving the snowstorm/wolf, which was to have occurred some days earlier on 27 April. Stoker's manuscript, however, contains an excised reference to the woman 'in the tomb on Walpurgis Night'. When did Stoker make this change, and what is the connection with the Dead House encounter, also scheduled for that day?

This uncertainty pertaining to the timing and original contents of 'Dracula's Guest' is heightened by consideration of its published format. To begin with, the narrative style employed in the short story is different from that found in *Dracula*. 'Dracula's Guest' is not easily identified as a diary entry, being a first-person account that contains much short, sharp dialogue. In addition, the central motifs of the two tales are quite distinct. In *Dracula* the 'wolf' is shown as savage and destructive: the animal familiar of the Count. In 'Dracula's Guest', by contrast, a wolf warms the body of the insensible guest to protect him from the cold.

More critically, the unnamed 'guest', although identified in Stoker's notes as Jonathan Harker, is unrecognizable from the Harker of the finished novel. In the course of the various drafts Harker's personality undergoes a radical change. In 'Dracula's Guest' he is aggressive, almost rude, sufficiently foolhardy to go sauntering off on his own on Walpurgis Nacht — an act quite out of keeping with the introverted Harker of the novel. Crucially, Dracula's guest does not speak any German: the Harker of *Dracula* does. This discrepancy is significant because Stoker originally intended to base his novel in German-speaking Styria. In a note scribbled in March 1890 Stoker remarks that the Count will insist that his English go-between cannot speak (or understand) German. Otherwise, of course, the locals will be able to warn him of his peril and convince him of the need to return home. By the time Stoker had relocated his Count to Transylvania — which he had done by early 1892 — there was no longer the same pressing demand for Harker's ignorance of German. Although many of that region's inhabitants speak German, their superstitious natures undermine the force of their warnings. It is, in any case, difficult for Harker to escape the all-seeing Dracula's powers once he has arrived in Transylvania (in 'Dracula's Guest' he was unable to escape them even in Munich). Besides, in his mature drafts Stoker clearly wanted Harker to be made aware of the risks he was running — by allowing him to communicate in German — and so contribute to his dire predicament by disregarding them.

It can, in summary, be maintained that if at some very late stage a chapter of Stoker's final manuscript was excised, that chapter could not have been identical in form to that published posthumously seventeen years later under the title 'Dracula's Guest'. More probably that particular tale, as it stands, is a self-contained episode reworked from the earliest, 1890-2, phase of Stoker's ideas. It is not clear how, or when, 'Dracula's Guest' came by its name.

## Van Helsing

A second outlet for Stoker's own personality is Professor Abraham Van Helsing, who is significantly allowed to borrow Stoker's Christian name. He is the only character other than Dracula to warrant a careful physical description. He is

> a man of medium height, strongly built, with his shoulders set back over a broad, deep chest and a neck well balanced on the trunk as the head is on the neck. The poise of the head strikes one at once as indicative of thought and power; the head is noble, well-sized, broad, and large behind the ears. The face, clean shaven, shows a hard, square chin, a large, resolute, mobile mouth, a good-sized nose, rather straight, but with quick, sensitive nostrils, that seem to broaden as the big, bushy eyebrows come down and the mouth tightens. The forehead is broad and fine, rising at first almost straight and then sloping back above two bumps or ridges wide apart; such a forehead that the reddish hair cannot possibly tumble over it, but falls naturally back and to the sides. Big, dark blue eyes are set widely apart, and are quick and tender or stern with the man's moods (D 14:218-9).

His countenance is repeatedly described as 'of iron'. Van Helsing is old (we are not told how old), grey, and lonely — his wife is insane and his son is dead (D 13:210,12). He remains faithful to his wife's memory and finds a substitute for companionship in work, though he comes to 'love' each and every one of the little band afflicted by Dracula, and views them as his sons and daughters. He treasures old-fashioned virtues, and (evidently like Bram Stoker) is unsettled by the sceptical, selfish late-Victorian age in which he lives (D 14:226). He fulfils similar functions in Dracula to Baron Vordenburg in Carmilla, and his name is similar to Dr Hesselius in another of Le Fanu's tales 'Green Tea'; though in view of his battle with Dracula, Van Helsing has also been identified with 'Hell Singer'.[7]

Van Helsing is the remote, aged specialist. Like Father Lankester Merrin in The Exorcist, he is the Catholic scientist, the superbrain waiting for the inevitable call for one final battle against the forces of evil. Both these wise men appear on their respective scenes only when ordinary 'medicine' has failed to cure the patient and it is necessary to seek recourse in the 'witch doctor' who has access to less orthodox remedies.

Many readers see Van Helsing as the hero of Dracula, which was probably Stoker's intention. The Dutch professor is the repository of worldly wisdom; the guru and shaman without whose intervention Dracula's schemes would doubtless have succeeded. As a Doctor of Medicine, of Philosophy, and of Letters — and a lawyer into the bargain — he is portrayed as the all-round intellectual and free thinker. His philosophical breadth of mind may reveal how Stoker thought of himself. Van Helsing knows something of many languages and has 'revolutionised therapeutics by the discovery of the continuous evolution of brain matter' (*D* 18:292). When he is introduced, the reader is left in no doubt that here is the man to do battle with the Count. Van Helsing

> knows as much about obscure diseases as anyone in the world . . . He is a seemingly arbitrary man, but this is because he knows what he is talking about better than anyone else. He is a philosopher and metaphysician, and one of the most advanced scientists of his day; and he has . . . an absolutely open mind. This, with an iron nerve, a temper of the ice-brook, an indomitable resolution, self-command and toleration exalted from virtues to blessings, and the kindliest and truest heart that beats — these form his equipment for the noble work that he is doing for mankind — work both in theory and in practice, for his views are as wide as his all-embracing sympathy (*D* 9:137).

He is, in other words, almost too good to be true: a paragon of professional and personal virtues.[8] He is the Sherlock Holmes who will tackle Moriarty. Both the professor and the sleuth share the qualities of being detached, purposeful, the possessors of a superior intellect, and able to make their views prevail — as well as showing tenderness and concern for others. Likewise both the Count and Moriarty are coldly and cunningly evil, have total control over their underlings, and possess brilliant, if twisted, minds.[9] For all its supernatural content, *Dracula* is as much a tale of detection as of horror, so it is not surprising that Stoker's super-hero started out, in the early drafts of the novel, as several different people: a German philosopher and historian, a psychical research agent, and a detective. Such is the range of talents necessary to offset the Count's mastery, that all three seem to have been encapsulated in one composite embodiment of power, knowledge and virtue — Abraham Van Helsing.

Unfortunately, Van Helsing is not always the inspiring presence Stoker intended him to be. Despite having been a student in London, his spoken English is heavily accented. This often makes him difficult to understand, and because it is Van Helsing's crucial function to elucidate the behaviour of vampires the reader is put to some inconvenience every time he speaks.

Although capable of discretion and sensitivity towards the sufferings of Dracula's victims, Van Helsing is not immune to thoughtless remarks, and his sense of humour can be distasteful, even macabre. At times, he seems to be taunting the others with

the perilousness of their position. On one occasion he reminds
Mina, needlessly and tactlessly, that the Count has 'banqueted
heavily' from her body (D 22:352). An apologist for this side of
Van Helsing's nature would suggest that he must be permitted
some lapses, given the severe strain he is under. For he is fighting
for the redemption and salvation not just of his comrades but, in
all likelihood, mankind. A less indulgent interpretation would be
that because Van Helsing is central to the religious ideas that
underpin the book, he is acting as priestly condemner of lax
behaviour — particularly of sexual desire. His name 'Abraham'
is not only Stoker's, but was also that of the first biblical patriarch.
By combining his scientific eminence with his Vatican contacts,
Van Helsing has connections with the two (not necessarily
compatible) dominant forces of Western culture.[10]

Van Helsing, of course, is principally a medical man: he is not
a trained vampire hunter. He has to learn quickly the nature of
the crisis confronting him. He relishes the challenge presented by
Dracula's brain, and feels not a little intellectual affinity with him:
'I too am wily and I think his mind in a little while' (D 23:373).
Even when he fully comprehends, his secretive and conspiratorial
nature makes him resist the temptation to impart his understanding
to others until they are able to discern the light for themselves.
Through his own arcane researches he has a pretty shrewd idea
of what he is up against, but like the true initiate he refuses to tell.[11]
Although the professor cannot yet be sure, he evidently suspects
the presence of a vampire from the outset (D 9:139; 10:150).
However, he is slow to make use of his suspicions, and his tardiness
contributes to Lucy's death, which could have been averted given
the state of Van Helsing's knowledge at the time, although
afterwards he maintains that he had not guessed the horrific cause
of her malady (D 18:283).[12] He then compounds the errors made
over Lucy, operating a conspiracy theory when he learns of the
attack on Mina which, it turns out, could easily have led to a second
tragedy.

Van Helsing, the more the microscope is turned on him, entertains
somewhat unliberal attitudes and beliefs. What liberal-minded
doctor, for example, would refer to mental illness as a 'defect' (D
18:294)? Moreover, he is manifestly a Roman Catholic and the
upholder of the strictest moral values. He constantly urges 'trust'
and 'belief' in what he has to say about the nature and causes of
vampirism. His supposedly 'open mind' is in fact a sham. Everything
is seen through the narrowest spectacles of Christian dogma,

and Goodness and Evil interpreted in the light of Vatican strictures. He is basically a kindly, avuncular old man, but one for whom the path of righteousness is narrow and the consequences of deviating unthinkable.

Nor is he in the least constrained by the conventions of science and medicine, and is quite prepared to turn to non-scientific thinking for inspiration. When modern science and Christian faith prove inadequate for the task in hand he readily resorts to folklore and superstition. Van Helsing, of all people, should know that there is no such thing as systematic superstition or a homogeneous tradition of vampire legends. He turns vampire lore into vampire law, yet he solves that particular difficulty by declaring such superstitions to have their roots in 'faith' (D 24:390). As a consequence, Van Helsing leads the forces of Good with a bizarre combination of modern science and superstition, and he warns his fellows against the materialist scepticism provided by their bourgeois values and prejudices (D 18:285). By his use of garlic, not to mention Host and crucifix, Van Helsing takes science across the frontiers of witchcraft. Whereas Mary Shelley's Frankenstein, eighty years earlier, had been a 'magician-turned-scientist', Van Helsing becomes a 'scientist-turned-magician'.[13]

## Renfield

Occupying the strategically opposite position to Van Helsing in the novel is Renfield, an inpatient in a lunatic asylum. He stands outside the little band opposed to Dracula, being psychically in tune with the Count and, initially, anxious to serve him. In that sense he, too, like Harker and Van Helsing, can be viewed as a manifestation of Stoker — Renfield being the minion of a vampire, Stoker of an actor.

Renfield is fifty-nine, of ruddy complexion, and with pleading eyes. He possesses great physical strength; is selfish, secretive, and purposeful; and he is morbidly excitable, being prone to violent spasms (D 5:78; 6:87; 9:131-2). He is also, it later transpires, surprisingly well-educated and articulate.

As regard the novel's structure, one of Renfield's functions is to form a triangular relationship. He connects with Dracula, on the one hand, his pursuers on the other — which helps to clarify the reader's understanding of both.[14] A second function arises when Stoker attempts to use Renfield to expound a pseudo-scientific theory of vampirism. The patient gives the lie to those who would assume vampirism to be exclusively the product of simple-minded peasants in distant lands. Renfield is himself a living vampire, serving his vampire apprenticeship while confined within the walls of an asylum. He consumes blood by consuming life. Consider the children's song:

There was an old lady who swallowed a fly
  I don't know why she swallowed a fly — perhaps she'll die.
There was an old lady who swallowed a spider
[bird, cat, dog, goat, cow, horse].

Renfield is like that old lady, and throughout Stoker's notes he is referred to as the 'Flyman' or the 'Fly Patient'. Incarcerated in his cell he takes to catching flies and eating them, seeking justification and explanation in the scriptural phrase 'the blood is the life' (D 11:171; 18:280). Not content with flies he turns his attention to spiders, which have previously caught and digested flies — all to provide him, or so he thinks, with good, strong, wholesome life. Next he contrives to gorge sparrows, jubilant in the various accumulated lives he is ingesting. He asks for a cat — but does not get one — and even tries to kill a human solely for the purpose of lapping his blood. He believes that flesh and blood from living creatures will grant him immortality, and for his pains he is medically classified as a 'zoophagous (life-eating) maniac' (D 6:90).

Another role for Renfield is that of barometer of the Count's presence. As will be explored, Renfield takes on a John the Baptist identity, prefiguring the arrival of his 'Christ'. In this connection, one Dracula etymologist has suggested that 'Ren' means to 'clear a way for' a pastoral area (a 'field'). [15] Certainly, Renfield's eccentric behaviour starts attracting attention while the Count is still hundreds of miles from England, although it is not clear whether it is he who senses Dracula, or vice versa. His tantrums thereafter coincide with the times — dawn, noon, and dusk — when Dracula's powers are changing or at their weakest.

Finally, Renfield is included in the cast to highlight the issue of madness. Is it really he who is mad for acknowledging the existence of Dracula, when other, 'saner', persons must sooner or later come to the same conclusion? Like Harker, Renfield desperately wants to be able to distinguish between nightmare and grim reality. As with Harker, too, truth eventually wins through, confirming what Van Helsing once observed: 'I may gain more knowledge out of the folly of this madman than I shall from the teaching of the most wise' (D 19:305).

Strange to say, although Renfield is the most unusual and bizarre character in the novel (apart from Dracula), he is also, paradoxically, the most convincing.[16] The same could not be said of the three young, worldly heroes — Seward, Holmwood, and Morris.

## Dr Seward

Dr John (Jack) Seward shares with Jonathan Harker the facility of being a compulsive diarist. Many of the events of the book are seen through his eyes — or, rather, mouth, for Seward records his thoughts on to the newly invented phonograph. Seward functions as a link man, being the catalyst which brings four of the other male characters together. His relationship with Van Helsing and Renfield, for example, is central to the unfolding of the plot.

Seward is a twenty-nine-year-old psychiatrist, running a large, private lunatic asylum — a booming industry in late-Victorian England. He is of good birth, handsome, with a 'strong jaw and good forehead', and eminently marriageable. He has had his share of youthful adventures, hunting, and travelling the world, though he nonetheless appears inexperienced and nervous in the company of desirable women. Seward has studied under Van Helsing in Amsterdam (he was his favourite pupil), and the admiration evidently goes both ways. But the personal bond goes deeper than merely shared professional competence. Seward once saved his master's life, in circumstances which cast a shadow over an already deepening plot. Van Helsing suffered a wound, inflicted by a gangrenous knife, which Seward had to suck clean (D 9:138). Seward, in other words, has sucked Van Helsing's blood — a second instance of 'natural' blood-sucking, added to Renfield's, introduced by Stoker.

Seward is included as the representative of all that Van Helsing rejects: materialist, rationalist science — cure-all of the late-Victorian age. Seward finds it difficult to have faith or trust in anything. He does not trust people he does not know well (D 17:265), and in the case of Van Helsing not even someone he does. His role is also that of social commentator. Through him, for example, the reader is made aware of how Victorian manhood refuses to acknowledge emotion. Tearful breakdowns are considered unmanly, but if unavoidable are best performed in the company of women, not men (D 17:275).

Van Helsing, despite Seward's prejudices, presumably admires his ex-student's intellect, just as Sherlock Holmes respects Dr Watson's. The reader, however, is less impressed with Seward — though the doctor does occupy the same position *vis à vis* Van

Helsing as Watson does for Holmes. Seward's comparability to Dr Watson extends to possession of the same Christian name and membership of the same profession. Both characters are given to some 'half-baked philosophizing'.[17] In *Dracula*, Seward is the foil, the means by which Stoker can explain everything to the reader through someone who cannot, or will not, fully comprehend unless everything is elaborately reduced to first principles. Seward is the last of the characters to understand and accept the presence of the supernatural in their midst. *Punch*, in reviewing *Dracula*, summarized Seward as: 'the Inquiring, Sceptical, Credulous Noodle . . . the devoted admiring slave of the philosophic astute hero, ever ready to question, ever ready to dispute, ever ready to make a mistake at the critical moment, or to go to sleep just when success depends on his remaining awake'.[18]

Seward, in fact, is more than just a 'noodle': for one thing, his medical ethics are somewhat questionable. He admits to a certain cruelty in his handling of Renfield, who is his pet lunatic (*D* 5:78). Although familiar with Renfield's violent mania, Seward still encourages him to escape so that his behaviour while at large can be studied. Nor is Seward averse to offering Renfield the live cat that he earlier wanted to eat (though his patient this time declines it). Seward even demonstrates a happy disregard for the law when it is expedient to do so; for example, sidestepping the need for an inquest into Lucy's death — although he has at that time no inkling of what caused it.

Moreover, just as Van Helsing is partly responsible for Lucy's death, so Seward ultimately fails as Renfield's physician — both in the diagnostic sense, and by contributory negligence which results in his patient's death. When Renfield, with the unexpected lucidity of apparent sanity, tries to show others what he alone can see, he is disregarded — fatally for him. He is mortally wounded, but is abandoned by Seward, who does not even summon an assistant to care for him, and is left to die alone.

If Seward is a somewhat unprincipled doctor, he is even more pitiful in his private life. Early in the book he is driven to distraction by his love for Lucy. His proposal of marriage is turned down and within weeks he confesses to a 'savage delight' at the prospect of beheading her (*D* 16:253). Worse, as the hunt for *Dracula* nears its climax, this respectable man of healing comes to feel 'wild with excitement' as battle approaches. He naïvely imagines he now knows 'what men feel in battle when the call to action is heard' (*D* 25:399). Obviously unbeknown to Seward, that feeling is usually described as one of abject terror.

To compound matters Seward not only fails to appreciate his limitations, medical and otherwise, but instead harbours a somewhat disconcerting personal ambition. The fact that he runs his own lunatic asylum at such a young age presumably testifies to his conventional medical abilities and his entrepreneurial aptitude. Yet he yearns to promote his own claims to medical research, and sees Renfield as the key to his success. He even envies his patient's sense of purpose. Seward's ego is sufficiently developed for him to contemplate whether he might enjoy a congenitally exceptional brain (D 6:90). But eventually, depressed and unsettled by unrequited love, obsessed by Renfield's behaviour, and mentally tortured by the apparently supernatural intrusion into his tidy, scientific mind, he is forced to tackle the nature of sanity — his own and Van Helsing's — head on. His innate nineteenth-century belief in progress clashes with his increasing doubts about himself and his motives. Not surprisingly, given his inner torment, he is usually ineffectual when it matters.

## Arthur Holmwood (Lord Godalming)

The most shadowy and under-developed of the major characters is the Hon. Arthur Holmwood — Lord Godalming as he becomes. It is obligatory for Stoker's young heroes to be physically attractive, and Holmwood conforms, being 'tall, handsome and curly-haired' and possessing 'stalwart proportions'. Naturally 'buoyant', he is wrecked by the double death of his fiancée. Although he is good with dogs and steam launches he seems otherwise to have no worthwhile qualities at all — save those of inherited wealth, for which he is not responsible. True to his privileged upbringing he is preoccupied with his honour as a gentleman and his faith as a Christian (D 15:246) — though neither prevents him using his title or his money to win whatever favours he wants. His Lordship's practical suggestions are usually cause for some hilarity: to assist in the under-cover operation to unearth Dracula's whereabouts in the rundown East End of London he offers to provide his heraldic-adorned coaches (D 22:350); and when the action shifts to the primitive vastness of eastern Europe he enquires about the feasibility of hiring a 'special' train to transport his comrades around the Black Sea hinterland (D 25:402).

Holmwood, in fact, has only two justifications for being in the book at all. The first is his wallet. A six-person expedition across Europe chasing Dracula costs a great deal — but Holmwood happily and unquestioningly provides the money. The second is his title. Holmwood's elevation to the peerage immediately prior to Lucy's first death promotes him to a platform opposite Count Dracula: two aristocrats fighting for possession of the same woman.

In fact, both Holmwood's name and his title give insight into Stoker's thinking. The Christian name 'Arthur' highlights the chivalrous nature of his role as England's archetypal hero and saviour.[19] There is, furthermore, a suggestion that 'Holmwood' was taken from 'Ringwood' — a character in *Varney the Vampire*. In *Dracula* the Holmwood family home happens to be at Ring. An alternative source for the name 'Holmwood' can be found in an 1892 edition of *Lloyd's Weekly Advertiser*, wherein the story is told of a certain Mr Holm, who, in the company of a Mr Wood, broke into a vault in St Mary's churchyard, Hendon, to sever the head from his mother's body. This incident appeared on the same page as a review of Irving's *King Lear*, so was likely to have come to the attention of Stoker.[20] Whatever the source, Holmwood's title transforms him into 'LORD GOD . . . alming'. God has come to take on the devil. Indeed, the full title is nearly LORD GOD ALMIGHTY, and the '. . . alming' implies *noblesse-oblige* pedigree,[21] or alms to God.[22]

## Quincey P. Morris

Quincey P. Morris, the American from Texas, has deliberately been left to last because with him lie most of the persistent uncertainties pertaining to the male cast. As a personality he is painted by Stoker with almost invisible strokes. Almost nothing is known about him. He does nothing of note throughout the book: nothing, that is, until its concluding lines. Then he dies — giving his life in the successful assault on Dracula.

The reason for Morris' death is a major mystery. He is the most superfluous character in the drama, being neither a direct victim of the vampire's kiss, nor the grieving partner of a victim out to settle accounts. It is difficult to imagine the novel as being irreparably harmed were he to be struck from it altogether (several film versions fuse Morris and Holmwood into a single personality). Morris' role seems simply to complete the trio of Seward and Holmwood, all suitors of the same girl — to mirror Dracula's three vampire mistresses. Yet this nonentity is not only the one who plunges his knife into Dracula's heart: he is the only one of the pursuers to lose his life in consequence; and it is he who symbolically lends his name to the Harkers' subsequently born son — Quincey Harker.

Morris thereby gains vicarious immortality, and as a result takes pride of place in Stoker's puzzling climax.

The problem lies in seeking to unearth Stoker's intention. As Morris is the most peripheral of the initiates his sacrifice is neither as telling, nor indeed as logical, as that of any other of his companions. Dracula has no particular quarrel with Morris. Before the possibilities are explored it will be useful to recap what is known about Quincey Morris. He is pure cardboard, a complete stereotype; the fresh, breezy, all-American boy; the bubbling well of good spirits; the brash, vulgar Texas millionaire. He is somewhat in the mould of Teddy Roosevelt, conforming to Victorian Britain's condescending view of the raw-edged but genuine American — dependable yet banal. At the practical level, Morris, as the gun-totin', knife-waving campaigner, is expected to provide the brawn to complement the Europeans' monopoly of brain. (Significantly he is the only one of the pursuing party who can speak no foreign language [D 26:412].) He is the calm, phlegmatic, tobacco-chewing man of action in a gang otherwise composed of medical men, aristocrats, and city slickers; he is a born leader in hunting expeditions (D 16:251; 23:363). So stereotypical is he, in fact, that Morris actually appears, cloned almost, in one of Stoker's earlier short stories.[23]

In sum, Morris is much travelled and a man of countless adventures. This makes him, in a sense, the most attractive, the most romantic, the most uncomplicated, the most identifiable of the little group. He is the only one who can die a hero's death, for he has no personal axe to wield against Dracula. Perhaps, then, it is just those qualities of friendship, loyalty, and reckless courage that Stoker is trying to celebrate.

Of course, Stoker was notably fond of America and proud of the courage of her menfolk, though why Morris should have been made a Texan is less apparent. There are, in fact, extended similarities between Morris and that real-life Texan freedom fighter, Jim Bowie, which go beyond the mere arming of Dracula's attacker with a Bowie knife. Stoker might conceivably have constructed Morris around that earlier hero of the Lone Star State who met his end, along with William Barrett Travis and Davy Crockett, in the Mexican assault on the Alamo in 1836. There is the similarity of personality. Both Bowie and Morris were adventurers. Both were hunters who relished entertaining massive odds. Despite their frontier ethos both were urbane, polished, and rich. They were quietly spoken and gentle — qualities which stood in stark contrast to the more belligerent aspects of their personalities, and which made them appear all the more formidable when aroused. Each was pragmatic, generous, extravagant, immovably loyal to an espoused cause, and a born leader.

In the company of women both were shy and ill at ease. Both fell in love with a member of the local social élite (Bowie with a nineteen-year-old Mexican girl; Morris with the similarly aged, similarly privileged Lucy), and both later lost them in appalling circumstances (cholera in the case of Bowie's young wife and children; the bite of Dracula in the case of Lucy).

Thereafter both men dedicated themselves to combating the greatest malefactor to plague their lives. Jim Bowie took up with fellow Texan settlers to stand firm against Santa Anna, while Quincey Morris risked all in the hunt for Dracula. Not only did Morris wield the Bowie knife in a symbolic lunge against his tormentor but, like Bowie, he paid the ultimate sacrifice. In their respective campaigns both fell victim to the cold steel employed by their antagonist's troops/bodyguard.

In their financial affairs both men lived by somewhat questionable principles. Jim Bowie won his immense personal fortune by wheeler-dealing, slave trading with pirates, and indulging in fictitious or fraudulent land titles. [24] Similarly, for all his dashing heroism, Quincey Morris is also aware of not having always lived by the Book: 'I'm only a rough fellow, who hasn't perhaps lived as a man should', he admits (*D* 25:393). He is also a teller of tall stories which, less charitably, could be another way of saying he does not know truth from fiction.

At the very least, then, Morris bears more than a passing resemblance to Jim Bowie. As for the name 'Morris', Stoker may have learned that Bowie's youthful notoriety first came to prominence with the knifing of a Major *Morris* Wright, [25] or else that immediately following the Alamo's fall Senator Thomas *Morris* of Ohio presented a petition to Congress demanding the recognition of Texan independence. [26]

The difficulty with Stoker's borrowing from Jim Bowie is that by reincarnating the Alamo's first commander half a century later, the circumstances which gave rise to Bowie become much less amenable to the manufacture of similar heroes. Given that the year in which Count Dracula visits England is 1893, and that Morris is no more than twenty-five (Seward is twenty-nine and he refers to Morris and the others as younger men [*D* 25:403]), it is possible to pinpoint the time of Morris' birth as the late 1860s — hard on the heels of the American Civil War.

With his choice of Texas, Stoker alighted on an area so vast and the product of so many disparate human forces and influences that efforts to place Morris in his native environment are easily frustrated.[27] He comes, Stoker says, 'from' Texas; he does not specifically say that he is a Texan. He may have been a second- or third-generation Texan, or, along with thousands of others, been an immigrant from another State. Either way, the pre-Civil War methods of profiteering in Texas were succeeded by decades of comparative austerity — the product of the emancipation of slaves and the consequent disruption of the cotton industry. The value of land collapsed, and most Texans were more concerned with staying alive than with striking it rich; for there was the Indian menace and resentful, unpaid veterans of the war to guard against. The Ku Klux Klan also made their first appearance in Texan history at this time. The commonest Texan pastimes in these troubled years were said to be drinking, card-playing, and shooting.[28] Taken as a whole, Texas had to wait until the twentieth century before recapturing the money-making opportunities of its pre-Civil War heyday. Not long before Morris' death in 1893 Texas was viewed by many Americans as a marginal region almost at the edge of civilization.

To account for this, it is probable that much, if not all, of Morris' fortune was the product of his parents' or grandparents' endeavours, and that he was something of a globe-trotting playboy. This would not leave much time for money-making, other than by speculation of one kind or another, and it rules out any kind of professional career.

If, however, Morris was more than simply a playboy son of affluent stock, how did he come by his fortune in post-reconstruction Texas? Oil had little significance until the twentieth century, and manufacturing was only just becoming profitable by the 1880s. More plausibly, he might have been a cattle baron or a railroad entrepreneur. One television adaptation of *Dracula* casts Morris as a diplomat, exploiting the established tradition of Texan frontiersmen dabbling in politics — though 'politicians' were one species of American known not to have impressed Stoker.[29] Alternatively, in his working notes Stoker mentions an American 'inventor' from Texas, though this is crossed out.

The reason for this greater attention being paid to one of Stoker's minor personages is to prepare the ground for a radical conjecture. Several critics have been puzzled by the seeming incongruity of a nobody like Quincey Morris taking precedence in the final pages of *Dracula*. This incongruity is made congruous if the possibility is explored that Morris was in league with the Count. This hypothesis has been presented most forcibly by Moretti, who opens his argument by noting the inexplicability of Morris' death, and that it is totally extraneous to the logic of the narrative. Moretti then takes a closer look at the American's activities in the novel, for Morris is shrouded in mystery:

'He looks so young and so fresh that it seems almost impossible that he has been to so many places and has had such adventures' [D 5:74]. What places? What adventures? Where does all his money come from? What does Mr Morris do? Where does he live? Nobody knows any of this. But nobody suspects. Nobody suspects even when Lucy dies — and then turns into a vampire — immediately after receiving a blood transfusion from Morris. Nobody suspects when Morris, shortly afterwards, tells the story of his mare, sucked dry of blood in the Pampas by 'one of those big bats they call vampires' [D 12:183]. It is the first time that the name 'vampire' is mentioned in the novel: but there is no reaction. And there is no reaction a few lines further on when Morris 'coming close to me . . . spoke in a fierce half-whisper: "What took it [the blood] out?" ' But Dr Seward shakes his head; he hasn't the faintest idea. And Morris, reassured, promises to help. Nobody, finally, suspects when, in the course of the meeting to plan the vampire hunt, Morris leaves the room to take a shot — missing, naturally — at the big bat [but nearly hitting the people inside] on the window-ledge listening to the preparations; or when, after Dracula bursts into the household, Morris hides among the trees, the only effect of which is that he loses sight of Dracula and invites the others to call off the hunt for the night. This is pretty well all Morris does in *Dracula*. He would be a totally superfluous character if, unlike the others, he were not characterized by this mysterious connivance with the world of the vampires. So long as things go well for Dracula, Morris acts like an accomplice. As soon as there is a reversal of fortunes, he turns into his staunchest enemy.

. . . And at the moment when Morris dies, and the threat disappears, old England grants its blessing to this excessively pushy and unscrupulous financier, and raises him to the dignity of a Bengal Lancer: 'And to our bitter grief, with a smile and silence, he died, a gallant gentleman' [D 27:448] . . . These, it should be noted, are the *last* words of the novel, whose true ending does not lie — as is clear by now — in the death of the Romanian count, but in the killing of the American financier.[30]

Following up Moretti's lead it is possible to unearth several incidents in the novel which lend support to his contention. When Lucy dies upon receiving Morris' blood he abets her 'death' which the Count is trying to bring about. Again, once the decision is taken to exclude Harker's wife from the hunt for Dracula, it is Morris who ensures she is left alone, thereby enabling the Count to visit her without hindrance (*D* 18:290). It is then Morris who discovers (beckons?) Dracula's rats in the chapel (*D* 19:300-1). Dracula's advances to Harker's wife behind a locked door are actively encouraged by the Texan, who tries to avert Van Helsing's intrusion by *twice* protesting against violating a woman's bedroom (*D* 21:335) — the only occasion in the book in which he is concerned with propriety. In the ensuing chase Morris is in a position to give false directions to assist the Count in making good his escape. Later, after Renfield has tried to impede Dracula and has been abandoned by the doctors, the next person to see him is Morris, who 'reports' his death (*D* 21:340). Finally, when Dracula is almost cornered in a house in Piccadilly it is Morris' self-imposed function to prohibit escape through the window. How does Dracula escape? — through the window (*D* 23:365)!

Whatever the plausibility of Moretti's reassessment, it is worth noting that when Stoker was laying down the plot for his novel in an early formulation he left clues. His Texan (whose name went through several changes[31]) was forever turning up, then disappearing. Once, Seward was intended to receive two visitors: the Count and the Texan together. Significantly, chapters three and four of Book Three were supposed to have the Texan journey to Transylvania alone and at his own request. Although this was later scrapped from the finished novel, the question remains: what did Stoker intend should happen to him there?

# 8.

# 'SWEET, SWEET, GOOD, GOOD WOMEN'*

There is no head above the head of a serpent: and there is no wrath above the wrath of a woman. I had rather dwell with a lion and a dragon than to keep house with a wicked woman . . . All wickedness is but little to the wickedness of woman . . . What else is a woman but a foe to friendship, an unescapable punishment, a necessary evil, a natural temptation, a desirable calamity, a domestic danger, a delectable detriment, an evil of nature, painted with fair colours! . . . women are naturally more impressionable and more ready to receive the influence of a disembodied spirit . . . they have slippery tongues . . . since they are feebler both in mind and body it is not surprising that they should come more and more under the spell of witchcraft . . . Women are intellectually like children . . . she is more carnal than a man as is clear from her many carnal abominations . . . for the sake of fulfilling their lust they consort even with devils . . . she is a liar by nature.

*Malleus Maleficarum*, Part 1, Question 6.

**M**ALE hostility towards, and fear and suspicion of, women is as old as time. Was not the act of childbirth the greatest and most inexplicable act of magic of all? And why had women always lived longer than men (providing they survived childbirth) and been more immune, historically, to plagues and pestilence?[1] What other unknown powers of sorcery did they possess? While their menfolk fought and died in countless battles, women stayed at home to pass on their mysteries to their daughters. Classical Europe was not above contempt for women: Seneca (*Tragedies*) wrote of their lust, hatred, pride and evil; Cicero (*The Rhetorics*) complained of their avarice; and even Socrates referred

*Dr Seward's diary: '. . . of that sweet, sweet, good, good woman . . .' (*D* 23:367).

to them as a confounded nuisance, necessary only for producing heirs.

The Christian religion then lent a new dimension to misogynous persecution. From St Paul onwards women were accused as the temptresses of men. Woman, after all, was not created in God's image, but was a mere bent rib from Adam's breast. Eve was shown to be fickle and weak-minded, and these qualities were assumed to have been handed down to women in general. The Bible tends to discriminate against the weaker sex, and the extraordinary language of the *Malleus Maleficarum* (above) testifies to the official Church view of womankind in fifteenth- and sixteenth-century Europe. Women not only attracted the devil; they also had his mark on their anatomy. Just as the ancients could imagine the shapes of constellations when gazing up at the heavens, so the dissected woman's belly revealed two sweeping Fallopian tubes — surely the horns of the devil.[2] Woman, in short, was the source of all man's evil — soiling his 'reason' with her 'desire'.

The great problem for the Church was how to reconcile the perceived abomination of most women with the divine perfection of the Virgin Mary.[3] It was solved by cutting out the middle ground: women were either fallen creatures, with treacherous minds and lecherous bodies — a recruiting ground for the devil; or they were saint-like, obedient to the commands of men, and exalted for their spiritual and bodily purity. Women, in other words, knew no moderation: they were either sacred beyond belief, or whores from the pits of hell.

English literature has always reflected this dichotomy. Chaucer's Criseyde is fickle; Shakespeare's Hamlet sees Gertrude as weak and disgusting; Milton's temptresses are shown as iniquitous; and Restoration comedy depicts flirtatious behaviour by older women with contempt. By the eighteenth century, novelists such as Richardson and Fielding became custodians of public morality. Female innocence and purity were celebrated through their heroines stoically resisting seduction. In Fielding's *Tom Jones*, for example, the hero has his fling with loose women, but finally marries a 'pure' one. Pope and Swift look upon female sexuality almost with disdain, and Richardson conveys near paranoia at its very existence. His Clarissa, bereft of her virginity through rape, and as yet unmarried, has no recourse but to take her own life.

With the coming of the nineteenth century, sexual liaisons produce such embarrassment that it becomes almost impossible to express them openly in fiction. The division between the idealized angelic purity of 'good' women and the defiled untouchables is never so marked. Throughout Victorian literature flirtatious women rarely earn sympathy, and overt sexuality barely breaks the surface. One of the few Victorian novels to contain a rampantly sexual woman (and even here the suggestion is made obliquely) is *Jane Eyre*, in which Charlotte Brontë demonstrates utter loathing for the presupposed romps of Bertha Rochester, whose sexual appetite all but deprives her of her humanity. Naturally, Bertha's promiscuity can have just one explanation: she is deranged. Only the mad and the sick can behave as she does. Brontë's description of this lewd woman is revealing:

> I never saw a face like it! It was a discoloured face — it was a savage face. I wish I could forget the roll of the red eyes and the fearful blackened inflation of the lineaments! . . . The lips were swelled and dark; the brow furrowed; the black eyebrows widely raised over bloodshot eyes. Shall I tell you of what it reminded me? . . . of that foul German spectre — the Vampyre.[4]

Brontë only mentions the 'vampyre' this once, but it is clear that she, and her readers, were familiar with the psychological association between female lasciviousness and demonic blood-sucking. The implication could hardly be more explicit: sexually active women were associated in the Victorian mind with mental derangement and devilry.

Typical Victorian heroines are the opposite of Bertha Rochester. They are pure souls existing only to be loved, and rescued from malicious adversaries, by good, brave men. This holds true for *Dracula*, although the novel on many occasions expresses a view of female inferiority. Seward, speaking of Van Helsing, says:

> He laughed till he cried and I had to draw down the blinds lest anyone should see us and misjudge; and then he cried till he laughed again; and laughed and cried together, just as a woman does. I tried to be stern with him, as one is to a woman under the circumstances; but it had no effect. Men and women are so different in manifestations of nervous strength or weakness! (*D* 13:209-10)

Van Helsing, upon first meeting Harker's wife, says: 'Ah, then you have a good memory for facts, for details? It is not always so with young ladies' (*D* 14:219). He is obviously used to scatterbrained females, but he is relieved to find 'that there are good women still left to make life happy' (*D* 14:222). One of the book's minor characters is given the words: 'you can't trust wolves no more nor women' (*D* 11:167).

*Dracula*, in fact, turns out to be a fusion of contempt for women, adulation of them, and an overdose of female sexuality. In the novel we meet two young ladies, both targets of the Count, and both acting as windows on the tensions aroused by male-female relations in the 1890s. Lucy Westenra is nineteen and, despite being cast as a joyous *ingénue* — a worthy prize for any worthy man — she comes over to the modern mind as almost totally devoid of admirable qualities. She is a pampered, upper-middle-class child with the silver spoon still showing — the perfect damsel in distress. One critic describes her as 'silly, transparent, gushy, giggly, beautiful and good';[5] another as 'a fragile, porcelain, simple-minded creature'.[6] All Lucy seems concerned about is her own pleasure. She is a kept woman whose idle life involves no more than trivial recreations: picture galleries, walking and riding in parks; rowing, tennis and fishing (*D* 5:71; 9:131). She is overburdened even by writing regularly to her best friend. The only aspect of her life to arouse curiosity is infuriatingly left unexplained. Stoker tantalizingly lets slip that she — like her late father before her — was in childhood an habitual sleepwalker (*D* 6:91; 9:137). Dracula sensibly takes advantage of this habit to make her acquaintance during their mutual nocturnal jaunts.[7] So inclined, she makes an ideal 'Eve' for the visiting serpent, for as her friend says of her: 'She is of too super-sensitive a nature to go through the world without trouble' (*D* 7:110).

If her sleepwalking is the key to her relationship with Dracula, it is her good looks that spark the emotional entanglements which bind the central characters together. No less than three men — Dr Seward, Arthur Holmwood and Quincey Morris (friends for many years) — fall hopelessly in love with her. This, in itself, says much about courtship patterns a century ago, when marriage was frequently a matter of economics, social class and arrangement. Many a modern man will see Lucy — despite her beauty and financial resources — as less than a desirable companion for the rest of his days, and will feel little sympathy for Seward and Morris, whose proposals are turned down. Holmwood is the (un)lucky one. He himself is so unremarkable that the cynic might say they make a good match.

Throughout, Lucy shows such a dearth of character that the notorious *Malleus Maleficarum* might have had her in its sights when it castigated women. She is, as it declared of her sex, totally gullible. She is duped by Quincey Morris, of all people, into believing — on account of his tall stories — that he 'is really well educated'. She confides: 'We women are such cowards that we think a man will save us from fears, and we marry him' (*D* 5:74). She is forever reminding Mina of how happy she is with her own love-life, selfishly oblivious to the stress her friend is experiencing without news from Jonathan in Transylvania. Nor has Lucy the slightest intention of remaining faithful to her beloved. She might love Arthur: but she hardly hinders the amorous Count. She *can* have her cake and eat it.

Here, not for the first time, the author's intentions and the modern reader's perceptions diverge. Stoker intends his stricken characters to be the embodiment of Victorian virtue, not realizing that their plastic, antiseptic goodness repels more than it attracts. Lucy somehow has men fawning all over her and she revels in it. She almost admits to being a 'horrid flirt', and acknowledges feelings of 'exultation' at collecting proposals (*D* 5:75). Perhaps it is a form of power she is exercising, an insatiable appetite for counting suitors. Certainly there were Victorian women who collected marriage proposals and flaunted them as a sign of their worth and desirability — as Lucy herself admits (*D* 5:73). Some male readers may identify her, euphemistically, as a 'phallic' teaser.

To be fair, Lucy does have a rebellious streak. After all, she chooses her husband for herself, without discussing the matter beforehand with her mother. She also sighs with frustration that she cannot marry all three suitors. This might be seen as a glimmer of hope: that somewhere deep in her unconscious lies a latent dissatisfaction with her dull conformity, and a yearning to rebel and allow her as-yet-poorly-developed sensuality free rein.[8] A girl with no destiny, she finds one only through Dracula's kiss. She would have passed through life leaving no shadow until a chance encounter turns that metaphor into reality.

Attention is often turned to that most unusual of surnames — 'Westenra'. Possibly it is an amalgam of 'the West' (being under attack from the East) and 'Ra' (the pagan sun-god). Lucy, in other words, is meant to be the Light of the West. Other critics have fastened on her Christian name, which can perhaps be treated as a derivative of Lucifer: she does indeed become a servant of the devil.[9]

It is curious how Stoker resists all temptation at detailed physical description where his heroines are concerned, confining his descriptive efforts to the two central antagonists, Dracula and Van Helsing. All we are told is that Lucy is pale and thin long before Dracula gets near her, and Quincey Morris speaks of her 'little shoes', so she may have been of slight build. She has rippling black hair to offset her fragile countenance.[10]

Her friend Mina is made of sterner stuff. Christened Wilhelmina Murray, she marries Jonathan Harker, whom she has known since childhood, during the course of the novel. Mina is referred to as a 'sweet-faced, dainty looking girl' (D 17:26).[11] She is merely attractive, whereas it is Lucy who is blessed with the stunning, eye-catching looks. Mina wears her hair long and loose, so that she can pull it round to hide her face if upset (D 22:353). On one occasion she loans Lucy her shoes, so the two girls were presumably of similar size, both slender creatures. Mina is no weakling, however, chasing around Whitby in the middle of the night, up and down its cliffs, in a way that would tax a trained athlete. She is deeply religious, offering a prayer of thankfulness after surviving the slightest adventure.

The two girls have been intimate friends since childhood, though when considering their differences this is somewhat surprising. Mina is, unlike Lucy, a working girl (probably an orphan, she knew neither her father nor her mother); a productive member of society and of lower social caste than her friend. Their respective pairings underline their class positions: Lucy becomes betrothed to the aristocracy (twice — to a future Lord, then a Count); while Mina takes on a humble solicitor's clerk. When the reader meets her, Mina is an assistant school-mistress teaching 'etiquette and decorum' in Exeter. She must be a year or so older than Lucy, and may even have taught her, for she was once Lucy's 'friend and guide when [she] came from the schoolroom to prepare for the world of life' (D 9:130).

The girls' personalities are also markedly different. Mina is as resourceful as Lucy is resourceless. What Mina sees in Lucy to warrant her patient affection is almost as mysterious as the male trio's infatuation with her vacuous friend. Mina shows considerable forbearance, probably acting out of a sense of duty towards her ill-fated companion — though, given her caring, maternal nature towards everybody, it would be in keeping for her to overlook Lucy's faults and see only her good qualities. Mina is the nearest thing to a saint that Stoker can conceive of. She has shown no hint of malice throughout her life. She cuddles and comforts all the men in their distress over Lucy, always puts the welfare of others before herself, and even in her own direst agonies can say this of her tormentor, Dracula:

Jonathan dear, and you all my true, true friends, I want you to bear something in mind through all this dreadful time. I know that you must fight — that you must destroy . . . but it is not a work of hate. That poor soul who has wrought all this misery is the saddest case of all. Just think what will be his joy when he, too, is destroyed in his worser part that his better part may have spiritual immortality. You must be pitiful to him, too, though it may not hold your hands from his destruction (*D* 23:367).

Here she almost resembles the Virgin Mary, interceding with God on behalf of sinners. She is using her womanly power of pity to insist that even Dracula can be redeemed.[12] All the male characters think of Mina as an angel here on earth, though it is Van Helsing who customarily speaks for them all: 'She is one of God's women, fashioned by his own hand to show us men and other women that there is a heaven where we can enter, and that its light can be here on earth . . . so true, so sweet, so noble, so little an egoist' (*D* 14:226). This may make the modern reader squirm, but it should be stressed that Stoker was not unusual in handling his heroines in this fashion. He was in good company. When Charles Dickens describes Rose Maylie in *Oliver Twist* he could easily have had the future Mina as his model: '. . . cast in so light and exquisite a mould: so mild and gentle; so pure and beautiful; that earth seemed not her element, nor its rough creatures her fit companions'.[13]

Mina's virtue (as with many of Stoker's later heroines) is such that she must be exposed to the existence of evil, in order that she may consciously choose 'good'.[14] Her faith is to be tested to the utmost. For such a 'sweet, sweet, good, good woman' (*D* 23:367), chivalrous men will move heaven and earth to alleviate her suffering. Many female readers find Van Helsing's (Stoker's) repeated insistence that women cannot endure pain and hardship difficult to accept: 'We are men and are able to bear, but you [Mina] must be our star and our hope, and we shall act the more free that you are not in danger such as we are' (*D* 18:289). When, in the postscript to the novel, he looks back on the nightmare and surveys Mina's son, he declares: 'Already he [the child] knows her sweetness and loving care; later on he will understand how some men so loved her that they did dare much for her sake.' Not many books — even in the Victorian age — could exalt women for nothing other than being passive inspirations to men.[15]

But Mina is much more than the living embodiment of purity and virtue: unlike Lucy, she has a mind. Mina is, in fact, the real star of the show: the moral honours go to her, not to Van Helsing.

For all the Dutchman's brain-power, the pursuers are outfoxed by the Count until Mina's intuition and practical thinking turn the tables against him. Van Helsing reveals more about his own prejudices (and Stoker's) than about Mina's talents when he concedes: 'Ah, that wonder Madame Mina! She has a man's brain — and a woman's heart' (D 18:281; also 25:404). She must in any case be almost unique in surviving the vampire's bite.

It is this slightly unexpected attribute of Mina being able to think for herself that highlights Stoker's confused, ambivalent attitudes towards women. Part of the recent interest expressed in *Dracula* has been sparked by the growth of feminist concern for the ways in which women have historically been portrayed in the English novel. In *Dracula*, Stoker's perceptions of women are so convoluted that while one feminist critic identifies him as a fellow feminist,[16] others perceive a deep hostility towards female sexuality,[17] together with a desire to control women.[18] It is no accident that Dracula is the single male vampire in the novel, whereas the assortment of she-vampires are collectively displayed as aggressive, inhuman, wildly erotic, and motivated solely by an insatiable craving for blood/sex. (The term 'vamp' is used today to refer to a highly sexed woman.) Not surprisingly, a reading of the first half of the novel has been interpreted as demonstrating a pathological aversion to, or hatred of, women.[19]

It is Stoker's complex treatment of Mina that invites a reassessment. She is the mouthpiece for an exploration of a social phenomenon of the 1890s — the emergence of the so-called 'New Woman'. During the decade in which *Dracula* was written, English social and moral decadence was probably at its peak. Matthew Arnold observed that those years were 'wandering between two worlds, one dead, the other powerless to be born'.[20]

The New Women were the Victorian equivalent of today's feminists. They took issue with a whole range of social restrictions brought about by male dominance and male prejudice. They objected to their physical mobility being impaired through being encased in whalebone. Some of them dared to pedal around openly on newly available bicycles — necessarily dispensing with petticoats, and chaperons.[21] More importantly, certain women were striving for financial independence and careers of their own, which meant deferring or abandoning the traditional Victorian roles of marriage and motherhood. Motherhood had been held to constitute a woman's natural function; it was the manifest destiny of Victorian women. Now, these New Women were turning their backs on their 'rightful' place — in the home — and were opting for what were then considered novel forms of vocation, such as medicine or business.[22]

All this was radical enough, but what really created controversy, and made the New Women targets for accusations that they were destabilizing society and contributing to moral decay, was their challenge to the accepted precepts on sex. The New Women were hardly a homogeneous body — they embraced varying degrees of opinion — but what united them in the public image was their expressed need, and preparedness, to speak out on sexual matters from a female perspective more frankly than had hitherto been deemed possible.[23] Astonishingly, they would openly contemplate sexual liaisons prior to marriage. They were not coy about discussing contraception or even that greatest of Victorian taboos, venereal disease. Popular novelists of the time, many of them women, fuelled the movement, highlighting the perceived drudgery of the average woman: sexually repressed, and subservient in marriage.[24]

Mina's background and personal circumstances make her a potential New Woman. She discusses New Women readily in the novel, but is far from convinced about their values. She feels them to be more intolerant than men. Moreover:

> If Mr Holmwood fell in love with [Lucy] seeing her only in the drawing room, I wonder what he would say if he saw her now. Some of the 'New Woman' writers will some day start an idea that men and women should be allowed to see each other asleep before proposing or accepting. But I suppose the New Woman won't condescend in future to accept; she will do the proposing herself. And a nice job she will make of it too! There's some consolation in that (D 8:111).

Here, Mina's almost sarcastic tone clearly distances her from the New Women. Yet she, herself, is not only educated but has also embarked on her own teaching career. Such combined opportunities would not have been widely available to women much older than Mina, so it might be expected that she would have more sympathy with the New Woman ethos.

Nonetheless, she is no subservient, stay-at-home housewife. True, she does sacrifice her career upon marriage (this is never explicitly stated, but assumed unquestioningly), but then makes good use of her skills to assist her husband in his legal work. In today's terms, she would make an outstanding secretary: she has considerable organizational talents; she learns railway timetables off by heart (just as Stoker would have done for Irving); and becomes proficient in the stenographic arts — typing and shorthand. These aptitudes were novel for women in the 1890s, and her wanting to assist her husband other than through domestic chores was almost revolutionary for the time. [25]

All in all, it is only at the intellectual level that Stoker is prepared to grant Mina any kind of equality with men; 'etiquette and decorum' scarcely being the most radical and socially disruptive of subjects. One feminist critic has contended that Stoker reveals Mina at her most liberated only when she is imitating masculine pseudo-rationality and gentlemanly stoicism. [26]

Mina, then, is constructed as a dual-faceted creature. She adopts some of the modernist trappings associated with the New Woman, while remaining at heart a devoutly traditional female. Mina knows the proper place of women: she refers to the taste of the original apple that remains in all women's mouths (D 14:220). On matters of personal morality and sexual expression Stoker keeps the wraps firmly around her. Her represssion is typically Victorian: she even feels it improper for Jonathan to take her arm in public (D 13:207). Whereas Lucy presents not the slightest obstacle to Dracula's every advance, Mina resists with all the mental powers she can muster. The two girls' after-reactions to the Count's visitations could not be more contrasting. Lucy recalls only the bitter-sweet sensation of his presence, yet looks and feels refreshed for the experience (D 8:115). Mina, however, with her greater intelligence, strength of character — and repression — refuses to countenance what she has done. She is filled with revulsion, and never becomes wantonly sexual in the manner of Lucy. Mina's anguish, it is important to note, is not the anguish of rape, for she (like Jonathan and Lucy before her) knows the all-powerful temptation of the vampire. Mina admits: 'I did not want to hinder him' (D 21:342). As her spirit slowly succumbs during the following weeks, she is compelled to adopt a more inert, passive role, falling back on remarks straight from Stoker's heart: 'Oh, thank God for good brave men!' (D 23:370).

If the time should come, she instructs that the others destroy her according to the prescribed ritual, rather than allow her to join the undead; but even here her courage has been observed to possess a faintly sexist element. She assumes it is the duty of men to kill those they love to prevent their falling into the hands of an enemy. She does not recall that other women — Cleopatra, for instance — were quite capable of taking their own lives when faced with a fate worse than death. [27]

Lucy, the privileged but sexually liberated (fallen) woman, is shown to be a poor comparison with the intellectually superior, yet socially and morally more inhibited, Mina. In the context of the New Woman, Lucy's wish to sleep with/marry three men (four, if we include the Count) marks her down as guilty of that most venal of the New Woman's sins — promiscuity. To Stoker, and to common decency as he saw it, she must pay the ultimate price for her depravity. Van Helsing turns her body into a moral battlefield. She has stepped out of line. For her overt sexuality, her stepping beyond the bounds of chastity and showing 'desire', she must be persecuted, even destroyed.

This is not to say that Stoker conceives of Lucy as a villainess. Rather, she is a woman/angel violated by the devil. The memory of the 'real' Lucy never fades, although her vampire existence is significant in that, by being both dead *and* erotic, she defies not only the law of nature, but also the unwritten law of Victorian moral behaviour. In the actual Victorian world men effectively dominated women, but in the vampire world the unthinkable happens: women turn the tables and try to enslave the men who once enslaved them.[28] Perhaps this is why Seward yearns to decapitate Lucy.

But Stoker's moral indignation goes deeper than this. At the heart of his strictures against the so-called freedoms of the New Woman lie deeply embedded parables concerning motherhood. The maternal instinct, that most hallowed of female Victorian attributes, was often assumed to be the only aspect of life women truly cared about. Influential medical opinion of the period could state: 'Love of home, children and domestic duties, are the only passions [women] feel.'[29] Stoker seems to be suggesting that the traditional family structure can survive the threats posed by New Women/vampirism, and he does so by contrasting Lucy's and Mina's acquiescence to the 'delights' of motherhood.

The plot of *Dracula* hinges around the fate of these two women. Some critics have gone so far as to say that essentially it is the same story told twice:[30] first through Lucy, then Mina — both totally different mother figures. By way of preamble Stoker introduces the Count's three lady consorts in Castle Dracula. It is through them that Stoker establishes his claim that women who are flauntingly sensuous are on a par with child molesters. These three she-vampires, deprived of Harker's blood, are appeased only by the gift of a small child. Blessed children, in other words, are not to be cherished: they are to be eaten! Lucy, likewise, commences her career as a London vampire by snatching children, preparatory to graduating to adult males. This callousness towards helpless infants is meant to appal the reader; to insinuate the consummate reversal of the proper female function. It is not only the sex roles that are reversed in New Women/vampires, but the mothering roles too. It is conceivable that some deep-seated trauma is being hinted at here: a mute protest at the intolerable strains large numbers of children put on the average Victorian family.[31] A more straightforward view, however, is that by rejecting the prescribed feminine social role, New Women/vampires are social outlaws — even 'sexual sociopaths'.[32]

When Lucy is finally laid to rest the novel could logically have been concluded.[33] (Upon her 'first' death Seward utters 'Finis' [D 13:212]). But now Dracula turns his attentions to a different calibre of woman. Unlike Lucy, Mina does not reject men: on the contrary, she accepts and comforts them all — like a mother. Soothing Arthur in his grief she says: 'We women have something of the mother in us that makes us rise above smaller matters when the mother-spirit is invoked; I felt this big, sorrowing man's head resting on me, as though it were that of a baby that some day may lie on my bosom, and I stroked his hair as though he were my own child' (D 17:275).

There is nothing sexually threatening about Mina. Even the child which eventually does grace her life is named after those who fought Dracula on her behalf, as if a multi-platonic love affair is responsible for the child. This is another link with the Virgin Mary, for Mina's son can be seen as the product of immaculate conception, without her having defiled her body or spirit through succumbing to the sexual act. Whatever the circumstances, she crowns the novel by bearing a son on its concluding page. The little band return to England to live happily ever after, closing their minds to the brief threatening interlude when women tried to rise above their station. The maternal has beaten off the challenge of the carnal.

Mina's all-round purity stems from her knowing her place vis à vis men, and her absence of active 'appetites'. She blends the best in what is traditional and what is modern. In his conscious mind, Mina is probably Stoker's perfect woman: in his unconscious mind it is probably Lucy. It seems almost superfluous to draw attention to the near obsessional fixation which he had for women: the conflict between what was right and proper and what was illicit and irresistible, and the need to keep both lives apart. In this connection, not only was Stoker's life surrounded by strong,

challenging women,[34] but beginning with *Dracula* his fiction turns
increasingly to portraying heroines who are anything but meek
and submissive — though they uniformly relinquish their
independence for the supposed pleasures of marriage (his
villainesses, by contrast, radiate eroticism). Further, it is noticeable
that in the literature of the 1890s onwards greater sexual expression
was permissible — but not for Bram Stoker. Nowhere in his fiction
is explicit sensual pleasure experienced by any of his chaste heroines.

Now that the characters of *Dracula* and their functions have been
introduced, the ground has been prepared for tackling some of
the underlying themes of the novel. In view of the foregoing
discussion of Lucy and Mina it will be apposite to begin by
examining *Dracula*'s sexual symbolism.

# 9.

# SEXUAL SYMBOLISM

I was afraid to raise my eyelids, but looked out and saw perfectly under the lashes. The fair girl went on her knees and bent over me, fairly gloating. There was a deliberate voluptuousness which was both thrilling and repulsive, and as she arched her neck she actually licked her lips like an animal, till I could see in the moonlight the moisture shining on the scarlet lips and on the red tongue as it lapped the white sharp teeth. Lower and lower went her head as the lips went below the range of my mouth and chin and seemed about to fasten on my throat. Then she paused, and I could hear the churning sound of her tongue as it licked her teeth and lips, and could feel the hot breath on my neck. Then the skin of my throat began to tingle as one's flesh does when the hand that is to tickle it approaches nearer — nearer. I could feel the soft, shivering touch of the lips on the supersensitive skin of my throat, and the hard dents of two sharp teeth, just touching and pausing there. I closed my eyes in a languorous ecstasy and waited — waited with beating heart.

Jonathan Harker's Journal,
*Dracula* 3:52.

THAT *Dracula* has a certain sexual content will by now be evident, though the very suggestion sounds, at first, preposterous. What, on the face of it, could be less erotic than a mouldering corpse; less enticing as a nest of love than a cobweb-infested coffin or a crumbling castle? Further, given the paranoia experienced by Victorian society at the very mention of the word 'sex', how could an erotic book ever have been published, let alone sold by the thousands? For erotic *Dracula* certainly is. 'Quasi-pornography' one critic labels it. [1] Another describes it as a 'kind of incestuous, necrophilious, oral-anal-sadistic all-in-wrestling match'. [2] He is being reticent. A comprehensive search of the novel unearths the following: seduction, rape, necrophilia, paedophilia, incest, adultery, oral sex, group sex, menstruation, venereal disease, voyeurism — enough to titillate the most avid sexual appetite.

Of course, Count Dracula was hardly the first vampire to exude sexuality. The ancient lamias of folklore did so; as did several of the literary vampires of the nineteenth century. But the question remains: how could explicit sexual behaviour (despite the pretence at vampire subterfuge) come to be portrayed at this period? No nineteenth-century writer could depict sex *as* sex. There were obscenity laws; strict control over the contents of the circulating libraries; and the invisible jury of public opinion to regulate what was publishable and what was not.[3]

Yet what could not be conveyed directly could be explored allegorically, and at this level *Dracula* is alive with sensuality. As dead people cannot logically indulge in sex, there was no fear of Stoker being accused of prurience, and *Dracula* was not acknowledged for its eroticism among readers of the day. It is revealing that not a single contemporary reviewer questioned *Dracula*'s sexual or moral content, though there had been a near-hysterical reaction just a few years earlier when Ibsen's *Ghosts* had dared to allude to sexual relationships and even venereal disease. Evidently, it was all a matter of effective camouflage; and evidently Stoker camouflaged his eroticism effectively. Nevertheless, *Dracula* can be seen as the great submerged force of Victorian libido breaking out to punish the repressive society which had imprisoned it.[4]

The novel, in fact, epitomizes what Twitchell has to say about vampirism: 'The myth is loaded with sexual excitement; yet there is no mention of sexuality. It is sex without genitalia, sex without confusion, sex without responsibility, sex without guilt, sex without love — better yet, sex without mention.'[5] The erotic preoccupation is obsessively oral, for vampires tend to be sexually inoperative from the neck down.[6] Their 'kiss' is the euphemism for deeper intimacy, and throughout Stoker's notes he refers to vampire 'kisses', not 'bites'. Several lengthy episodes alert the reader to the erotic undercurrents of *Dracula*. The first is when the imprisoned Jonathan Harker strays upon the Count's three 'mistresses'. Outwardly, their objective is (as befits vampires) to take Harker's blood, but the entire sequence is overlaid with unmistakable sexual imagery. The extract quoted at the opening of this chapter is taken from this particular episode, but let us look at how Stoker first introduces Harker's erotic encounter:

I suppose I must have fallen asleep . . . In the moonlight opposite
me were three young women, ladies by their dress and manner
. . . Two were dark, and had high aquiline noses, like the Count's,
and great dark, piercing eyes, that seemed to be almost red when
contrasted with the pale yellow moon. The other was fair, as fair
as can be, with great, wavy masses of golden hair and eyes like pale
sapphires. I seemed somehow to know her face, and to know it
in connection with some dreamy fear, but I could not recollect at
the moment how or where. All three had brilliant white teeth, that
shone like pearls against the ruby of their voluptuous lips. There
was something about them that made me uneasy, some longing
and at the same time some deadly fear. I felt in my heart a wicked,
burning desire that they would kiss me with those red lips. It is
not good to note this down, lest some day it should meet Mina's
eyes and cause her pain; but it is the truth. They whispered together,
and then they all three laughed — such a silvery, musical laugh,
but as hard as though the sound never could have come through
the softness of human lips. It was like the intolerable, tingling
sweetness of water-glasses when played on by a cunning hand. The
fair girl shook her head coquettishly, and the other two urged her
on. One said:-
'Go on! You are first, and we shall follow; yours is the right to
begin.' The other added:
'He is young and strong; there are kisses for us all.' I lay quiet,
looking out under my eyelashes in an agony of delightful
anticipation. The fair girl advanced and bent over me till I could
feel the movement of her breath upon me. Sweet it was in one sense,
honey-sweet, and sent the same tingling through the nerves as her
voice, but with a bitter underlying the sweet, a bitter offensiveness,
as one smells in blood (*D* 3:50-2).

There is not much of the squalid, pig-grunting vampire of
Montague Summers here. In any other language, Harker is being
seduced. If the she-vampires wanted only his blood they would
simply have come and taken it, but they are obviously desirous
of something else. Indeed, the passage reveals far more than a thinly-
veiled focus on seduction. This is a woman making explicit
advances to a man! — unheard of according to the Victorian code
(except in pornography), although probably the ultimate male
fantasy. It is the stuff of dreams, and sure enough Harker does
think he is dreaming. Note, too, the ambivalence of his response,
the 'longing' coupled with a 'deadly fear'. This conflict is crucial
to vampire sexuality: attraction versus repulsion. Coleridge wrote
of it a century previously in an exquisite phrase: 'desire and loathing

strangely mixed'.[7] Harker's head tells him he must resist. He describes his desire as 'wicked' and thinks of how hurtful his moment of pleasure would be to Mina — should she find out. But his physical yearning, as inevitably happens when faced with vampire temptation, is bound to triumph.

Intriguingly, the exchange of sex roles even extends to Harker's manner: peering out from under the eyelashes is what one has popularly come to expect from any coy female who does not wish to 'encourage' her lover. Moreover, there are *three* women vampires, all queueing up to get at him — a kind of demonically inversed 'gang-bang': 'There are kisses for us all.' Harker must be virile indeed. To the Victorian mind Harker's anguish provides a mirror on the suffocating repression which consumed his society. He is being offered, on a plate, instant sexual gratification, no strings attached — the utopia of the permissive society. His culture, however, has conditioned him to wait until marriage, and the somewhat matronly Mina is hardly the type of woman to lighten these frustrations.[8] Moreover, throughout the book it is the vampire women who are shown as pleasure seeking, sexually motivated, and endowed with greater potency. This constitutes another dramatic reversal, this time of the common prejudice that men were the ones with insatiable sexual appetites, while the female function was to passively appease it.[9]

On this point it is appropriate to mention another of Stoker's long-standing puzzles. Setting eyes on the blonde vampire, Harker later writes: 'I seemed to know her face, and to know it in connection with some dreamy fear, but I could not recollect at the moment how or where.' Harker never does recollect, so who was she? Some critics have suggested the arch-temptress Lucy (although Lucy was dark-haired, and in any case it is not clear from the novel whether Harker had ever actually met her), or a fantasy view of his beloved Mina: not as she is, but how he subconsciously wants her to become. Van Helsing, however, later destroys the blonde vampire and he offers no recognition of any resemblance to Lucy or Mina (*D* 27:440). Others have proposed that Harker is confronted with the face of a mythological temptress, either Medusa or, alternatively, the original wife of Adam, Lilith — the first and archetypal lamia.[10]

Only with the unearthing of Stoker's manuscript has the riddle been solved. The fair beauty is she whom Harker had encountered in the tomb of Countess Dolingen of Gratz, in the episode 'Dracula's Guest': 'I saw, as my eyes were turned into the darkness of the tomb, a beautiful woman, with rounded cheeks and red lips, seemingly sleeping on a bier'.

Whatever the source of Harker's vision, nothing more complex has yet been suggested about his experience than a reversal of traditional heterosexual (if necrophilious) role-play. But when the Count intervenes to protect Harker from the ravages of his three companions, a whole range of new relationships emerge. Two of the women are said to resemble Dracula: this would indicate that they are biologically related to him in some way — probably his daughters. The third (whom Harker recognizes) has the right to head the queue and is presumably their mother.[11] The Count's fury, expressed in human terms, is that of the jealous husband and irate father; in vampire terms it is an expression of incest. His women taunt him: 'You yourself never loved; you never love!' To this he rejoins: 'Yes I too can love; you yourselves can tell it from the past. Is it not so (D 3:53)'?

With this exchange Stoker would seem to be reinforcing two points: first, that the vampire's lack of sexual inhibitions extends even to indulgence in incest — a rigid taboo; and second, that the Count, by not having 'loved' his creatures, except in the distant past, is not particularly motivated by 'kisses' or 'love', except when they further his schemes for power. His 'love' is restricted to the warm-blooded living.

Only once in Harker's experience does he hint at something other than straightforward seduction, when he describes the vampire's breath as possessing 'a bitter offensiveness as one smells in blood'. Here, too, his language has hidden meaning. In many societies blood is held to be an aphrodisiac, and it is not uncommon to find people who derive sexual satisfaction from shedding blood.[12] The most obvious instance of this is the love-bite, which can, in extreme cases, draw blood. More generally, the colour 'red' can produce an awakening of sexual consciousness, as illustrated by the application of lipstick to the mouth and rouge to the face, not to mention the popular name for the haunts of prostitutes — 'red light' districts.[13]

Dracula's women prepare the reader for the kind of promiscuous behaviour exhibited by Lucy. It is a scenario that has to be resisted by all the forces available to Van Helsing et al. That is why the battle to save Lucy from Dracula's clutches is so protracted and critical to the novel's structure. During these particular sequences blood becomes a direct analogy for semen. The association of one with the other in vampire mythology is not arbitrary. The vampire's craving for blood is due to its life-giving properties, yet semen is also a fluid without which procreation cannot take place. The lamias and succubi of folklore depend on this ambiguity — sucking the 'vital spirits' out of man. More recently, the convertibility of the two fluids has been calculated: forty ounces of blood is needed to recompense the loss of one ounce of semen.[14] Cold-blooded demons, moreover, possessed cold semen. In the annals of folklore it was always theoretically possible to detect seduction by the devil (incubus), for his sperm was as cold as ice. The whole question of the psychological relationship between blood and semen has been summarized by Ernest Jones:

> The explanation of these fantasies is surely not hard. A nightly visit from a beautiful or frightful being, who first exhausts the sleeper with passionate embraces, and then withdraws from him a vital fluid; all this can point only to a natural and common process, namely to nocturnal emissions accompanied with dreams of a more or less erotic nature. In the unconscious mind blood is commonly an equivalent for semen.[15]

Harker's fantasy does allude to the surreal nature of a 'wet dream'; for when a male awakes to find himself having emitted sperm in his sleep it is easy for him to imagine that 'someone' took it out.

With all this in mind, it is now possible to turn attention to the battle for Lucy's life. Her admirers and the medical men are obliged to put in what Dracula has taken out — blood. She receives no fewer than four blood transfusions: from her fiancé, the two rejected suitors, and Van Helsing — who despite his age retains a keen eye for female beauty, and can rise to the demands made upon him. Psychologically, the giving of blood has been known to instil feelings of pride and wonder on the part of the donor, who may feel s/he has metaphysically escaped the confines of his/her body and become part of another's.[16]

Pursuing the theme of Lucy's sexual liberation, this sequence of blood transfusions can be taken as symbolizing successive acts of sexual intercourse, as she attains the freedom she dreamt of in life ('Why can't a girl marry three men?'). On her deathbed her wish comes true, and she take a series of 'lovers'. Holmwood, due to marry Lucy but foiled by her death, is the first to give her his blood/semen. In his later grief he interprets the mingling of his blood with hers as a symbol of marriage in God's eyes. Their relationship, in other words, had been consummated before her death. Holmwood knows nothing about the later transfusions, and his friends agree to silence regarding their contributions to save him pain and jealousy (*D* 10:156; 13:209).

But Van Helsing (and Stoker) knows perfectly well what has really happened. Using Holmwood's analogy of marriage, Lucy has become a polyandrist and he, Van Helsing — still married in the eyes of the Catholic Church, though his wife is deranged — an adulterer and bigamist. Worse, he had described Lucy as like a daughter to him. It is apparent, then, that even though there is no vampire component to the above episode, blood exchanges are still portrayed as though charged with sexual potency. Nor would Stoker claim anything novel in this metaphor. In the seventeenth century John Donne's poem 'The Flea' was dependent on the understanding that the mingling of two people's blood *was* sexual intercourse.[17]

Lucy, we know, was beautiful when alive. She must also have possessed a certain erotic presence, judging from her effect on the men she came across, though Stoker plays this down. In her living death, however, her beauty changes from the pure innocence that her virginity symbolized to the wanton voluptuousness of male fantasy. Her 'sweetness was turned to adamantine, heartless cruelty, and the purity to voluptuous wantonness': indeed the apparition is 'like a devilish mockery of Lucy's sweet purity' (*D* 16:252-3). Lucy's attacks on small children smack of paedophilia. Even her apparel reflects her new-found liberation: gone is the restricting corset she presumably wore in life; instead she wears the symbolic, free, flowing, unhampering shroud.[18]

Lucy's nocturnal existence comes to a gory end in another of Stoker's passages saturated with sexual meaning. On that day, had she lived, she was to have married Holmwood. Now she taunts him: 'Come, my husband, come!' and the following night Holmwood is given the task of setting his wife's soul free by driving a (phallic) stake through her:

He struck with all his might.

The thing in the coffin writhed; and a hideous, blood-curdling screech came from the opened red lips. The body shook and quivered and twisted in wild contortions; the sharp white teeth champed together till the lips were cut and the mouth was smeared with a crimson foam. But Arthur never faltered. He looked like a figure of Thor as his untrembling arm rose and fell, driving deeper and deeper the mercy-bearing stake, whilst the blood from the pierced heart welled and spurted up around it. His face was set, and high duty seemed to shine through it . . .

And then the writhing and quivering of the body became less, and the teeth ceased to champ, and the face to quiver. Finally it lay still. The terrible ordeal was over.

The hammer fell from Arthur's hand. He reeled and would have fallen had we not caught him. Great drops of sweat sprang out on his forehead, and his breath came in broken gasps (*D* 16:258-9).

This incident is not merely a thinly disguised account of passionate intercourse, which is indicated by Holmwood's post-coital exhaustion (the tradition whereby a vampire is destroyed by a solitary thrust is conveniently overlooked). Stoker's language also dares to portray another of the Victorian unmentionables — the female orgasm. In probably no other literary form of the period could such a taboo subject have been depicted. Even though Dracula has presumably had sexual access to Lucy previously (thereby enslaving and freeing her simultaneously), her reactions to being 'staked' are suggestive of the painful deflowering of a virgin, followed by her first and last orgasm. The passionate display is also performed onstage, so to speak. Lucy's and Arthur's only moment of intimacy is not a private affair. All his friends are gathered around, admiring, and cheering him on. The violent mutilation of an unresisting female body provides the clearest act of sexual sadism in the book; contrasting with Lucy's own masochistic self-destruction as she repeatedly yielded herself to Dracula.

The notion of a 'pecking order' surfaces again. Just as one of Dracula's three women had the first 'right' to kiss Harker, so Holmwood has the 'right' to stake Lucy. Despite the obvious sadism, there is something uncomfortably civil and organized about the behaviour of these distinguished gentlemen: all except Holmwood must take their pleasure vicariously, voyeuristically. Later, Mina will force a pledge from her husband that his loving hand will be the one to set her free, should the need arise (*D* 25:394). Once again, 'love' is equated with 'staking'.

Attention now switches from Lucy to Mina. Although her relationship to Jonathan is fundamental to the story-line, no aspect of their physical relationship is ever touched upon. She is totally sexless, until the Count awakens her submerged instincts. Whereas Lucy had merely to await his amorous touch, Dracula has a fixed purpose in mind for her friend. He wishes to immobilize his enemies by striking at Mina, symbol of all their values. By so doing he also takes revenge on Harker, who escaped his clutches in Transylvania and who has provided invaluable information for Van Helsing. Rather than go for the troublesome solicitor, Dracula inflicts greater suffering by making for his wife:

Kneeling on the near edge of the bed facing outwards was the white clad figure of [Mina]. By her side stood a tall, thin man, clad in black . . . With his left hand he held both Mrs Harker's hands, keeping them away with her arms at full tension; his right hand gripped her by the back of the neck, forcing her face down on his bosom. Her white nightdress was smeared with blood, and a thin stream trickled down the man's bare breast, which was shown by his torn-open dress. The attitude of the two had a terrible resemblance to a child forcing a kitten's nose into a saucer of milk to compel it to drink. (D 21:336).

This incident is so packed with erotic meaning that Stoker wants his readers to hear it twice, for Mina then tells of her ordeal in her own words:

[Dracula] pulled open his shirt, and with his long sharp nails opened a vein in his breast. When the blood began to spurt out, he took my hands in one of his, holding them tight, and with the other seized my neck and pressed my mouth to the wound, so that I must either suffocate or swallow some of the — Oh, my God, my God! what have I done?(D 21:343)

Mina's reaction is to rub her lips as though to cleanse them from pollution. Significantly, it is the victim who is now sucking from the vampire, something for which there is apparently no precedent in folklore.[19] One can only speculate what the Victorian public, starved (except for underground pornography) of erotic literature, must have made of these passages. Not content with voluptuous ladies breathing down Harker's neck and Holmwood hammering into Lucy until she climaxes, Stoker is now emboldened into describing enforced fellatio. Lapping a saucer of milk lends visual strength to the analogy.

The posture of Mina's husband adds to the intrigue. He is lying on the bed, flushed and breathing heavily. Is Dracula responsible for his stupor, or is it Mina, acting under instruction, who 'exhausts' her husband during love-making? If the latter, then Mina has become a succubus, draining Jonathan in order to nourish her own incubus, Dracula. She thereby assists in the process of energy exchange between her two 'husbands'. It is now that Harker's hair begins to turn white. But there is more symbolism to come:

She shuddered and was silent, holding down her head on her husband's breast. When she raised it, his white night robe was stained with blood where her lips had touched, and where the thin open wound in her neck had sent forth drops. The instant she saw it she drew back, with a low wail, and whispered amidst choking sobs:-

'Unclean, unclean! I must touch him or kiss him no more. Oh that it should be that it is I who am now his worst enemy, and whom he may have most cause to fear.' (*D* 21:338-9)

Here, her words, 'Unclean, unclean!' are indicative of something other than the product of a vampire bite. They are strangely suggestive of the ancient taboo of menstruation. Even Stoker's description of her wound conveys a distinct change. Hitherto in the novel, Dracula's canine teeth have left, as one might expect, twin puncture marks, but in this instance Mina bears a 'thin open wound'. Such a 'wound' penetrated by an elongated canine tooth is as near as Stoker can come to describing intercourse, for he is describing a narrow slit as presented by a menstruating vagina. In this instance blood imagery is not used as a substitute for semen, but refers more directly to the menstrual flow itself. [20]

On the face of it, this might seem a gratuitous diversion by Stoker. On closer inspection it is not. The ancients saw a connecting relationship between menstrual blood and semen. The seemingly miraculous circumstances of childbirth could be explained by simple observation. A child habitually emerged nine months after the injection of one fluid (semen) and the ceased emission of another (menstrual blood). Hence, logic dictated that a baby was a product of the mixture of the two: menstruation was to women what ejaculation was to men. On this point we might adduce Freudian psychoanalysis, which features in the following chapter:

The primitive cannot help connecting the mysterious phenomena of the monthly flow of blood with sadistic ideas. Thus he interprets menstruation, especially at its onset, as the bite of a spirit-animal [vampire?] or possibly as the token of sexual intercourse with this spirit. Occasionally the reports reveal this spirit as one of an ancestor, and then from other knowledge we have gained we understand that it is in virtue of her being the property of this spirit-ancestor that the menstruating girl is taboo. [21]

Count Dracula might not be an *ancestor* of Mina, but he does claim her as his *property*. It is also his bite which has caused the unclean flow of blood — token sexual intercourse according to a Freudian interpretation. There is, in addition, a social consequence from combining the idea of semen with that of menstrual blood, namely experiencing coitus during the time of a monthly period. By so doing, Mina could benefit from a kind of calendar liberation, so important to Victorian women, for they could then enjoy their sexual liaisons without fear of pregnancy. Again, the onset of menstruation is frequently accompanied by temporary personality changes — and it is the case that Mina is now acting rather differently to what is expected of her.

But why should Stoker have been driven to incorporate menstrual imagery in *Dracula?* One theory, aired to explore his deeper impulses in writing the book, concerns his wife. Florence, so the popular histories would have us believe, was frigid from the time of her son's birth.[22] If this is true, then she might, as with many other sexually dissatisfied women, have experienced troublesome periods. The hypothesis continues: 'Was it some image of these that gave Stoker's subliminal mind the hint that formulated a myth of formidable power, out of the ferocity of a frustrated bleeding woman crackling with energy and unackowledged sexuality?'[23]

The further one probes *Dracula,* the more sexual allegories are unearthed. Stoker even provides alternative methods of destruction for male and female vampires. Lucy and Dracula's women are extirpated by the application of the stake/phallus. Their destruction, and release, is accompanied by expressions of quasi-orgasm. Dracula is the only male vampire in the novel, yet in his case transfixion does not appear to be mandatory. The decapitation of the women is performed almost as an afterthought, once the full poignancy of their having been violently penetrated is exhausted. The decapitation of the Count, by contrast, is shown as much more crucial. Harker's knife goes for the throat, not for the heart.

The knife-blade has psychological connotations as a phallic symbol in that it can sadistically imitate the act of bodily penetration by the penis. It is notable that Harker strokes the blade of his knife as he contemplates the final assault on Dracula. The solicitor's own sexual responses have come full circle. The deeply masochistic instincts as he yielded himself to the Dracula harem are replaced by gross sadistic impulses as he sets about mutilating his tormentor.[24]

In this connection, psychologists note that in nightmares that involve fears of castration, the head can sometimes come to represent a penis-substitute.[25] Dracula is thereby neutralized, symbolically castrated, suffering the ultimate sexual revenge. Reaffirming this interpretation, Van Helsing's occasional use of the term 'sterilize', in the sense of ridding the world of Dracula's menace, hints at a sexual operation[26] — as applied to the Count, severing his head. Not to be overlooked is Harker's escape from Castle Dracula as illustrating his own fears of castration. In climbing down the castle's sheer walls, rather than let the vampire women capture him, his valedictory diary entry reads: 'At least God's mercy is better than that of these monsters, and the precipice is steep and high. At its foot a man may sleep — as a *man*' (*D* 4:69; author's italics). As for Dracula's own anxieties, it has been suggested that his great wooden boxes filled with native earth from Transylvania might be seen as womb-substitutes — as necessary as blood for sustaining the vampire's life in death. [27] His tomb becomes the womb.

Notwithstanding its perversions and inversions, in one respect *Dracula* remains within the bounds of traditional literary eroticism. Its sexual framework is rigidly heterosexual. [28] Dracula acquires she-vampires, who in turn pursue males. In fact, although Dracula is undead at the preternatural level, he is, on a more earthly plane, no more than a continuation of a discernible stereotype of eighteenth- and nineteenth-century literature. Just as Lucy and Mina start out as embodiments of sainthood, in the tradition of fictional women from Richardson through to Hardy, so too the Count is recognizable as the archetypal rake — the classic Gothic villain emanating from his mist-shrouded castle with its locked and secret rooms. He even looks the part, right down to the 'glittering eye' of the sexual tyrant. In this, he is aligned with other corrupt but courtly seducers of fiction, such as Lovelace in Richardson's *Clarissa*. For such men sexual conquests are almost to be expected: they would hardly be men otherwise. Dracula's visits to Lucy pre-empt the claims of her fiancé, and have been described as an echo of the medieval *jus primae noctis* — the Count is a feudal lord exercising his *droit de seigneur*. [29] If blood is an aphrodisiac, so is power.

Dracula and his fellow rakes of literature have the capacity to ruin respectable women and suffer no retribution themselves. In this Dracula is the envy of other men, who are jealous of this outsider's erotic power. He seduces their women with a sexual potency they cannot equal and then moves on to further conquests. It is the classic expression of the 'love them and leave them' ethos. It is noteworthy that both the rake of the popular novel and the vampire of folklore pass on their condition to their victims — moral depravity and acquired vampirism respectively. Both sets of victims become social outcasts, doomed in their differing ways to what amounts to a nocturnal existence. Dracula's mistresses stalk the land under cover of night, while the fallen women of fiction frequently turn to prostitution, or else serve as the chattel of their seducer [30] — both becoming in their respective ways creatures of the night. Dracula is, therefore, a moral degenerate, a disciple of carnal fun without responsibility.[31] He offers a glimpse into another world, the Eastern world — a leisured potentate selecting his harem.

This harem is socially discriminating. Dracula is not interested in low class women. His mistresses are, as Harker observes, not common whores but 'ladies by their dress and manner'. Lucy conforms to this pattern — as does a mysterious beautiful girl wearing a fashionable cart-wheel hat whom Dracula sets eyes upon in London (D 13:207). Mina, however, does not conform, for as already indicated the Count's interest in her is less erotic than strategic. In any case her bourgeois repression prevents her welcoming his embrace. To a member of the nineteenth-century middle classes (like Stoker) it often appeared that both the upper and the lower tiers of society enjoyed greater sexual licence than themselves.[32]

Moreover, it is not simply well-born women who interest Dracula. He also appears to be notably fastidious about their marital status. This emphasizes his moral offensiveness, for when he seduces Lucy and Mina one is betrothed and the other newly married. It is as if the awakening of female sexuality on the threshold of marriage makes them more vulnerable, and unlocks the key to his and their desires. He not only duplicates their marriage — symbolically taking them for his own — but he increases the sense of outrage on the part of their menfolk, emasculating those males who dare to challenge him. Harker has, in all probability, been rendered impotent by his ordeal in Transylvania: in which case, does Mina's 'frustration' weaken her resistance? In the case of Holmwood, it has been suggested that the novel needed to have Lucy destroyed before she could properly enslave her 'husband' — for that outcome would have been more than a Victorian readership could stomach.[33]

Throughout the novel, sexuality is portrayed from the male perspective. The ritual slaughter that befalls Lucy and the three vampires reinforces a consistent dichotomy: sexual passion is bad, and must be self-righteously persecuted; while sexual innocence is good and must be defended. Sex is evil, and evil is sex. The message is that erotically aroused women will annihilate if they are not first destroyed.[34] Victorian culture assumed that men bore the onus for sexual 'depravity': the responsibility of women was simply to submit to their husbands' 'bestiality' in order to reproduce. This male dominance was even 'confirmed' by Victorian science. Biologists of the time theorized that female children were the product of a passive, dormant energy cell, which left all responsibility for sexual aggression with the male.[35]

Despite, or perhaps because of, this institutionalized male superiority, there is evidence of a Victorian reaction against it, and not just on the part of the New Women. Many men must have felt burdened by their sexual responsibilities, and would have wished, like Harker, to simply lie back passively and soak up the pleasure. Victorian prostitutes frequently pandered to male masochism, not to mention sadism and homosexuality; and underground pornography often catered for masochistic activities, such as flagellation.[36]

From the perspective of its sexual symbolism *Dracula* conforms to the timeless Christian crusade against indulgence in physical pleasure. Yet the vocations of Dracula's principal assailants lend a new dimension to the sexual theme. On the surface vampirism is portrayed as supernaturally induced, to be countered by supernatural procedures — the efficacious armaments of Church and superstition. Vampirism is shown as a type of demonic possession that requires spiritual as well as practical antidotes. But by introducing medical men into the arena, Stoker opens up a further interpretation. Vampirism, in Victorian terms, is revealed as a disease, a physical and mental disorder which can be 'cured' by doctors rather than 'exorcised' by priests.[37] Stoker labours this point in several passages: Lucy and Mina are afflicted by a 'disease'; are 'infected'; and have 'poison' in their veins (*D* 9:140; 24:380-1,383). It is up to society's good doctors to uphold ethical standards and counter any sexual affliction.

The sexuality with which *Dracula* seethes was able to titillate its Victorian readers by being symbolic and hidden. It could therefore be enjoyed without admitting the source of the enjoyment. But it still remains to be considered to what extent Stoker was aware of all this. Was he writing pornography, confident that he had found the key to its possible expression? Or was he totally oblivious to *Dracula's* eroticism, in the same way that its reviewers were? From one vantage point, there is nothing known about Stoker's life and background to suggest that he would consciously write debauched fiction. Others take this view to be typical modern arrogance, with its implicit, patronizing belief that each new generation assumes that it has discovered sex for the first time. This latter view asserts that it is beyond the bounds of plausibility to claim that Stoker had no appreciation of *Dracula's* sexual underpinnings.[38] Thornburg, for example, insists that on every other criterion (folklore, occult, Christian, etc.) Stoker shows himself to be totally in control of his material. So why the exception when it comes to sexual imagery?[39]

To some extent this is undoubtedly valid. Unconsciously, Stoker's mind was evidently replete with hallucinatory sex. But on the conscious level he would have denied any suggestion of deliberate prurience. Indeed, so incensed was he at the smutty literature issuing forth in his later years that, in 1908, he launched a vehement attack on the moral standards of fiction. He came close to advocating formal censorship, at times his language straying closer to that of the pulpit than of the critic:

A close analysis will show that the only emotions which in the long run harm are those arising from the sex impulses . . .

Within a couple of years past quite a number of novels have been published in England that would be a disgrace to any country even less civilized than our own. The class of works to which I allude are meant by both authors and publishers to bring to the winning of commercial success the forces of evil inherent in man . . . As to the alleged men who follow this loathsome calling, what term of opprobrium is sufficient, what punishment could be too great? . . . For look what those people have done. They found an art wholesome, they made it morbid; they found it pure, they left it sullied . . . In the language of the pulpit, they have 'crucified Christ afresh' . . . such works as are here spoken of deal not merely with natural misdoing based on human weakness, frailty, or passions of the senses, but with vices so flagitious, so opposed to even the decencies of nature in its crudest and lowest forms, that the poignancy of moral disgust is lost in horror. This article . . . is a deliberate indictment of a class of literature so vile that it is actually corrupting the nation.[40]

Inconceivable as it may seem, this article was written by the same person that wrote *Dracula*. The contrast surely lends credence to the notion that *Dracula* was a work stemming from pronouced sexual repression. Let us then subject the novel and its author to some of the insights of psychoanalysis.

# 10.

# PSYCHOANALYTICAL APPROACHES

Complex and . . . fundamental emotions are at work in the
construction and maintenance of the vampire superstition. It is one
more product of the deepest conflicts that determine human
development and fate — those concerned with the earliest
relationships to the parents. These come to their intensest expression
in anxiety dreams and . . . a number of features . . . point
unequivocally to the conclusion that the terrible experiences there
must have played an important part in moulding the beliefs in
question: . . . the occurrence of the supposed events during sleep,
the evident relation of the events to nocturnal emissions resulting
from sexual — particularly perversely sexual — experiences, the
vampire's capacity for transformation, his flight by night, his
appearance in animal form and, finally, the connection between
the belief and that in the return of dead relatives . . . The essential
elements are . . . repressed desires and hatreds derived from early
incest conflicts . . . [especially] hate and guilt.

Ernest Jones, 'On the Vampire', in Christopher Frayling (ed.),
*The Vampyre: Lord Ruthven to Count Dracula*, p. 330.

THE 1890s witnessed the climax of Victorian decadence and
the dawn of psychoanalysis: 1897, in fact, was the year both
of *Dracula's* publication and the commencement of Freud's
psychoanalytical researches. For advocates of psychoanalysis
*Dracula* yields a rich harvest. Indeed, one critic insists that *Dracula*
must be seen from a Freudian standpoint: 'from no other does the
story really make any sense'.[1] Another sees *Dracula*, in its
relationship to our darkest fears and desires, as presaging the
attempts of psychoanalysis 'to dissect the human soul and penetrate
into its arcana by a secret door opened by a magic key'.[2]

A central hypothesis of Freud's complex model of human
behaviour is that the erotic drive cannot be overlooked when

considering the principal sources of psychic energy. When that drive is repressed, unless other 'healthy' defence mechanisms come into operation, guilt and neuroses may be the outcome. His arguments confronted Western society with the neurotic expression of its suppressed erotic impulses. Freud postulated that in the psychosexual development of every child several overlapping stages can be discerned, each distinguished by preoccupation with certain parts of the body. The infant first enters the 'oral' stage, whereby it explores the world and derives its pleasurable sensations through the mouth and teeth. It takes delight in suckling the breast and, following the arrival of teeth, in attempting to eat it.

That this 'oral' phase is not pre-sexual, but intensely sexual, is not hard to explain. *Dracula*, of course, derives much of its impact from its 'orality', and in this sense can be seen as illustrative of regressive infantilism. The English language is rich in the expression of how sexual and digestive pleasures are often related. Colloquial terms for a lover include: 'honey', 'sweet', 'sugar'. The admission of sexual desire can take the words 'I could eat you up'. The practice of the love-bite probably stems from the unconscious urge to devour the partner. More subtly, 'sex' and 'food' may be substituted for one another, as when a person falling helplessly in love may experience loss of appetite.

Following the 'oral' stage comes the 'anal' stage, when the child acquires physical gratification through withholding and expelling faeces. Then, according to Freud, at some point between the third and fifth year the male child will begin to exhibit a fixation with his penis. This 'phallic' stage is accompanied by the child maturing beyond its early narcissistic perspective on the world, and entering the realm of the Oedipus complex. The emotions of young boys towards their mothers develop sexual overtones, with corresponding sensations of rivalry and hostility towards their fathers. A consequence of this jealousy is the harbouring of deep-seated fears on the part of the child that he will be physically deprived of that part of his anatomy which makes him a rival to his father, and that he will be 'castrated'.[3] Applying Freud to *Dracula* will highlight the novel's obsession with intense, infantile sexuality, together with its preoccupation with death, for he maintained that morbid dread (of the kind produced by the fear of vampires) is likely to signify repressed sexual instincts.

In folklore, vampire visitations are largely confined within the family. Incest, therefore, is written into the very expression of vampirism. Likewise, the triangular Oedipal configuration of mother, father, and son is redolent of incest and the threat of parricide. (Compare the function of the dhampire, who suffers no pangs of guilt from destroying his vampire father.) *Dracula's* use of intricate family metaphors, and particularly its handling of competing father-figures, sets it up as a clear demonstration of the Oedipus complex. There exists in the book an endogamous motif which connects nearly all the main characters, other than the Count, as members of one large figurative family.[4] Most of the couplings can be slotted into parent-child or brother-sister relationships. Even Dracula's women approach Mina with the words 'Come, sister' (*D* 27:436). Quasi-ceremonies on several occasions bind Dracula's pursuers together, for example in Lucy's blood transfusions and in the bundle of names given to Harker's son, so that the whole book takes on an incestuous quality.

The Count himself is the obvious father-figure, endowed as he is with enormous potency. He is the patriarch of his domain, having one family resident in his castle while concurrently seeking to extend his blood-ties by acquiring colonies of subservient vampires. He will sire them not through his sperm but through his bite.

Van Helsing is also recognizable in the father role. He thinks of the young men and women around him as replacing his own lost son. However, one critic has suggested that by having two omniscient father-figures in the novel, Stoker allows Dracula's contempt for the family unit to spill over on to the professor, who thereby becomes tinged with a certain moral ambiguity.[5] Seen from another perspective, the existence of two competing 'fathers' enables the Oedipal complex to be resolved satisfactorily. The 'sons' are simultaneously allowed to kill the one, while respecting and obeying the other.[6]

Nor must it be overlooked that there exists an obvious sibling rivalry between some of the 'brothers' (the rivals for Lucy's hand), though this is effectively masked. Any hint of mutual jealousy is expunged so that their aroused emotions can be channelled against the evil father who steals their women. In so doing these Victorian avengers are reminiscent of Freud's 'primal horde',[7] in the sense that they concert their energies against the 'father' who desires to take all the females for himself.

Yet when Dracula is destroyed he is not the first father-figure to lose his life. The theme of parricide is endemic in the novel. Old Mr Swales, who had conveyed his accumulated wisdom to Lucy on the Whitby cliffs, is killed; Holmwood's father also passes away; as does Harker's employer and 'second father' Mr Hawkins. In his bereavement, the 'fatherless' Harker begins to doubt his own capabilities (D 12:190). He is then 'adopted' by Van Helsing, but his Oedipal trauma is finally resolved only with his slaying of Dracula.[8] To compound matters, Quincey Morris then also dies, to become a retrospective 'father' in giving his name to Quincey junior. What is curious, as MacGillivray has noted, is that some of these instances of father-death seem to be gratuitous; they are not central to the storyline, tending in fact to detract from it.[9] It is as if Stoker is driving home his own Oedipus complex: anybody remotely 'fatherish', other than Van Helsing, must be destroyed.

Actually, it is truer to speak of parenticide rather than parricide. Mother-figures die too. The first to do so is a peasant woman, pleading for the return of her child outside Dracula's castle, but upon whom he summons the wolves. The second to lose her life is Lucy's mother, followed by Lucy herself. The teenage beauty who rejected two of the novel's 'sons' and later molested toddlers is herself a victim of quasi-matricide.

Of greater consequence is the intended fate of the central mother-figure, Mina. The idea has been proposed that Stoker's apparent need to dispose of mother surrogates extends even to the goddess Mina. Alongside the expressed need to guard her from evil lies a submerged instinct to visit destruction upon her. How else, the argument goes, could her protectors so persistently expose her to the Count's predations, almost inviting him to win access to her, unless they unconsciously do so deliberately?[10] She resembles in the novel the purity of the Virgin Mary, and if her husband is still sexually incapacitated following his Transylvanian ordeal then she would still be a virgin. For the above interpretation to have any credence, one need only recall the practice of sacrificing virgin wives to the aristocracy — a deeply ingrained social custom in many cultures.[11]

The many instances of parenticide in Dracula are matched by infanticidal parallels. The Count is the clearest example of a murderous parent, for he must kill before he can recruit vampires into his 'family'. He even provides a living child to be consumed by his wife/daughters. But there are other, less obvious, instances. Lucy's mother, for example, is the immediate cause of her daughter's death when, in her ignorance, she removes the garlic that protected Lucy; and Dr Seward's negligence promotes the death of the 'child' in his care, Renfield. One commentator has suggested that perhaps Quincey Morris' demise can be seen as a reflection of his being the most independent of the pursuers. In Freudian terms Morris is punished for his non-conformity, figuratively castrated, and then reinstated into family-based social relationships via Harker's son. [12] Even the downfall of Dracula, on one level the climax of the father-son confrontation, is on another a further case of infanticide — this time supervised by the good father, Van Helsing. Not for nothing has the professor insisted on treating the Count as a 'child-brain' who, the previous chapter proposes, looked upon his crates of Transylvanian soil as surrogate wombs — to which he is tied as effectively as by an umbilical cord.

The child-like aura which Van Helsing perceives as surrounding his adversary is abetted by consideration of the Count's sexual proclivities. Dracula is not only a child-brain: he is also distinctly childlike in his psychosexual development. His sexual activity is not yet phallic, for it has not progressed beyond the oral and anal stages. To this preoccupation with biting and sucking can be added Stoker's repeated references to the foul odour which exudes from the Count's places of rest, which suggest the stench of excrement — to use Richardson's phrase, 'the mephitis of cloaca and the charnel house'. [13] It seems that the only aspect of Dracula that is not infantile is his age — he is over 400 years old.

In view of his all-encompassing 'infantility', perhaps it is misleading to attribute to Dracula the source of the pervasive terror induced by the novel. More persuasively, that accolade should fall to the vampire women. Harker clearly knows (as does Stoker) where the source of his own terror lies: 'It is maddening to think that of all the foul things that lurk in this hateful place the Count is the least dreadful to me' (D 3:49-50). The male reader, one suspects, agrees with him. What is most to be feared, unconsciously, is the devouring woman; the mother-figure who threatens by being desirable. This view can be supported, firstly, by referring to Stoker's three other horror novels. In each the supernatural presence is erotic and feminine. Secondly, it is necessary only to recall Mina's mouth being pressed down upon Dracula's breast. With that image it is *he* who becomes the threatening mother, forcing Mina to suckle from him. Roth has summarized the terror of women as manifested in *Dracula*:

> The threatening Oedipal fantasy, the regression to a primary oral obsession, the attraction, and destruction of the vampires of *Dracula* are, then, interrelated and interdependent. What they spell out is a fusion of the memory of nursing at the mother's breast with a primal scene fantasy which results in the conviction that the sexually desirable woman will annihilate if she is not first destroyed. [14]

More generally, Moretti has offered a perceptive explanation for the threats engendered by the male, as opposed to the female, vampire in literature. Those poets and writers who utilized vampire imagery and aimed their work at a more sophisticated readership have usually cast their vampires in the female mould (for example, the vampires of Goethe, Keats, Poe, Le Fanu). The vampires of mass, popular culture, on the other hand, were more usually male (Sir Francis Varney and Count Dracula being the obvious examples). From the foregoing discussion it would appear that literary vampirism is founded on the ambivalent impulses felt by the male child towards its mother. Therefore to present the source of the threat as a woman is appropriate, for the sex of the threatening mother and the threatening vampire coincide. By deploying a male vampire, however, the nature of the parental threat is softened because 'the unconscious source of perturbation is hidden'[15] — the conscious mind enjoys greater protection by being made less aware of the sexual dimension of parenthood. In short, 'the vampire is transformed into a man by mass culture, which has to promote spontaneous certainties and cannot let itself plumb the unconscious too deeply'.[16]

This central hypothesis, that it is really the female vampire which evokes terror, is associated with the expression of unconscious guilt — particularly sexual guilt — on the part of the male child. Freudian psychoanalysis propounds that the urge to perform incest is probably the primordial sin from which all others derive, and that the adult's unconscious sensations of guilt owe their origin to infantile incestuous desires. Those males who are most strongly in the grasp of the Oedipus complex — those who have not come to terms with their infantile desire for incest with their mother and who cannot cope with the rivalry with their father — are often the most jealous when it comes to exclusive possession of their women.[17] In extreme cases this guilt complex might be projected from the living on to the dead, who, it is supposed, in their torment, cannot rest in their graves but feel compelled to return in order to resume their love for the living. Those resting in peace, however, are permitted an incestuous relationship of their own — measured by their decomposition and integration with 'Mother Earth'.[18]

Those individuals most afflicted by visions of the vampire are, it is claimed, those most afflicted by feelings of sexual guilt. Sexually rejected, their initial love for the mother turns to hate, in turn leading to fear of retribution undertaken by the mother after her death. This illustrates the fundamental warring triangle — love, hate, guilt

— through which Freudian psychoanalysis postulates each of us must pass in infancy. In later life, whenever healthy sexual outlets are repressed, there is a tendency to regress to an earlier stage — oral sadism being one of the most frequently noted. Unresolved tensions may lead not only to repressed sexuality, but also to dread, both of which might then link up with the aggressive instincts to be expressed as oral sadism.

Of course, central to the whole vampire phenomenon lies a preoccupation with teeth. The notion of 'oral sadism' stems from an infant's discovery of his ability to inflict pain once he has grown them. The mouth that first sucked the breast is later able to bite it and try to eat it — in other words, to practise cannibalism (and draw blood, not milk). This is the first opportunity a baby has to cause physical pain and to demonstrate its aggressive instincts. The original sucking impulse is not abandoned, but stays throughout adult life in the form of kissing, so it always retains its sexual significance. Suckling at the breast has obvious parallels with sexual intercourse. Both acts involve the swelling of an organ, the emission of a precious white liquid, followed by a physical and mental sense of well-being in both participants. (This adds to the deep-seated psychological association between milk and semen.) The cutting of a child's teeth, however, comes to assume a critical place in his emotional development, for if teeth can inflict pain on the mother, her teeth can also inflict pain on the child. When he later comes to expect retribution for his earlier cannibalistic tendencies, it is castration that is his unconscious fear.

Here it is appropriate to introduce the concept of *vagina dentata;* the clinical term for a sexual myth found in many folk tales around the world, and which is bound up with the castration complex as described by Freud. The male's infant obsession with teeth and with his mother's love gives rise to a process of psychological displacement, leading in the mind to an unconscious fusion between her mouth and her genitals. The vagina is envisaged as mouth-shaped, complete with lips and 'teeth'. During menstruation the horrific image is intensified. (As blood is so precious its loss without visible injury is historically one of the most traumatic of human experiences.) The menstruating 'mouth' becomes bloodied, presenting a horrific image of the after-effects of castration following the devouring of the penis by the mouth/vagina. (The concept has parallels at the plant level, as when a splendidly coloured specimen, such as the Venus Flytrap, tempts insects inside before snapping shut around them.) Almost every culture in the world regards coitus during a woman's menstrual period as taboo: the thought of blood on the penis being too fear-provoking for most men to entertain. Likewise, many societies regard women as being in some way castrated men. They are viewed as less worthy for that reason, and it is hardly surprising that the notion of 'penis-envy' on the part of women became a fashionable notion.

Psychoanalytically, the *vagina dentata* concept is conditioned by the experience of one's own mother when she is menstruating, which invokes both sexual excitement and extreme terror.[19] The implicit threat of castration cannot be neutralized until the 'teeth' are extracted — symbolically (or actually) removed. Edgar Allan Poe, for example, in 'Berenice', demonstrates a morbid obsession with her teeth and the need to extract them from her dead body:

> The teeth! The teeth! They were here, and there, and everywhere, visibly and palpably before me, long, narrow and excessively white, with the pale lips writhing about them . . . I shuddered as I assigned to them, in imagination, a sensitive and sentient power . . . I felt that their possession could alone ever restore me to peace in giving me back my reason.

Teeth, it will by now be obvious, like any sharp elongated instrument (such as Harker's Kukri knife, Morris' Bowie knife, Seward's lancet, or Van Helsing's stake), represent a powerful phallic symbol. Berenice must undergo the symbolic castration that Poe's narrator fears for himself. And Bram Stoker unwittingly wrote about *vagina dentata* long before *Dracula*: the Iron Maiden torture device in 'The Squaw' takes the shape of a woman filled with spikes (teeth) to embrace any man who 'enters' her. But in *Dracula* the vampire women's assault on Jonathan Harker provides a classic display of *vagina dentata*. One critic has written:

> The danger of sexuality, the punishment that threatens all who yield, is shown by the manner in which [he] is obsessed by her teeth. And, indeed, in psychoanalysis, many cases of male impotence reveal, though more or less buried in the unconscious the notion of the female vagina being furnished with teeth, and thus a source of danger in being able to bite and castrate . . . Mouth and vagina are equated in the unconscious: [he] yields both the yearning for the mother's organ, and to be revenged upon it; since the dangers that hedge it about make him sexually avoid all women as too menacing. His act is therefore a sort of retributive castration inflicted on the mother whom he loves, and yet hates, because obdurate to his sex-love for her in infancy . . . The memory, or rather the phantasy of biting the mother's breast must become charged, in

the unconscious with past feelings of wickedness [and guilt]. And the child, having learnt by experience what is meant by the law of retaliation when he infringes the code . . . begins, in his turn, to fear that the bites he wished to give his mother will be visited on him: namely retaliation for his cannibalism.[20]

This passage actually refers to Poe, but its substance could equally apply to Stoker and to his hero, Harker, at the hands of Dracula's wife. It is a demonstrable statement of the Oedipus complex and *vagina dentata* intertwined. The reference to the conflicting emotions of love and hate is another way of recognizing the simultaneous attraction and repulsion of the vampire. As Jones put it: 'All the beliefs about the nightmare in whatever guise proceed from the idea of the sexual assault that is both wished for and dreaded.'[21] This ambivalence is not confined to sexual matters: it surfaces in many forms. On the question of death, for example, desire for oblivion co-exists with a yearning for immortality: the wish that our loved ones walk again conflicts with the hope that the dead stay where they are. Always, projection is at work: it might be the living who want to be reunited with the dead, but more usually it is the dead who are seen as seeking reunion with the living.

Perhaps then, when all is said, the real source of the novel's terror springs neither from Count Dracula nor his vampirellas, but from inside the human mind. The *real* monster resides within us, the readers. People create for themselves the monsters they fear out of their unconscious and repressed yearnings and anxieties. Fear of sexual punishment and of death mean that — because sexual expression is linked to the body, which will eventually die — fear and sexuality come into common focus. Sexual repression in the mind becomes metamorphosed, transforming itself into visions of frightful beings. The Dracula image operates as a filter through which the novel can reflect submerged desires. In other words, it somehow makes bearable to the conscious mind those desires and fears recognized as being unacceptable, and therefore unacknowledged to oneself.[22]

It is arguable that the entire Gothic genre is about the discovery of self-horror. Perhaps readers saw, and see, in *Dracula* faint echoes of themselves, because a close bond between any two people involves, however tangentially, the taint of vampire exploitation — be it economic, intellectual, emotional, or whatever. It is no trite observation that 'you always kill the thing you love', for only the intensity of that particular emotion can lead to the spiritual proximity to another person that can produce lasting damage. In *Dracula* that over-used phrase is given a savage new twist, for illimitable desire turns love, literally, into possession and an eternity of enslavement.[23]

Two other psychological motifs permeate *Dracula*: the world of dreams and the issue of insanity. Upon finishing the novel the reader may never be entirely convinced that the extraordinary episodes disclosed are not the products of sleep. Perhaps the whole book should be interpreted as a dream — or rather a nightmare — for Stoker weaves a narrative whereby terror and dream are never easily distinguishable. Harker, to begin with, experiences bad dreams even before he reaches Dracula's castle; his carriage journey is described as dream-like unreality; and later he is tempted to dismiss his entire ordeal as a grotesque nightmare. Dracula had previously warned him that 'there are bad dreams for those who sleep unwisely' (*D* 3:46). Lucy then recollects her sleep-walking as weird dreams, and is eventually too terrified to fall asleep for fear of what night may bring. Mina's encounter with the Count is similarly expressed as a surreal dream: 'I thought I was asleep' (*D* 19:308), and her hypnotically induced trances reinforce the view that only the unconscious mind is receptive to Dracula's presence. He is powerless without the consent of the unconscious mind, for his victims have only to wake up to experience a feeling of salvation and a lightening of their mental burden. Throw in Renfield's madness, Van Helsing's graveyard vigils, and the vampires' nocturnal powers, and the whole novel seems to be pitched into the twilight zone between waking and sleeping.[24] Throughout, actual happenings are phrased in the language and imagery of dreams.[25]

Linked to the fear of dreams is the novel's overpowering obsession with madness, a common enough theme in Victorian fiction. Harker, on many occasions, assumes he has gone mad; Seward entertains similar ideas about himself; and Lucy gives every appearance of derangement ('she makes a curious psychological study' [*D* 5:72]) long before Dracula gains access to her. Even then Seward can only diagnose that 'it must be something mental' (*D* 9:137). Van Helsing has tried to widen his ex-student's horizons by suggesting that 'all men are mad in some way or the other' (*D* 10:145), but Seward soon begins to harbour doubts about his mentor, who is so abnormally clever that even he could be 'off his head' (*D* 15:245).

Stoker is offering nothing original in this soul-searching of his characters. Polidori's Aubrey also questioned his own sanity; as did Stevenson's Jekyll. What is a departure from Victorian literary convention is that Stoker seems almost to be saying that madness is nothing to be afraid of. There *are* worse things in life. This notion emerges clearly in an exchange between Seward and the professor: ' "Dr Van Helsing, are you mad?" . . . "Would I were! . . . Madness were easy to bear compared with truth like this" ' (D 15:233). Stoker is attempting to show that whatever terrors lie in store for the insane they are nothing compared to the horror of everlasting hell as a vampire. Or, rather, madness in itself is not really at issue: it is the vampire that produces it,[26] just as it is Dracula who gives that extra twist to Renfield's unhappy mind.

Renfield is the focal point of madness as explored in *Dracula*. He represents the split personality that was a common literary device in Victorian fiction, as well as being an example of the 'victim' who must suffer the excesses of mental torment before being released into the calm waters of sanity. In places, the novel comes close to insisting that Renfield is anything but mad. Seward and company originally operate from the belief that only the mad can believe in vampires, yet their prejudices lead to some unpalatable conclusions. Dracula *does* exist, demonstrating that Renfield, who knows as much, has clearer perception than the doubters, whose mental faculties cannot comprehend the awful reality. Crucially, once the dying Renfield is freed from Dracula's power, and he returns briefly to 'sanity', he does not dismiss his earlier experiences as delusions. Renfield when sane is just as sure of Dracula's existence as when insane. When his mind is dispossessed it does not result in the banishing of his supposed hallucinations.[27] In other words, sanity and insanity are not mutually exclusive categories where the existence of Dracula is concerned. As detailed elsewhere, it is 'belief' and 'faith' that matter.

It is appropriate that these brief psychoanalytical attempts to fathom *Dracula* conclude with an attempt to fathom his creator. Two scholars have tried to probe Stoker's formative years with Freudian instruments.[28] He was, it will be recalled, sickly for his first seven years, and it is through a closer investigation into the handling of his early disability that insights might be gleaned regarding his major fictional work. *Dracula*, mirroring Stoker's illness, is a 'tale of medical detection of puzzling illnesses, of obscure diagnoses, and unusual cures'.[29]

Medical care in Ireland during Stoker's infancy was such that surgery was comparatively rare. Many disorders that today would warrant surgery or pharmacy were treated by the practice of blood letting — the presumption being that the illness was caused by 'bad' blood. Yet whether Stoker's malaise was tackled by the releasing of his blood or actual surgery, it is likely he would have suffered protracted surgically-induced trauma. Anna Freud (Freud's daughter) has written:

> Whenever we have to prepare a child for surgical experience, we find that the greatest difficulty is to keep the event down to its 'real' significance. The extraction of a tooth, the removal of tonsils or of an appendix would not be so frightening in itself. They become horrifying when the child's imagination turns them into amputation, castration, annihilation, etc., i.e. into dangers which existed previously as threats in his conscious or unconscious mind. [30]

The mechanics of hospitals are frightening enough today, for an adult as for a child. The extent of the trauma involved has been vividly described in this account, written in the 1930s:

> Certainly there is nothing in the practice of medicine so barbarous and so fraught with psychological danger as the prevalent custom of taking a child into a strange white room, surrounding him with white garbed strangers exhibiting queer paraphernalia and glittering knives and at the height of his consternation pressing an ether cone over his face and telling him to breathe deeply. The anxiety stimulated by such horrors is probably never surpassed in the child's subsequent life. [31]

According to Shuster, a child's terror of doctors stems from a fantasy that the physician has lost out in the sexual-aggressive battles of the primal bedroom, has become insane, and is seeking to alleviate his misery either by castrating the child or by emptying his/her body of its content. [32] Perhaps the child's emotional response is accountable for the introduction and popularity of the fictional 'mad doctor'. Doctors also play a large part in children's games. In 'doctors and nurses', for example, children act out the experiences they have been through as patients, but in reverse. It is conceivable that some comparable role reversal manifested itself in Stoker when, in later years, he came to write *Dracula*. The Count can, then, be seen as a reincarnation of the 'cruel' doctors encountered by Stoker in his childhood, while he himself identifies with the good doctors, Van Helsing and Seward. Nor can Stoker's mother be eliminated from his feelings of terror, for she might have taken him, struggling, to the doctor and then 'abandoned' him to whatever horrors lay in store. To a terrified young patient, the mother is guilty of complicity, or worse, regarding his suffering.

To proceed with this conjecture: the first phase of the novel — Harker trapped in the castle — can be perceived as a re-enactment of a child being abandoned by its mother in a huge hospital to suffer surgery and/or blood letting. Dracula, lying in his coffin gorged with blood, therefore takes on the role of the wicked doctor trying to fend off his fear of emptiness/death by drinking the blood of children.[33] The entire scene could be interpreted as autobiography at the level of fantasy. In the early chapters Stoker projects himself through the unfortunate 'child', Harker. Later in the novel he turns to portraying himself through the good doctors — especially Van Helsing — to redress his past suffering.

Reviewing the first section of the book to mirror Stoker's possible early disability, the castle becomes the hospital, with Harker naturally apprehensive about entering a nineteenth-century medical institution. An old woman (another mother-figure) tries to warn him and protect him. Once inside, he seeks to escape from his 'prison', as may the hospitalized child. The Count dressed in black and the doctors in white present stark images of absolute terror. Just as Dracula waits upon Harker hand and foot, and so disguises his menace, so the surgeon is all smiles and reassurances prior to picking up his knives. The threat of both is thus displaced, adding to Harker's/the child's terror and confusion. Nightmares are common to both the castle and hospitals. The vampires' injecting teeth correspond to the nurses' injecting needles. The special room where Harker lapses into unconsciousness matches the operating chamber where anaesthetic is administered, and when Harker/the patient wakes up he finds himself mysteriously transported back to his own room/ward. Harker's lashing out at the Count with a shovel suggests a child bouncing its little fists off the chest of the surgeon, and his near-miraculous escape from the castle might be Stoker's way of denial that the surgical nightmare ever happened at all.[34]

Later, Harker undergoes a period of convalescence in Budapest, where his 'mother'/wife is warned that he will suffer long-term trauma — as often happens after a child leaves hospital. Thereafter doubt pervades his consciousness until rationalization can take place, when Van Helsing eases Harker's mind by reassuring him that his experience was not nightmare, but real. Only with that comfort can Harker/Stoker come to terms with his trauma and lay it to rest.

Needless to say, many people who were severely traumatized in childhood from surgery never become aware that they were ever traumatized. Yet the wretched experiences that Stoker possibly endured in his earliest years might have been awakened in adulthood in his fiction. Traces of these experiences appear long before *Dracula*: in fact, they are manifest in his first published fiction, the collection of fairy tales in *Under the Sunset*. Themes from the anthology reappear throughout much of Stoker's later fiction, as though he felt compelled to relate them again and again. In view of this, an attempt has been made to use two of the tales to hypothesize upon a link between Stoker's childhood and his conception of *Dracula*. They 'help explain the blood sucking, madness, the psychiatrist and the insane asylum, the sleep disturbances, of . . . *Dracula*'.[35]

Of principal interest in this respect is Stoker's little cameo 'How 7 Went Mad', which incorporates nightmares, insanity, and blood letting with not a little wit and humour. A little boy — Tineboy (tiny boy?) — who has trouble at school with his arithmetic, wishes that the troublesome number seven had never been invented, whereupon his wish comes true in a dream. The Alphabet Doctor, whose job it is to treat sick letters and numbers, uses his instruments, including a horoscope ('horrorscope' to Tineboy), to examine the patient, who complains of callous treatment because of his being an orphan. As a prime number, he has no relatives, no kith and kin. The tormented digit succumbs to insanity and prompts a passage from Stoker worthy of *Catch-22*: 'You surely are not mad enough to insist upon being mad? . . . if you are mad enough to insist upon being mad, we must try to cure your madness . . . and then you will be unmad enough to wish to be unmad, and we will cure that too.' It is worth noting that the insane digit, who is foaming at the mouth, is restrained by a nurse who is trying to bleed him — further evidence that this was standard medical treatment at the time.

But why the number '7' in particular? Bierman points to the seven Stoker children. Four of them were younger than Bram and were born while he was still disabled. Bierman perceives intense sibling jealousy on Bram's part, even identifying death wishes towards his younger brothers. This is evidenced by the various instances of infanticide in *Dracula* and the borrowing of their names — Tom and George — for various minor characters.[36] Also of interest to Bierman is the fact that no less than three of Stoker's brothers entered the medical profession, one of whom, George, became an ear, nose, and throat doctor.

The second relevant tale from *Under the Sunset* is 'The Wondrous Child', another story of sibling rivalry and dreams. In this tale we find birth expressed in oral terms: to conceive, the girl opens her mouth, into which is poured 'scarlet' milk. The 'child', who dies and is reborn, is then able to control wild beasts such as dragons and snakes. Later, in *Dracula*, the Count is referred to as both a 'child' and as 'wondrous'.

What is common to both short stories and to *Dracula*, according to Bierman, is the theme of death wishes towards younger brothers nursing at the mother's breast, together with primal scenes expressed in nursing terms. He is impressed by the psychoanalytical concept of the 'oral triad' — the wish to eat, to be eaten, and to sleep.[37] In *Dracula*, as in the human mind, the interrelationship between these wishes causes them to be reactivated together: 'Sleep, as expressed in Harker's stupor, would be a first line of defense against being awakened by the primal sounds, but the wishes to eat and be eaten would also arise; and thus the stage would be set for intercourse being seen in terms of sucking and being sucked.'[38] As applied to the infant Irishman, Stoker would have been irritated by his younger brothers' crying, which prevented him sleeping, while also being aroused by their suckling at his mother's breast. Through being bed-ridden he would have been unable to dissipate his aggression in normal ways, but would have had to express it orally. The act of 'killing' his brothers would have been seen as eating them (as in 'How 7 Went Mad', when the raven eats all the number 7s). This in turn would have triggered the other parts of the triad — the wishes to be eaten and to sleep — which themselves generate fear of sleep and death. Bierman explains:

> Being bled must have been interpreted by young Stoker as being eaten up. Sucking blood and eating are equated in *Dracula*. After the Count has sucked Mina's blood . . . Van Helsing remarks, '. . . last night he banqueted heavily and will sleep late . . .' Due to the generic linkage of the wish to be eaten and the wish to eat and to sleep, being bled would have become linked to the latter two wishes. Milk would no longer have been white, but blood red.[39]

Is it purely coincidence, Bierman asks, that the collection of stories for *Under the Sunset*, though written over a period of years, were gathered for publication shortly after the birth of Stoker's only son — his new rival in the Oedipal triangle?[40] Having earlier experienced a lessening of his mother's attentions following the arrival of his younger brothers, Stoker now faced the loss of his wife's affections after the birth of Noel.

The application of psychoanalytical techniques to *Dracula* is necessarily speculative and contentious, particularly those that seek a direct correlation between his life and his fiction. But the questions they raise are nevertheless important: was Stoker reliving his infancy in the form of Jonathan Harker? Was he embodied in the good doctor Van Helsing? Or was he fantasizing as the Count, able to take vicarious sexual pleasure from other men's women? Whatever the value of the psychoanalytical approach, the world of the vampire has been described as a 'twilight borderland where psychopathological and religious motives intermingle'.[41] Therefore let us turn to reflect upon some of the Christian and moral insights to be gleaned from *Dracula*.

# 11.

# *DRACULA* AS
# CHRISTIAN PARODY

'Now let me guard yourself. On your forehead I touch this piece
of Sacred Wafer in the name of the Father, the Son, and —'.

There was a fearful scream which almost froze our hearts to hear.
As he placed the Wafer on Mina's forehead, it had seared it — had
burnt into the flesh as though it had been a piece of white-hot metal
. . . she wailed out: 'Unclean! Unclean! Even the Almighty shuns
my polluted flesh! I must bear this mark of shame upon my forehead
until the Judgment Day.'

Jonathan Harker's Journal, *Dracula* 22:353.

IT MIGHT seem superfluous to claim that *Dracula* is a Christian
parody. Everything that Christ is meant to be, Dracula either
inverts or perverts. Christ is Good: Dracula is Evil — an agent
of the devil. Christ was a humble carpenter: Dracula a vainglorious
aristocrat. Christ offers light and hope, and was resurrected at dawn:
Dracula rises at sunset and thrives in darkness. Christ's death at
the 'stake' was the moment of his rebirth: for the vampire the stake
heralds 'death' and oblivion. Christ offered his own life so that
others might live: Dracula takes the lives of many so that *he* might
live. The blood of Christ is drunk at the Eucharist by the faithful;
Dracula reverses the process and drinks from *them*. Both preach
resurrection and immortality, the one offering spiritual purity, the
other physical excess. The link between Christ and Dracula is made
explicit through the Count's recoiling from crucifixes, holy wafer,
and other symbols of Christianity.

It can be proposed that one of the basic lessons of the novel was
to reaffirm the existence of God in an age when the weakening hold
of Christianity generated fresh debate about what lay beyond death.
The marshalled diary extracts and letters are themselves endowed
with the status of scripture. Instead of the Gospels according to
St Matthew and St Mark, we find Gospels according to Mr Harker

and Dr Seward. Taken with Van Helsing's concluding remarks, 'We
want no proofs' (*D* 27:449), they constitute a 'revelation' of Dracula's
existence, as the Bible offers a 'revelation' of Christ's.

In the novel, faith in God is rewarded by incontrovertible evidence
of His power, and the provision of tangible means whereby to defeat
the evil creature who seeks to usurp it. The book offers an exercise
in syllogistic logic: a supposedly immortal being is destroyed by
the defenders of Christ, armed above all with faith in God — the
conclusion therefore follows that God exists. What might not be
so apparent are the depths to which the biblical allegory reaches.
*Dracula* is replete with Christian imagery, so it is pertinent to
commence this chapter by examining a selection of passages that
relate in some way to the Bible or to Christian liturgy.

Jonathan Harker dominates the book's opening sequences. His
proposed coach journey to Castle Dracula invites local
consternation, particularly fear of the 'evil eye' (the sign of the devil),
which must be averted at all costs. The expression has biblical
origins: 'The light of the body is in the eye . . . But if thine eye
be evil, thy whole body shall be full of darkness' (Matthew 6:22-3).
Harker's pilgrimage happens to be planned for St George's Eve,
acknowledged by the Romanian Orthodox Church at that time
as falling on 4 May. St George, a mythical 'saint', was, according
to legend, as difficult to dispose of as vampires. Several times he
was chopped up, buried or incinerated, but each time was
resuscitated — presumably by God. This early reference in the novel
to St George enables the interconnections between 'Dracul' —
meaning 'dragon-slayer' — and 'Christian warrior' to be forged at
the outset: Harker's sojourn will provide the spark for a Christian
crusade against Dracula/the devil. Interestingly, Harker has to
*ascend* to Dracula's castle, a curious reversal of the classical *descents*
into hell of such mythical figures as Odysseus, Proserpine, and
Orpheus.[1] But once Harker is imprisoned, the Count's vampirellas
provide him with a glimpse of heavenly experience — not fire and
brimstone but an eternal dreamy ecstasy.

Dracula is all things to all people. To Lucy he is principally an
irresistible lover; to Harker he is a feudal tyrant come to subvert
Britain; to Van Helsing he is in the service of the devil. He might
even be the Antichrist. There is some irony in this association for,
as Dracula reminds Mina, he once (in his earlier existence) waged
war and intrigued against the Turks on behalf of Christianity (*D*
21:343). The real Vlad Tepes, it will be remembered, actually died
for that cause.

Nonetheless, there are grounds for supposing Dracula to be cast as a figurative Antichrist, even though the notion of such a being probably plays a greater role in the Christian faith than its emphasis in the Bible might warrant. Only briefly does the term appear explicitly, in the first and second letters of John (1 John 2:18,22; 4:3; and 2 John 7), although the Antichrist has also been identified with the strange beasts and demons to be found in the Book of Revelation. There we encounter further reminders of the 'dragon-devil' connection: 'And the great dragon was thrown down, that ancient serpent, who is called the Devil and Satan' (Revelation 12:9). Some Christian scholars conceive of the Antichrist not in personal terms but as an attitude of mind; a collective evil inherent in all those who deny the teachings of Christ. Those inclined to believe in a 'personal' Antichrist view him as a being 'who opposes and exalts himself against every so-called god or object of worship, so that he takes his seat in the temple of God, proclaiming himself to be God' (2 Thessalonians 2:4). Count Dracula fits the description.

On the one occasion that Dracula is permitted by Stoker to quote scripture he alludes to the alienation of an Antichrist. In Transylvania he is a ruler, a boyar, but he would be a nobody in London — 'a stranger in a strange land' (D 2:31), the very words of Moses' son, Gershom. Possibly, too, there is a connection here with Stoker's insistence that Dracula can sleep only in consecrated ground. The elaborate safeguards that the Count makes to ensure his daily rest are open to a variety of interpretations. Perhaps his daily imitation of the true Christian dead is an indication of his inner torment: he yearns to rest permanently among Christ's believers. [2] Perhaps, more subtly, Stoker is hinting at the powerful proximity between good and evil. Just as a thin line divides love and hate, genius and madness, so 'evil' is intimately allied to 'good'. More likely, Dracula's hotel arrangements are an innovation by Stoker designed to highlight the sense of blasphemy. The Count is not cast out from sacred places, but is a parasite upon them.

The Antichrist is usually depicted as the offspring of a consenting living woman and a male demon. This inevitably focuses attention on young Quincey Harker, who is born thirteen months after Dracula's visits to his mother. Is Stoker alluding to the possibility that the twentieth century must experience collective terrors when this infant reaches manhood?

If the novel does hint at the Antichrist, then Renfield emerges as a sort of anti-John the Baptist. Both lunatic and prophet are described as impatient, wild-looking figures, for whom the Messiah is not merely coming — he is here. Also relevant is that in Christian chronology John the Baptist is 'the operative agent who sets the whole thing in motion'.[3] So it is with Renfield, who prepares the way for Dracula's coming and provides his means of entry into Seward's residence/asylum. The fate of the two men is also similar: John loses his head, while Renfield also dies of a head wound.

To reinforce his biblical credentials Renfield is given most of the passages containing quasi-Christian symbolism. 'The blood is the life' is his clarion call, but as previously noted his blood-drinking takes a literal view of what is a theological minefield. The Bible contains numerous references to the power of blood,[4] but Renfield conveniently overlooks one of their primary purposes as prohibiting the imitation of pagan sacrificial practice. Deuteronomy 12:23, for example, demands 'Only be sure that you do not eat the blood; for the blood is the life, and you shall not eat the life with the flesh.'

On other occasions Renfield is less careless as to the wider context of his scriptural borrowings. He pronounces: 'The bride-maidens rejoice the eyes that wait the coming of the bride; but when the bride draweth nigh, then the maidens shine not to the eyes that are filled' (*D* 8:125). Here he seems to be giving a loose rendering of John the Baptist's words when witnessing the coming of Christ: 'He that hath the bride is the bridegroom: but the friend of the bridegroom, which standeth and heareth him, rejoiceth because of the bridegroom's voice . . .' (John 3:29). There are several explanations behind this reference in *Dracula:* possibly the Count is to be seen as the radiant bride, with Renfield the groom, and all his spiders the bride-maidens — made redundant by the coming of the bride.[5] Alternatively, and more logically, it is Dracula who is the bridegroom, with Lucy his future bride and Renfield the rejoicing bridesmaid.[6] Whatever the case, the union of two people in marriage in the sight of God is to be violated by Satan, a theme to which we shall return.

Renfield is ingenious enough to escape from his asylum, and is discovered speaking through the adjoining chapel wall: 'I am here to do Your bidding, Master. I am Your slave, and You will reward me, for I shall be faithful. I have worshipped You long and afar off. Now that You are near, I await Your commands, and You will not pass me by, will You, dear Master, in Your distribution of good things?' (*D* 8:126). Here Renfield is clearly at prayer, and Stoker's use of capitalizing pronouns when the lunatic is referring to Dracula gives emphasis to the Count's divine status. When Seward recaptures his patient after a further escape, even he cannot resist reference to a biblical episode: he interprets Renfield's craving for flies and spiders as 'loaves and fishes' — except that they are gathered solely for Renfield's selfish purpose.

When Renfield comes to reflect on his own position with regard to his messiah, it is not with John the Baptist that he draws a parallel, but with an Old Testament figure. 'I am, so far as concerns things purely terrestrial, somewhat in the position which Enoch occupied spiritually!' (D 20:321). Enoch, the father of Methuselah, was said to have 'walked with God' (Genesis 5:18-24). Renfield expects to be Satan's/Dracula's minion and to be granted immortality — as God presumably granted Enoch.

Throughout, Renfield is tempted by the devil, as was Christ. The Count, holding up his hands to control the rats, says to Renfield: 'All these lives will I give you, ay, and many more and greater, through countless ages, if you fall down and worship me!' D 21:333). Here Stoker is repeating Satan's exchange with Christ in the wilderness:

> Then was Jesus led up by the Spirit into the wilderness to be tempted by the devil . . . Again the devil took him to a very high mountain, and showed him all the kingdoms of the world, and the glory of them, and he said to him: 'All these I will give you, if you will fall down and worship me' (Matthew 4:1-9).

Jesus declined *his* offer with the rebuff 'Get thee hence, Satan'; Renfield responds with the reply: 'Come in, Lord and Master!' But later, angered by Dracula's attacks on Mina, he is prepared for martyrdom. He grapples with the Count, who has slipped into his cell as mist, knowing that lunatics are reputedly endowed with superhuman strength. His efforts here seem to be a dark analogue of Jacob wrestling with the angel of the Lord (Genesis 32:24-5). Jacob's efforts are beneficial both for himself and the people of Israel, and even Renfield attains a spiritual, if not physical, victory from his struggle.[7]

Van Helsing, as the obvious shaman/priest of the book, frequently resorts to biblical language. He makes use of the parable of the seed and the sower (D 10:145-6; cf. Luke 8:5-8) to explain to Seward that with regard to Lucy's ghastly malaise all will be revealed in good time. The parable ends with the words 'He that hath ears to hear, let him hear', and as if to drive home the message Van Helsing gives his colleague's ear a playful tweak. Faith, of course, is of the essence to the Dutchman; but it is a curious kind of faith, as one might expect from a priest-figure who believes in vampires and the efficacy of pagan antidotes such as garlic. Few modern Christians would accept Van Helsing's definition of faith: 'that which enables us to believe things we know to be untrue' (*D* 14:232), for it comes close to suggesting that the intellect and the intuition can never act in concert. To Van Helsing, the existence of Dracula seems to be on a par, logically speaking, with that of Christ.

Further indication of Van Helsing's oblique, eccentric view of his God comes with his (mis)use of Catholic beliefs and relics. His application of certain tools of the Catholic faith is disrespectful at times, futile at others, and on occasions blasphemous.

Especially damaging are the liberties taken with core Catholic precepts. According to Catholic dogma, the sacred wafer *is* the body of Christ, and cannot be used in any profane manner, no matter what the ulterior motive.[8] The Host, which represents the risen body of Jesus, is intended as food for the faithful — not to be used by the laity for their own purposes. Worse, Van Helsing makes a feeble attempt to legitimize his more extreme acts. Preparatory to the staking of Lucy he claims to have an indulgence (*D* 16:252), to which he refers almost as if he has received Vatican *carte blanche* to desecrate graves and mutilate corpses. In Catholic theology an indulgence is a remission from temporal punishment for sinful behaviour which has already been perpetrated and forgiven. Van Helsing is claiming his indulgence for something he is about to do. Whatever discredit had already fallen upon the practice of indulgences when granted by Catholic clergy in previous centuries, their use for the purposes Van Helsing has in mind could not possibly have been sanctioned.

There is also a general point here. The 'powers' of the crucifix and Communion Host (when it is not specifically employed during the Eucharist) are symbolic only — they serve to remind the faithful of Christ. When they are used as 'weapons', as if they possessed divine energy in themselves, they then become objects of magic rather than religion. That is why Van Helsing acts more as a magician than a scientist/priest.

Lucy's re-entry into the Christian fold heralds more than the climax of Van Helsing's manipulation of Catholic dogma. It provides further instance of Stoker linking pagan gods with the Christian God. The act of staking her is not described as Christ-like, but as Thor-like (*D* 16:259). Thor, the Norse God of Thunder, happens to wield a hammer as his symbolic weapon. From reading Baring-Gould's *A Book of Folklore* Stoker would have learned of an anecdote, linking the Norse gods Thor, Wodin, and Loki with the Father, the Son, and the Holy Ghost, in which the devil is nailed to a post with a hammer — the equivalent of staking a vampire.[9]

Evidence that Van Helsing is at heart a more orthodox Catholic than some of his activities might suggest, surfaces when the stricken Mina talks about ending her own life. The professor's prohibitions are uncompromising: 'You must not die by any hand; but least of all by your own' (D 22:346). In this he is referring not only to her immediate transference to the land of the undead once she dies: he is reminding her of the uncompromising Catholic doctrine that suicide is a mortal sin. Nor would he have overlooked that, according to folklore, suicides are candidates for vampirism. Mina would be merely precipitating her own fate.

Mina, herself, is not a Catholic.[10] Yet when she marries Jonathan in a Budapest convent/hospital she wraps his as-yet-unread diary and ties it with a blue ribbon as 'an outward and visible sign for us all our lives that we trusted each other' (D 9:129-30). This has been interpreted as conforming to Catholic symbolism, wherein the sacraments are outward (visible) signs instituted by Christ to give grace.[11] Mina is deeply devout, reaching for biblical passages to assist in the expression of the world as she sees it. Early in the novel she prepares the ground for deeper Christian allegory when she notices distant figures on the beach at Whitby, who are 'men like trees walking' (D 6:93) — the words of a blind man whose sight is restored by Jesus (Mark 8:22-5).

When she is first visited by Dracula she again refers to vision that is somehow impaired. The Count arrives disguised as mist, prompting her to recall the scriptural phrase 'a pillar of cloud by day and of fire by night' (D 19:309; cf. Exodus 40:34-8), with the assistance of which the Hebrews were guided across the desert. Mina, likewise, is unsure of the reality behind her vision. Her brain begins to whirl. Is the spectre beneficent or malevolent? Too late she realizes it is not God who materializes, but the devil.

It is the graphically described blood exchange between Dracula and Mina that climaxes her 'religious' experience. The forcing of her mouth upon his open breast is reminiscent of the medieval use of the pelican to symbolize Christ's passion; the pelican being fabled for its supposed habit of opening a vein in its chest in order to feed its young. By imbibing the blood of a man-god, Mina is performing the most ritualistic form of cannibalism.

This blood exchange is the second marriage 'ceremony' performed in the novel. First, it was Lucy who took four 'husbands' by receiving their blood; now it is Mina who 'marries' Dracula by receiving his. The Count, on this occasion, performs a demonic corruption of the Christian marriage service. Mina has become 'flesh of my flesh; blood of my blood; kin of my kin; my beautiful wine-press for a while; and shall be later on my companion and my helper' (*D* 21:343). He is paraphrasing the words of the Catholic marriage service, taken from Ephesians 5:28,31.

> So also ought men to love their wives as their own bodies . . . for we are members of His body, of His flesh, and of His bones . . . For this cause shall a man leave his father and mother, and shall cleave to his wife; and they shall be two in one flesh.

Dracula's words also hint at a re-enactment of the Adam and Eve story. God, deciding that Adam should not live alone, created a 'helper'; similarly Dracula wants Mina as his 'helper'. When Eve is created out of Adam's ribs it is he himself who says: 'This at last is bone of my bones and flesh of my flesh'. Mina, like Eve before her, has become, literally, a 'biological' wife. Furthermore, just as Christ's blood was shed to save humanity, so here Dracula feeds Mina with his own blood to grant her immortality. In effect, he is performing communion with the solitary member of his congregation, reversing the process of transubstantiation. Instead of wine being converted into blood, blood is transubstantiated into wine (Mina being his wine-press). By fusing the profane marriage service with the simultaneous enactment of Mina's 'baptism of blood', Stoker emphasizes the Count as an agent of the devil out to pervert all the Christian sacraments.[12]

Mina's torment has an even more terrible sequel. Her spiritual anguish is caused less by the fact of her sin than by a visible reminder of it. Christian symbols in *Dracula* are not confined to the use of weapons against the Count, but extend to marks on the body. Not content with stealing Harker's wife, Dracula wishes to settle accounts with the solicitor who earlier had inflicted an unsightly scar on his forehead. That mark makes Dracula resemble an image of the 'beast' (Antichrist?) from the Book of Revelation, who is sent to earth by the devil and who can be recognized through a mortal head wound which has apparently healed (Revelation 13:3).

When Van Helsing applies the sacred wafer to Mina's forehead it brands her. From now on she is visibly identified with Dracula, and again Stoker seems to have borrowed from Revelation: 'If any one worships the beast and its image, and receives a mark on [her] forehead . . . [she] shall drink the wine of God's wrath . . . and shall be tormented with fire and brimstone in the presence of the holy angels' (Revelation 14:9-10). The Old Testament offers parallels of its own, for both Dracula and Mina now display the mark of Cain, one of the two sons of Adam and Eve. The other — Abel — was killed by his brother, the first act of murder by mankind. Because Cain refused to repent, God decreed that he should become a fugitive and wanderer of the earth (undead?), and to prevent anyone putting an end to his misery God placed a distinctive mark upon him (Genesis 4:1-15). That mark is traditionally thought to have been on the forehead.

Mina's desperate cry of 'Unclean, Unclean!' was, in a previous chapter, linked with menstruation. Now, upon having her flesh seared, she utters the words again, provoking reminders in her husband (D 22:353) of the biblical leper:

> The leper who has the disease shall wear torn clothes and let the hair of his head hang loose, and he shall cover his upper lip and cry 'Unclean, unclean'. He shall remain unclean as long as he has the disease; he is unclean; he shall dwell alone in a habitation outside the camp. (Leviticus 13:45-6).

This seems to reflect Mina's predicament precisely. She is an outcast from God, and will continue to be so for as long as the cause of her disease remains at large. She seems aware of the leper analogy herself: 'Even the Almighty shuns my polluted flesh.' Over the next weeks she comes to feel abandoned and shunned by God: 'As for me, I am not worthy in His sight. Alas! I am unclean to His eyes, and shall be until He may deign to let me stand forth in His sight as one of those who have not incurred His wrath' (D 27:430). The modern reader may be puzzled by this. Mina, the walking angel, would appear to have done nothing intentionally to incur God's wrath. She takes a very severe view of Christianity; perhaps she assumes that because she 'did not want to hinder' Dracula she is culpable of her adulterous union, even though it is manifestly beyond human capacity to resist the advances of the vampire. (Stoker's notes show that Dracula is able to induce evil thoughts in others.) As Lucy had discovered previously, in God's eyes innocence is no defence. In the tribunal of heaven there is apparently no such thing as a plea of honourable intent. The battle now turns to save Mina's soul, and one wonders whether Stoker was entirely oblivious of the fact that, spelled backwards, the name 'Mina' comes close to the Latin word for 'soul' — 'anima'. (Le Fanu had earlier employed anagrams for his vampire, Carmilla.)[13] Mina's soul will be saved and the mark will disappear only at the climax of the novel, when Quincey Morris takes on the Christ-like role of dying for her sin.[14]

The fight for Mina's soul is waged with Catholic implements. Stoker might take liberties with the uses to which they are put, but it is nevertheless the Catholic Church which, in the end, is vindicated. The 'open mind' which Van Helsing demands — something which can embrace superstition, science and faith — leads not only to a literal belief in vampires, but also to a demonstration of the *de facto* power of Catholic relics in overcoming them. The path to God is thereby shown to be not that of Luther, but that of Rome. The question is not asked, let alone answered, but what must this devout Protestant community have believed when all was over? Harker once held crucifixes to be 'idolatrous' (*D* 1:15), and Seward for much of the book refuses to believe anything that is unverifiable by the appliance of modern science. Yet Harker soon comes to appreciate the gift of a little cross (*D* 3:40), and when in possession of crucifix and holy wafer during a confrontation with the Count, Seward admits to experiencing 'a mighty power fly along my arm' (*D* 23:364). Are Harker and Seward converted to the Catholic faith once they discover its tangible power? Perhaps it is as well that Stoker, likewise a confirmed Protestant, chose not to confront the issue.

There is another aspect concerning the religious inferences of *Dracula* that deserves attention. Christianity is predicated on the fact of Evil. Dracula is the naked presence of that Evil. He is not like the other wicked characters of Victorian fiction: Fagin is a saint by comparison. Dracula *is* Evil, and the perceived need to combat his threat permits, indeed commands, no half-measures. The 'mercy-bearing' staking of Lucy to free her soul has nothing to do with caring, but everything to do with expediency: unless Lucy is staked she will continue to snare wandering children before maturing as a vampire to stalk her loved-one, Arthur. Moreover, Christianity is not evoked merely to exorcise the threat of the undead; Christian justification is also provided to rationalize the 'murder' of the vampires. Van Helsing is the Witch-Finder General returned. The self-assurance is overpowering: Christ *must* be on the side of Dracula's hunters. Therefore they *must* be right, and have been granted divine licence to perform whatever atrocities they please. A diabolical foe demands diabolical counter-measures. Van Helsing sets out on his quest with the zeal of a nineteenth-century Inquisitor — as he admits (*D* 17:262).

At this point let us take a closer look at what Van Helsing takes to be the malevolence that Dracula performs. Stoker's skill lies in creating an aura of absolute evil around his master demon, which it is useful to put into clearer focus. It is what Dracula *is*, rather than what he *does*, that strikes terror into the hearts of these representatives of decent, civilized England. Stoker is playing to a public gallery culturally conditioned into accepting the sources of its fears. In the opening section of the novel Harker's alarm stems from the realization that he is confronted with an unnatural (he is not yet sure it is 'supernatural') presence. No ordinary man can command wolves, or is eccentric enough to climb face down the castle wall rather than use the stairs. Dracula's appearance is of course unusual, but the solicitor's steadily mounting unease is occasioned by very 'human' observations in his host, such as a volatile, capricious personality. Dracula is all charm and grace interspersed with spontaneous outbursts of hatred and anger. As proposed in the previous chapter, Harker's real anxiety is aroused by the vampire women: Dracula has no premeditated malice in mind where his guest is concerned.

Paradoxically, Dracula actually *does* very little to merit the vendetta against him. Instances of his physical cruelty mostly take place in or around his castle, where he is not answerable to the law: he *is* the law. Like Vlad Tepes in life, the fictional vampire-king is lord and master of his native environment, and rules with an iron hand. Once in England, however, Dracula is the perfect law-abiding citizen, because to be otherwise would make him conspicuous and threaten his purpose. He has laboured to learn British values and customs. His house purchases are meticulously above board. It could almost be said he performs no violence (except in self defence when under direct personal attack)[15] or indeed any other offence. His only crime is to 'seduce' women who are not at all determined to resist him.

Furthermore, once they have become vampires the women he recruits do not seem remotely displeased with their new existence, so why the obsessional crusade to 'release' them? On the face of it, the prospect of immortality and perpetually aroused libido do not warrant feverish dread: quite the contrary. Van Helsing, however, insists that he alone knows what is right and proper: Lucy cannot really want to be a vampire, though a closer reading suggests she might. Although the reader is conditioned to sympathize with a distressed God-fearing community, from another perspective Dracula is being hunted for no other reason than for doing what comes naturally to him — as foxes are hunted because their natural activities are inimical to the interests of the farmer. Over the years foxes have come to be associated with unflattering human qualities — slyness, cunning — simply because they are in competition for the farmers' livestock and because they sensibly keep out of the way of his guns and undertake their marauding at night. There is something comparable in the circumstances of the 'cunning' Dracula.

In Van Helsing's world view there is no room for 'foxes', or for radical, heretical minority groups as epitomized by Dracula and his acolytes. Would they not expand their numbers by vampire proselytization — just as the Church once feared heretical sects might do — unless they are rigorously persecuted? *Dracula* derives its impact because Christian precepts of heaven and hell, good and evil, are to be found not only in the book: they are also to be found in its readers. The horror of the former depends for its effectiveness on the preconceptions of the latter. Another age or another culture less imbued with Christian dogma might well fail to appreciate the religious threat posed by Count Dracula. Indeed, his global appeal operates less from the Christian angle and more from the psychological: he epitomizes fear of darkness and of the unknown.

It is to the Christian context of Victorian Britain, and in particular of the 1890s, that we must now turn. When Stoker was still a child, Charles Darwin's *Origin of Species* was published. Darwin's theory of natural selection contributed to a widespread crisis of faith in late nineteenth-century Britain. The actual mechanics of Darwin's thesis were almost a side issue: what was at stake was the previously unquestioned belief in the Bible as the direct word of God. By the 1890s many educated Protestants had come to accept that a literal interpretation of the Bible was incompatible with the findings of science, although the Catholic Church remained more outwardly sceptical of evolutionist principles.

The influence of Darwinian thinking on *Dracula* can be observed at several levels. The Count is nature personified — red in tooth and claw. He does not 'love his neighbour' in the way that Christian *agape* is espoused by his pursuers. Later evolutionists, moreover, like T. H. Huxley came to believe that all living things were reducible to a basic chemistry. Man is not separate or unique. Trees, plants, insects, birds, animals, and humans all share a common protoplasm that is the physical basis of all earthly life. Any living entity, it was contended, can obtain nourishment from consuming any other living entity. Now, at last, Renfield's behaviour becomes more comprehensible. It can almost be said that Huxley prefigures

Renfield's insight: 'I used to fancy that life was a perpetual and positive entity, and that by consuming a multitude of living things, no matter how low in the scale of creation, one might indefinitely prolong life' (D 18:279-80). Renfield, like his patron, is embarked on an idiosyncratic quest for the survival of the fittest through the cannibalistic absorption of living tissue. The vampire women, sometimes described in this book as 'vampirellas', similarly devour living beings. As an aside, Victorian research into protoplasm tried to identify life forms within primordial ooze; one imaginary species of which happened to be termed 'vampurella'.[16]

Philosophically, Huxley and other evolutionists preached 'materialism'; the belief that everything is reducible to matter. There is no God, nor is there a soul. Mental activity is not separate from, but is equivalent to, brain activity. Materialism contradicted the very essence of Christianity, which depends on the notion of personal dualism: each individual is comprised of a physical component which perishes, together with a non-physical soul which does not. Dracula can be seen to invert Christian teaching, and particularly that of St Paul. The Count dares to offer, and to provide, immortality — not of the soul, but of the body. Even theologians and dualist philosophers experience difficulty with the concept of 'soul', so it is no wonder poor Renfield's mind cannot cope with its implications (D 20:320-2). He, imitating Dracula, is preoccupied only with immortality of the body, and it is towards that goal that his ingestion of protoplasm (flies and spiders) is directed, until the philosophical repercussions of his actions leave him bewildered and confused.

Dracula, of course, is an active materialist, for whom all phenomena are simply examples of matter in motion. Like all vampires Dracula is shorn of a soul, physical existence being all that concerns him. Stoker, in contrast, self-evidently does believe in souls, and his novel takes on the appearance of a protest — however veiled — against the blasphemies of Darwin and Huxley. Materialists denied the existence of free will and immortality, viewing brain activity as nothing more than chemical turbulence, with no detached soul or spirit to direct this activity. But while Stoker would have dismissed materialist notions, as they applied to humans, with contempt, he is bound to admit them for his vampires. Lacking a soul and operating entirely at the physical level, Dracula, in common with all lower forms of life, *is* deprived of free will. The sexual predilections of vampire courtship have even been likened to the amoeba, in which the victim 'sinks deeper and deeper into the soft yielding mass, and becomes dissolved, digested and assimilated in order that it may increase the size and restore the energy of its captor'.[17]

Even to a dualist, Dracula's active choice to become a vampire upon his natural death would have signalled his last act of conscious volition. As a vampire he is like a driven machine, with Satan behind the wheel. Van Helsing's crusade, however, is directed against someone he thinks is a deliberate perpetrator of evil, although according to Stoker's premise Dracula can possess no free will. In the courts of Britain Count Dracula would escape culpability (because he is 'child-like', and not accountable for his actions) on the grounds of diminished responsibility. Perhaps it is because Van Helsing knows the futility of legal redress that he feels compelled to take the law into his own hands.

One of the controversies arising from evolutionary debate was the focus on apes, from whom, it was maintained, man was descended. Apes thus became objects of ridicule. Civilized man was demeaned by the association, for apes were 'characterised primarily by hairiness and horniness'.[18] The myth of the virile male ape can be found in many cultures — King Kong being an example from our own. What was true of apes, it seemed, was also being levelled at humans: 'the male of the species is characterised by cupidity, pugnacity and a simian inclination for the other sex'.[19] For decent folk, it was not merely the claimed biological relationship to apes that appalled, it was disgust at being reminded of their rampant and undisciplined sexuality.

Not surprisingly, Christian opponents of evolutionism tried to impede the popularizing of science. Zoos were particularly suspect, offering an open window on monkeys perennially playing with themselves — or one another. Darwinism was seen as responsible for the encouragement of vice and licentiousness. Lust was held to stem directly from idleness. No wonder the devil found work for idle hands. Count Dracula, with his ape-like hairy palms and pointed ears, also shares with apes the lack of a soul and the possession of highly developed erotic instincts.

There is no reason to suppose Stoker was aware of it, but in 1889, the year before he commenced work on *Dracula*, a scientific work appeared which seemed to propose a further link between Darwin and the coming Count. The biological arguments can be omitted here, but they contributed to the contention that evolution is not necessarily progressive. Retrogressive metamorphosis can occur, leading to the creation of parasitic forms. As applied to higher animals:

Any new set of conditions occurring to an animal which render its food and safety very easily attained, seems to lead, as a rule, to Degeneration; just as an active, healthy man sometimes degenerates when he suddenly becomes possessed of a fortune; or as Rome degenerated when possessed of the riches of the ancient world . . . It is possible for us [humans] to reject the good gift of reason with which every child is born, and to degenerate into a contented life of material enjoyment accompanied by ignorance and superstition. [20]

Dracula is such a degenerate, 'offering to his followers the power of pleasure, eternal carnal fun, here and now — not as in Christian eschatology, spiritual integration later and somewhere unmapped. In the kingdom of heaven which the Count endeavors to establish there are no disembodied souls strumming on harps, but rather fleshy beings whose business is pleasure'. [21] To its critics, there was moral danger in materialist philosophy; Dracula's degeneracy seems to epitomize that danger.

Blinderman describes Count Dracula as being part Vlad Tepes, part Elizabeth Bathory, part lamia, part werewolf, part bat — and part 'Darwinian Superman'. [22] Carried to its ultimate degree, social Darwinism could pave the way for the emergence of a literal 'superman'. The survival of the fittest' could almost be Dracula's anthem: the strong and the brave survive, while the weak and the cowardly perish. This was, it should be noted, as true of Vlad Dracula as of Count Dracula.

The 'superman' concept is fundamental to the writings of Stoker's contemporary, the German philosopher Nietzsche. The key element of Nietzsche's superman is a celebration of the aristocrat, who is seen in Darwinian terms as biologically superior to the masses on account of bloodline, education, and environment. The common people are of no consequence, being like Dracula's 'sheep in a row', and have no purpose other than to assist in the excellence of the élite. Their suffering is of no importance if it contributes to the well-being of that élite. 'Trivial people suffer trivially: great men suffer greatly.' Nietzsche espoused the purifying virtues of war, ruthlessness, and aristocratic *noblesse oblige*, while abhorring wishy-washy British liberalism and the celebration of compassion as preached by that 'fatal and seductive lie', Christianity. Human progress was achieved solely by the singleminded 'will to power'. Dracula could almost have been Nietzsche's prototype 'superman'.

Professor Van Helsing, Stoker's prototype medico-scientist-philosopher, would obviously have read Nietzsche, and, more essentially, Darwin; in which case, part of his long-term fear in dealing with Dracula would have been prompted by the prospect of a biological catastrophe. The Count's intended 'family' ties in England, if successfully extended, would result in the propagation of an incestuous community genetically interrelated through his blood. His immortality and his evil would be disseminated far and wide through a genetically deformed sub-species. At the same time, Van Helsing also pays respect to the principle of 'species improvement': when he selects the blood donors for Lucy's transfusions all are intelligent, moneyed, and privileged. Never does he turn to the parlour-maids to help out by opening their veins. Stoker, too, acknowledges Darwinian sentiments. Charles Darwin had written: 'There is apparently much truth in the belief that the wonderful progress of the United States, as well as the character of the people, are the results of natural selection.' Stoker would have agreed emphatically, as Seward's evaluation of Quincey Morris confirms: 'If America can go on breeding men like that, she will be a power in the world indeed' (*D* 13:209).

Blinderman sums up the evolutionist angle on *Dracula*. The novel 'presents a contest between two evolutionary options: the ameliorative, progressive, Christian congregation, or the Social Darwinian superman in the form of the ultimate parasitic degenerate, Count Dracula'. No doubt Stoker viewed Dracula as morally offensive in the same way that many Victorian Christians felt about Darwin. The novel can thus be seen as a microcosm of decadent late nineteenth-century England faced with the threat of an evolutionary apocalypse.[23]

# 12.

# THE TAROT AND THE GRAIL

*Dracula* is, like most major Gothics, a book given to symbols and images archetypal in its design. Like the other big Gothics, it is a book of myth, a book which mirrors consistently and insistently in its use of metaphor and in its meaning certain truths of the human spirit . . . Most Gothics end happily, and *Dracula* is no exception . . . The happiness of [its] ending is that [it] ends in knowledge — thus the happy ending of *Dracula*, of the Fool's Quest in the Tarot, of any story in which the Quester comes home.

Thomas Ray Thornburg,
'The Quester and the Castle', pp. 167-8.

TO PRESENT the religious dimension of Dracula as simply a parody of biblical events is to over-simplify. There is another aspect to the religiosity of the novel which transcends any straightforward God-devil, good-evil dichotomy. Thornburg has suggested: 'As a compendium of ancient arcana, *Dracula* knows few rivals in fiction, and as a work of art which demonstrates the properties of world myth and archetype, and the diabolical reversal thereof, the book has no equal.'[1] Through *Dracula*, Bram Stoker delves into the world of the arcane and of myth, illustrating his deep familiarity with its occult and literary expression.

Where better to begin the search for some of Stoker's hidden meanings than in the mysteries of the Tarot cards?[2] No one can feel completely confident about the time and place of their origins, nor their visual representations, far less their meanings. It is probable that the modern packs evolved from various sources and traditions: Christian, gnostic, Islamic, Celtic and Norse, although one school of thought claims that the Tarot offers a compendium of arcane wisdom that stemmed from ancient Egypt. Bram Stoker's involvement with Egyptology was given full expression in *The Jewel of Seven Stars*, and his wider occult interests remove sensible doubts about his familiarity with the Tarot.

The cards themselves can be put to several uses. Most familiar is their occult reputation as guides for divination, for predicting the future. They can, however, also be used for games, being the precursors of the modern pack of playing cards. A Tarot deck is comprised of seventy-eight cards divided into two series. It is the larger, the Minor Arcana, which resembles the familiar modern pack, being arranged into four suits each numbered one to ten, plus Jack, Knight, Queen, and King.

For the purposes of relating the Tarot to *Dracula*, we must turn to the twenty-two cards which make up the Major Arcana — the Trumps. Many occultists are of the opinion that these cards taken as a whole embody a systematic key to the mysteries of mankind, God and the universe, and the path to be taken to acquire this knowledge. The Major Arcana lays down a system of initiation harbouring a secret language of symbolism, the unfathoming of which is the task that befalls the quester after self-knowledge. These cards are numbered 1-21, with an extra card — *The Fool* — unnumbered, but usually placed first. The negative side of *The Fool, The Joker*, survives, also as an 'outsider', in the modern pack of cards. The Major Arcana of the Tarot is as follows:

|      |                      |       |                          |
|------|----------------------|-------|--------------------------|
|      | *The Fool*           | XI    | *Fortitude*              |
| I    | *The Magician*       | XII   | *The Hanged Man*         |
| II   | *The Papess*         | XIII  | *Death*                  |
| III  | *The Empress*        | XIV   | *Temperance*             |
| IV   | *The Emperor*        | XV    | *The Devil*              |
| V    | *The Pope*           | XVI   | *The Tower (of*          |
| VI   | *The Lovers*         |       | *Destruction)*           |
| VII  | *The Chariot*        | XVII  | *The Star*               |
| VIII | *Justice*            | XVIII | *The Moon*               |
| IX   | *The Hermit*         | XIX   | *The Sun*                |
| X    | *The Wheel of*       | XX    | *The Day of Judgement*   |
|      | *Fortune*            | XXI   | *The World*              |

These cards, if taken sequentially, are symbolic of the classical gnostic quest, of the kind featured in the myths and legends around the world and exemplified by the divinely assisted quest of Jason and the Argonauts for the Golden Fleece. The 'hero' journeys forth, encountering hazards and perils of every conceivable kind, progressing stage by stage on a voyage through life towards the goal of redemption. The cards are capable of multiple interpretation

— hence the enduring fascination with them — but it is possible nevertheless to extract some of the personalities and themes from *Dracula* and discuss them in the light of the symbolism of the Major Arcana. For one thing the cards feature the recurring image of a ruined castle, which dominates the novel's opening and concluding sections. The 'cross', too, is represented in the Tarot, as are cutting and thrusting images pertinent to the phenomenon of vampirism.

Let us start with *The Fool*. This card depicts a man standing on the edge of a precipice and surrounded by mountains. He is ready to step out into the supreme adventure, accompanied only by his 'Dick Whittington' bag on a stick and a small dog. *The Fool* is representative of Everyman, the ordinary person, faced with the trials and tribulations of encountering new worlds in his search for the meaning of life. Jonathan Harker is manifestly an archetypal example of the questing *Fool*. He is inexperienced, naïve, yet not without an inner sense of expectation that does not close his mind to unusual experiences — such as travelling alone to the primitive wastes of Transylvania. *The Fool* frequently embarks upon his quest for Wisdom through a blunder or by accident: the undertaking is rarely planned. Sure enough Harker has packed his bags only because gout prevented his employer making the trip himself (*D* 2:27). Likewise, *The Fool* is, at the outset, often given advice or warnings which he either fails to understand or prefers to ignore. Protective figures may appear, who provide gestures of godly assistance, such as the crucifix pressed upon the solicitor by a well-meaning old woman. In fact, his determination to keep his appointment with Dracula, when every instinct within him tells him to delay or flee, marks Harker down as a 'fool' in its everyday meaning, as well as that of the Tarot. Even when ensconced in the castle, he appears perversely oblivious to the peril he is in.

*The Fool* has a long path to tread in his spiritual journey. He may not yet even be aware that he is embarked on such a journey. To assist him, he encounters *The Magician* — card No. I of the Major Arcana. *The Magician* is something of an adept, a semi-wise man blessed with a degree of understanding, and therefore of benefit to *The Fool* in his quest. *The Magician* is confident, exceedingly so, believing that his wishes are those of God. He thinks he is the conscious link between the creative will of man and God, and he will appear at the appropriate hour, when *The Fool* has most need of him. *The Magician*, brandishing a wand (stake?), is Abraham Van Helsing, 'the scientist-turned-magician'[3] — armed with his faith in the practices of folklore and witchcraft. Only with

Van Helsing's intellectual support can Harker proceed with his quest.

Later, *The Fool* will encounter *The Empress*. This card is a blueprint for Mina. *The Empress* is the matronly mother goddess, descendant of other earth goddesses (such as Demeter). She presents a symbol of universal fertility, which can be construed as a further reminder of the multi-fatherhood of Mina's son. *The Empress* is suggestive of one about to become a mother, in the way that Mina restores 'life' in *Dracula*. The powers of the *The Empress* are passive, stereotypically feminine: she has not the active intellect of *The Magician*. She represents intuitive feeling and a highly developed sense of values. She is warm, helpful, and stable, gifted at handling people — as Mina is with Renfield.

Further along his questing path, *The Fool* must make the decision of *The Lovers*. In some versions this card depicts a young man alongside two women, one young and fair, the other older and dark. Possibly he must choose between the 'good' and the 'evil' woman. Possibly, too, he is making the decision between remaining at home with his mother or departing with his beloved — the classic Oedipal dilemma. It is the moment when the bird flees the nest, leaving comfort and security behind for the excitement of the unknown. His female companion (Mina) will provide dedication and support for *The Fool* (Harker). In fact, there are many 'lovers' in *Dracula*, and the card is able to refer to both the earthly love (*eros*), which centres around Lucy and Mina and their assorted menfolk, and also the more spiritual love (*agape*), which binds the whole group together by transcending sexuality. The card also posits a reversal of the pleasurable side of love, hinting at Adam and Eve and the evil which visited them in the Garden of Eden. This might be applied to the anguish of Lucy and Arthur, parted irrevocably from one another.

The next relevant card is No. IX. From Stoker's working notes it is known that Van Helsing was created as a composite figure, combining the qualities of scientist, philosopher, and detective. Appropriately, a further card from the Tarot can be applied to the Dutch professor, alongside *The Magician*. *The Hermit* is as solitary and austere as Van Helsing. He is the ancient looking down from on high, following the flame that burns within him, along the road that leads he knows not where. He seeks answers to the questions that plague him and, like the professor, feels driven by a high duty. Even more reminiscent of Van Helsing, *The Hermit*'s negative side is reflected in stubborn dogmatism. Neither of them is able to conceive of answers outside the existing framework of their thoughts. This sums up Van Helsing: magician, hermit, and bigot.

Thornburg has this to say about the card that follows: 'The Wheel of Fortune is significant for Dracula, and for the Gothic generally, in that this card shows the universal balance of things demonic and apocalyptic, diabolical and divine.'[4] The card depicts conflicting images, including the beast from Revelation, highlighting the cycles and rhythms of life and death, growth and decay. The Wheel of Fortune constitutes a major turning point in the ritual of the Tarot. Ahead of The Fool/Harker lie paths of darkness, the complete unknown, yet he must follow these if he wishes to unearth the truth. The card corresponds with a signal turning point in Dracula, when Van Helsing assures Harker he was not the victim of a nightmare or insanity. His mind is sound — and strong. Harker now joins the forces hunting for Dracula.

The Hanged Man is one of the most mysterious of the Major Arcana cards, for the 'victim' — hanging by one foot, not the neck — wears an expression of detachment rather than suffering, as if indicative of spiritual contemplation. Thornburg identifies this with the mental torpor that descends upon Harker after his Transylvanian escape.[5] On another reading, The Hanged Man can be taken as symbolic of bodily death as a prelude to the birth of the true self, the essential prerequisite of the gnostic quest. The Hanged Man might also be engaged in an act of personal sacrifice, thereby paving the way to rebirth and the immortality of the spirit. This is the function performed by Quincey Morris.

Faced with the card of Death the Count's pursuers each come to a new understanding of its force and meaning. The Tarot interpretation of Death, moreover, is sometimes seen not as a pronoucement of termination, but of transformation; the passage from one level of existence to another, which lifts the dead into new life. Death, in other words, is at one and the same time a process of destruction and creation — which is exactly how Dracula sees it. Some versions of the card, furthermore, reveal a skeleton behind which is a setting sun — the exact moment of Dracula's expiry.

The previous chapter speculated upon the relationship between Dracula and the devil. According to the Tarot, The Devil is portrayed as the purveyor of lust, pride, and ambition; the possessor of unbridled passions and seeker of mastery over earthly things. He is a symbol of misused power, as savage as nature, a fountain of temptation and the personification of evil. Visually, aside from having bat-wings, some versions include hairs on the palms of his hands and he bears marks upon his flesh, including an inverted pentagram on his forehead. The similarity to Stoker's scarred Count is striking. Further, *The Devil* depicts a man and a woman, apparently chained one on each side of him. In *Dracula* they are represented by Renfield and Lucy Westenra — Satan's assistants until such time as their release. It is the function of the card to remind *The Fool*/Harker that he must ultimately do battle with *The Devil*. If he wins he will enjoy a special relationship with God.

The concluding five cards of the Major Arcana all deserve brief comment. *The Star* is illustrative of all that is potentially good; the expectancy of a happy future after the encounter with *The Devil*. A young girl is shown on her knees, pouring water from urns held in each hand. She is Mother Nature, refurnishing the fountain of life. This situation is totally reversed in *Dracula*, for Harker has not brought 'life' to the barren land of Transylvania. Instead he has set free the powers of darkness that seek to despoil his native England.

*The Moon* has obvious inferences for Renfield's 'lunacy', for his moods come and go with the change from moonrise to sunrise, so that Seward comes to suspect their influence on him (*D* 9:143). Dracula, too, reverses the mythical solar god: it is darkness which lends him strength, and it is the moon which symbolizes his evil. One version of the card has what looks like a werewolf howling up at the moon, a graphic reminder of the primitive, unconscious fears associated with moonlight.

Next comes *The Sun*, characterized according to some traditions by a naked child riding a white horse bareback under a warm sun. This is the child of Enlightenment. He is rid of the trappings of conventional thought and identifies with the single Life process of the universe. The child is man: the man is a child, innocent and reaching out, confident and joyous. He is the reward for earthly love and the symbol of life's renewal. The child is the infant Harker. (Other versions of the card show two people in an enclosing ring, like the magic circle within which Van Helsing and Mina shelter as they approach Castle Dracula.)

One version of *The Day of Judgement* shows several coffins floating on water, from which a man, a woman, and a divine child are shown rising up with their arms outstretched. Above them is an image of an archangel and his summoning trumpet. This card is associated with renewal; death followed by resurrection. Thornburg takes this to reflect the destruction of the undead and the expression of peace which comes over them at that moment.[6]

The final card of the Major Arcana is that of *The World*, which symbolizes the culmination of *The Fool's* quest. It denotes release and fulfilment, the ultimate attainment of Knowledge and Understanding. The Harker who strides the land following his destruction of Dracula is a very different Harker to the one who began his travel journal on his fateful expedition six months previously. The card portrays a youthful figure within a circular wreath, the symbol of ultimate victory. The figure is androgynous, a veil draped across his/her groin. Its sex is immaterial, its self is unity, a symbol of psychic wholeness. In this respect many exponents of the Tarot prefer to interpret the Major Arcana not as a sequence, but as a circle. *The Fool* appears not only at the start, but also at the end, which is another beginning. This time it is young Harker junior who will one day embark upon the quest for Truth.

This has necessarily been a cursory excursion through the symbolism of the Tarot, yet what is apparent even from this brief reading is that in *Dracula* the ritualistic quest is reversed: it is diabolical rather than divine. The summons which sends Harker off on the journey to open Pandora's Box is issued by the devil, not by God. But as Thornburg notes: 'Although Harker seeks to refuse the diabolical call, the effect upon his psyche is virtually that which is visited upon those who refuse the divine call.'[7] Harker's mind begins to disintegrate once he has released evil on to the world, and the novel follows the gradual stages of its reintegration.

From the perspective of the Tarot, in other words, the focus of *Dracula* lies less with the malevolent Count than with a Fool's Quest, that of a young solicitor unknowingly sent out on an archetypal spiritual journey. A second, and even more evident, source for the quest motif in *Dracula* derives from quintessentially British origins. Victorian literature was intoxicated by the great Romantic myths, none more so than the quest of the Arthurian knights for the Holy Grail. What started out as simply a legend of military gallantry at a time when post-Roman Britain found a mythical warrior-saviour to fend off the Saxon hordes, became endowed over the centuries with ever more complex embellishments, as writers and poets contributed to the skeletal story: jousting, chivalrous knights; the Round Table; courtly romance; and the search for the Holy Grail. No longer did the knights do battle for earthly reward, but for the goal of spiritual truth.

The Holy Grail is identified with the chalice drunk from by Christ at the Last Supper, which was then used to collect some of his blood at the Crucifixion. Afterwards the chalice disappeared. In romantic fiction it became an object of intense desire for those who are prepared to search for it. Some versions declare that it gives off light and perfume, that it can heal the wounded, and, among its more spiritual benefits, that it can produce a sense of well-being similar to that induced by Holy Communion. Sinners can never set eyes upon the Grail; only Arthur's gallant knights can approach it, and they are bound by absolute secrecy. The Grail's mysteries are held to transcend life and death, and its awesome power brings dire misfortune upon anyone who betrays its secret. The tradition of the Grail presents a vivid expression of blood worship, and at some stage it evidently came into contact with that of the Tarot. Not only do they both represent archetypal quests for the seeker after hidden knowledge: the four fundamental symbols of Grail legend almost coincide with the four suits of the Minor Arcana. These are cups, batons, swords, and coins in the case of the Tarot; chalice, lance, sword, and platter according to the Grail quest.

The Grail legend evolved from pagan conceptions of the miraculous cauldron of fertility, and the entire theme is enmeshed with primitive preoccupations with life and death, as revealed by the cyclical effects of the seasons. It is nature itself which provides the inspiration behind the idea of resurrection following upon death. Every year vegetation sprouts, withers, dies, and then grows again as spring moves through autumn and back to spring. Man is utterly dependent on this cycle for his survival, and fertility rites came to be performed with crop-spirits revered and appeased as necessary. As corn was the staple diet of settled peoples, so corn-gods came to dominate communal religious practice.

Arthurian romance similarly wove itself into the cycle of nature. The Round Table, for example, is emblematic of cyclical death and rebirth. Central to this feature of the legend is the introduction of the 'Fisher King'. In some versions, the Grail is held in custody in a mysterious castle. The guardian monarch suffers a wound — a spear-thrust through the thigh, which is a polite description for castration. The king is unable to govern and his constituency is laid barren and waste (the 'wasteland'). The cycle of rebirth is broken: there is no more regeneration. His kingdom dies, so the king turns for solace to fishing — the Fisher King. His health and the fertility of his kingdom, which lies about his castle, can only be restored once his wound has been healed through the sinless touch of a quester after the Grail. Until the king is healed, the Grail's powers are held in suspension. In more recent accounts the title 'Fisher King' can loosely be applied to any ruler whose virility is somehow linked to the fertility of the land. Any misfortune befalling him — illness, injury, impotence — reflects his own sterility on to his kingdom. Only his restoration will bring verdure back to the 'wasteland'.

Many of these ideas can be discerned in *Dracula*. To begin with, Stoker makes use of the agricultural calendar, reversing the traditional death and rebirth cycle, so that the novel opens in the spring and concludes in the autumn. The Count, like some malign vegetation, begins to flourish in May and, like the leaves on the trees, returns to dust and is blown away in November. The novel's cyclical structure even extends to its geography; opening in Transylvania, blooming in London, and returning to its sources for the conclusion. So conscious is Stoker that the book's beginning and end should exactly coincide that, at the climax, he makes Van Helsing and Mina retrace the precise route traversed by Jonathan Harker six months previously.

Further indication of Stoker's thinking is gleaned from the name of the ship which carries Dracula to England: the *Demeter*. This is what Walsh infers from Stoker's choice of vessel:

> Demeter was an earth goddess [to be precise, a corn goddess] and the mother of Persephone; when Persephone was stolen by Hades, Demeter wandered over the earth in search of her, but when Persephone was found Demeter had to strike a bargain with Hades that Persephone stay with him for six months of the year. Thus one has a mythological rendering in the story of Demeter of the origins of the seasons, connected with the king of the underworld, Hades . . . Demeter and Persephone, before the Hades incident, lived in a pastoral garden, unspoiled by winter and want. Hades' interference changed the world from a pastoral summer paradise to its present seasonal alternation . . . The meaning of Dracula's passage by the *Demeter* underscores the dire threat of Dracula's intention to destroy the pastoral vitality, fertility, and beauty of the West. [8]

Dracula flouts nature through his every essence: 'as an undead he both transcends and subverts the order of natural law, the returning to dust of all mankind according to God's plan. Dracula exists apart from the chain of being: his is a kind of anti-creation opposing the natural life-to-death cycle of human existence'. [9]

These 'cyclical' dimensions to *Dracula* can be explored more deeply by returning to the imagery of Arthurian grail romance, and consideration of what Hennelly terms 'the gnostic quest and the Victorian wasteland'. [10] Gnosticism is a generic term for a variety of spiritual beliefs and practices having as their common focus a mystical quest for hidden knowledge of God and the universe; knowledge which cannot be realized through the confines of dogmatic thought. The grail legends are similarly about the search for psychic growth and spiritual emancipation, and, as shown with the Tarot, *Dracula* takes the form of a mighty 'quest'.

To illustrate this interpretation it will be helpful to reflect upon the moral decay of late nineteenth-century England, as portrayed in *Dracula*, and Stoker's apparent desire to rehabilitate this Victorian 'wasteland'. Although Transylvania is anaemic in one sense — a 'barren land' (*D* 24:380) drained by the blood-sucking of Dracula — London in the 1890s is anaemic in another. It presents a *fin de siècle*, smog-bound, decadent culture threatened with moral collapse and desperately in need of redemption before the fresh new century can be born. To Stoker, the Britain of his day was undergoing a profound philosophical and moral crisis. Van Helsing acts as Stoker's mouthpiece on this question, yearning for a return to pre-sceptical, pre-rationalist times. The traditional values of 'faith' have been eroded, and the novel unearths no less than six alternative ethical frames of reference, each competing for supremacy: scepticism, transcendentalism, empiricism, criminality, the value of superstitions, and scientific rationalism. As Hennelly says: 'the small central group of splintered selves is also searching for a new stockpile of communal and personal values'.[11]

Stoker suggests that Transylvania and Victorian London are both 'wastelands',[12] each desperately needing the vitality of the other to heal its own sterility. Irony of ironies, a sceptical community must come to belief in vampires, with their primitive energies and passions, if the tired, decrepit nineties are to be redeemed. To this end the novel concludes with a postscript, written seven years after the Count's demise (that is, in the turning year 1900), in which Stoker's heroes and heroine survey the carnage of the past and look forward with confidence to the hopes of the morrow. These hopes are built around the rediscovery of personal faith — not only in vampires, but in the God who provided the means to destroy them. 'Evidence', that accursed accompaniment of modern science, is of no account: 'We want no proofs, we ask none to believe us' (*D* 27:449).

To assist in the unfolding of this spiritual emancipation, Stoker cultivates an intimate identity between Transylvania and London, between vampirism and Christianity, which cannot be expressed better than in Hennelly's own words:

Dracula's castle is a schizoid dwelling with upper, fashionable apartments and even a Victorian library but also with lower crypts and vaults; while, analogously, Dr Seward's Victorian mansion conceals a lunatic asylum, complete with fledgling vampire, beneath it. Dracula has three lovers; Lucy has three suitors. Dracula hypnotises; Van Helsing hypnotises. Dracula sucks blood; Van Helsing transfuses blood; and once, in fact, Seward sucked blood from a gangrenous wound of Van Helsing. Dracula wears Harker's British clothes to steal babies and later in London even wears a 'hat of straw'. Additionally, there is a consistently stressed analogy between vampirism and christianity; and both, given the insights of Frazer . . . and Freud's *Totem and Taboo*, seem related to the Oedipal Fisher-King and the wasteland. Thus vampirism deals with 'zoophagy'; christianity with eating the body and drinking of the blood of Christ — the scriptural phrase 'For the blood is the life'. Both employ numerous rituals and complicated liturgy, for example 'the Vampire's baptism of blood'. And lastly, both are locked in a theomachy for control of the world (Crucifix and Host against Demiurge). [13]

Both this Demiurge (Dracula) and his antagonists engage in a climactic quest, journeying to strange lands with strange customs. First to do so is Dracula. In coming to Britain he is engaged upon a quest of his own for a personal gnosis. The wasteland of Transylvania can offer him no prospects, no battles, no blood. Dracula needs to move with the times. He therefore comes in search of exchanging his 'child-brain' for the 'man-brain' of modern self-awareness.

But his unsavoury activities unleash a counter-quest: the Dracula-hunters embark upon their own journey into the unknown with almost ritualistic secrecy and discipline. On no fewer than three separate occasions do Van Helsing and his disciples solemnly vow their determination to pursue the Count. Their quest formally commences once Lucy has finally been restored to peace. An oath is taken, with everybody in turn taking hold of the professor's hand, whereupon he pronounces: 'And then begins our great quest . . . there is a terrible task before us, and once our feet are on the ploughshare, we must not draw back' (*D* 16:261). On a later occasion the inquisitors all stand around a table and link hands in a circle. They then individually swear allegiance in a 'solemn compact' (*D* 18:284-5), suggestive of an initiation ceremony within an occult lodge.

By the time of the third oath, Mina has been 'compromised' by the Count. In this instance they all kneel on the floor, take hands, and swear to be true to one another — all except Mina then making a supplementary pledge ultimately to raise her veil of sorrow (*D* 22:354). The three oaths, in other words, are made first to Van Helsing, second to the group as a whole, and third by kneeling to God; at the conclusion of which the Arthurian connections are truly forged. Van Helsing speaks for all: 'We go out as the old knights of the Cross to redeem [Mina's soul] . . . we are pledged to set the world free' (*D* 24:381-2). They are not embarked on a quest for a literal Grail, but for a spiritual destiny that will grant them redemptive understanding: 'We shall go to make our search — if I can call it so, for it is not search but knowing [*sic*]' (*D* 24:374).

Indeed, the whole novel can be interpreted not so much as Gothic or Victorian, but as distinctly Arthurian and medieval. In *Dracula*, Arthurian chivalry is displayed through the antiquated notion of 'comitatus', whereby the retinue of a chieftain or prince would band together for a common purpose and set forth as warriors to fulfil their master's (Van Helsing's) quest.[14] The professor provides a Merlin-like presence. He is alone, without the love and comfort of a family, and has absorbed himself in his world of magic and medicine to offset a life 'barren' of human warmth. King Arthur surfaces as Arthur Holmwood, lending the young aristocrat not only his Christian name but also his wife: both Guinevere and Lucy are expropriated by rivals. The functions of the two Arthurs are also comparable. In earlier days they enjoyed adventures a-plenty; but now the centre of attention has switched to others, of lower social standing — respectively, King Arthur's knights and Holmwood's commoner acquaintances. Turning to the simple, good-natured Jonathan Harker, he is almost a reincarnation of Sir Galahad, the purest of the knights who discovered the Grail.

As for Count Dracula, he is both a corn-god and the Fisher King. Stoker refers to the Count, who can direct the elements just as the ancients supposed their gods able to do, as forsaking his own barren land to walk among the teeming millions of London, who are 'like the multitude of standing corn' (*D* 24:380). Dracula is, moreover, a manifestation of the Fisher King; a being who has anachronistically outlived himself. Yet he still exudes a primitive life force, something of which decadent, contemporary England, hidebound by its scientific rationalism, is bereft. He must therefore be slain and his energies and vitality re-absorbed if the London wasteland with its swarming population is to be rejuvenated. There is nothing novel in this concept. Since time immemorial man has slain his gods in order to 'absorb' their powers. And how does Stoker describe the Count's native land after his spectacular downfall? 'The castle stood as before, reared high above a waste of desolation' (D 27:449).[15] With the withering of Dracula comes the withering of his domain.

Van Helsing fully appreciates that Dracula's energies are in themselves neutral. They can be used for good or ill: 'For it is not the least of [Dracula's] terrors that this evil thing is rooted deep in all good' (D 18:288). It is hoped that the Count's powers can be absorbed and utilized to assist in the creation of a fresh, new twentieth-century totem, and one is reminded again that 'there have been from the loins of this very [Dracula] great men' (D 18:288). Once more this focuses attention on Jonathan's and Mina's son. Symbolically, the infant will grow to represent twentieth-century manhood, eventually inheriting the renewed wasteland: in Arthurian language he will inherit the mantle of a modern Fisher King.

What should be elaborated is the extent of this child's relationship to Dracula. Out of the ashes of one totemic being emerges the conception of another. Young Quincey Harker will certainly be unique, but not solely by virtue of his parents' extraordinary psychological experiences. Genetically, he is an alarmingly complex being. He is linked to the band of Dracula's adversaries in more than just their names: he also has their blood. Worse, he has that of Dracula flowing through his veins. His mother has sucked the blood of Dracula, who had previously sucked that of Lucy, who had already received transfusions from Seward, Van Helsing, and Holmwood. The only blood *not* in the boy is that of Quincey Morris, his nominal 'father', for Lucy died before she could transmit his blood to Dracula. Nevertheless, in his matrix of blood-ties, this is no ordinary child, and he will grow into no ordinary man for far more profound reasons than Van Helsing can suspect. This child of the future offers the hint of a demonic parousia.

It would appear, then, that the diabolical reversal of myth in *Dracula* suggested by the Tarot is reinforced through consideration of the Grail. Fundamental to the Grail myth is the interrelationship between the vitality of the ailing king and that of his kingdom. The purpose of the hero is to restore the former, and with it the latter. The point of Harker's journey to Transylvania, however, is not to heal the Fisher King/Dracula with the aid of the Grail. It is to release the vampire for the purpose of regaining his youth by draining the living of *their* blood. Throughout the rest of the novel Harker's fate hinges on that of Dracula: the destruction and dissolution of the one is the ecstasy and salvation of the other. In the postscript the reader is introduced to a child: not the heir of Jonathan Harker, but a representative of all the dark powers at Dracula's command. Here, as elsewhere, Stoker either reverses the classical myth or manipulates it to his own purpose; either way he acknowledges his debt to the profound mysteries of the Tarot and the Grail.

# 13.

# *DRACULA* AS SOCIAL AND POLITICAL COMMENTARY

From the bourgeois point of view, Dracula is . . . a manic individualist; from his own point of view . . . he is the bearer of the promise of true union, union which transcends death. From the bourgeois point of view, Dracula stands for sexual perversion and sadism; but we also know that what his victims experience at the moment of consummation is joy, unhealthy perhaps but of a power unknown in conventional relationships. Dracula exists and exerts power through right immemorial; Van Helsing and his associates defeat him in the appropriate fashion, through hard work and diligent application, the weapons of a class which derives its existence from labour.

David Punter, *The Literature of Terror*, p. 260.

IN THIS, a fifth and final perspective on *Dracula*, attention comes back 'down to earth'. The concerns of this chapter are not biblical or occult, but social and political. *Dracula* is a valuable period piece, mirroring the ideological strains and tensions that afflicted the Britain of Stoker's middle years. His attitudes towards the place of women in society have already been considered. In the following pages issues relating to, among others, social class, race, crime, Nazism, Marxism, and the Cold War will be explored, where they can usefully shed light on *Dracula*. In the process some understanding will be reached on how the *Dracula* myth has been manipulated for the purposes of twentieth-century propaganda.

Bram Stoker, as befits the age in which he lived and his own perceived place in the social hierarchy, was notably class conscious and socially prejudiced. The *dramatis personae* of *Dracula* are, with the exception of Renfield, all drawn from the well-to-do, the guardians of the Empire, and the book is shot through with social, class, racial, and sexual prejudices. The novel is unabashedly 'conservative', firstly, in that all those who die show qualities of rebelliousness or independence; secondly, in having the bourgeois characters at the conclusion revert back to the bliss of the opening without benefiting from any social, as opposed to spiritual, advancement in any form; and thirdly, in a more ideological sense. Stoker was writing an ostensibly non-political novel, yet he still manages to create a work which reinforces the prevailing establishment beliefs of the ruling classes. Jackson has remarked, with reference to Stoker's final fantasy novel *The Lair of the White Worm*: 'the shadow on the edges of bourgeois culture is variously identified as black, mad, primitive, criminal, socially deprived, deviant, crippled, or (when sexually assertive) female'.[1] Likewise in *Dracula*, Stoker's conscious world is rigidly middle class, monogamous, and male dominated — under an all-seeing God. When Renfield is introduced to Morris, Godalming, and Van Helsing he at once recognizes their prized virtues as stemming from, respectively, 'nationality, heredity, and the possession of natural gifts' (*D* 18:292): in other words it helps to be of Anglo-Saxon stock, to possess unearned riches, and to have taken advantage of an élitist (British) education.

Let us glance at some of the peripheral characters in *Dracula*. The existence of maids and servants is of course axiomatic, although the novel is concerned with the adventures 'above stairs', not 'below'. Stoker has little patience with those employed in domestic service: he denigrates the elaborate ritual of mourning rigidly observed by the 'lower classes' (*D* 12:179); he describes them as untrustworthy and lacking courage when it comes to finding suitable blood-donors (*D* 12:180); and includes among their number the obligatory thief — someone who could even stoop to stealing a crucifix from a corpse (*D* 13:200).

Stoker's real scorn, or rather contempt, is reserved for the 'harijans', the untouchables. He seems to flinch every time his demure ladies and gallant gentlemen are forced into social contact with the manual working classes. Their one redeeming feature is their uniform deference to their betters, but everywhere they are encountered they are shown to exhibit the same unspeakable characteristics: uncouthness, illiteracy, peculiar dialects riddled with expletives, excessive drinking, and preparedness to offer favours only for monetary or, better, liquid reward. (In this, their demands are merely parodies of Dracula's: 'First, a little refreshment to reward my exertions' (*D* 21:342). His blood is their liquor.) Harker, Stoker's principal alter ego, is of lower social standing than his acquaintances, and he is predictably the most disdainful of those of lower class than himself. He has 'an interview with a surly gatekeeper and a surlier foreman, both of whom were appeased with coin of the realm' (*D* 20:314), and when Harker does encounter a 'good, reliable type of workman' (*D* 20:311) it is only to underline his rarity and obsequiousness.

For their part, the social superiors live according to a kind of cash nexus. 'Money talks' is the dominant unwritten philosophy. Harker is grateful that 'Judge Moneybags will settle this case, I think!' (*D* 25:397), referring to Godalming's generous funding of their Continental trek. Mina sighs at the thought of 'the wonderful power of money! What can it do when it is properly applied; and what might it do when basely used' (*D* 26:423). Actually, Mina is not too fussy how it is used. Bribery, for example, is frequently resorted to, and draws no admonition from Stoker. Returning to Transylvania Harker remarks: 'Thank God! this is the country where bribery can do anything, and we are well supplied with money' (*D* 25:397). Ethically, England and Transylvania are on a par: the mere mention of Lord Godalming's title wins him favours from cowering peasants/proletarians in the manner to which Count Dracula has long been accustomed. 'My title will make it all right', his Lordship announces whenever he wishes to break the law or breach confidences (*D* 26:412).

Paradoxically, what might be termed a 'business ethic' surfaces in several places in the novel. On his first arrival in Transylvania, Harker is not deterred by the premonitions of the locals: 'there was *business* to be done, and I could allow nothing to interfere with it' (*D* 1:13). Later, when Seward is acquainted with Harker for the first time, he comments upon his 'quiet, *business*-like' quality (*D* 17:269), which is obviously to be taken as complimentary. Again, when one of the solemn vows is taken to pursue the Count, come what may, Seward notes that the oath was made 'as gravely, and in as *business*-like a way as any other transaction of life' (*D* 18:285; author's italics). Bram Stoker the Lyceum businessman was evidently imbued with the business world's ethos, and he was equally favourably disposed to the propriety of inheritance. Harker inherits Mr Hawkins' legal practice, and Godalming, despite his existing wealth, comes to acquire the Westenra family estate. The unspoken lesson that Stoker teaches is that wealth, and its acquisition, are morally virtuous.

Clearly, too, the novel provides a social lesson. It is a celebration of the middle classes at the expense of the aristocracy. Count

Dracula, of course, is a fiend incarnate, while Lord Godalming is a fringe character achieving little of note. Indeed, what he does achieve is to propose marriage to a commoner, Lucy Westenra, as if to reduce his class-laden threat to his bourgeois companions. Godalming has been labelled a 'safe', 'tamed', 'bourgeois' aristocrat.[2]

These archetypal representatives of respectable England implicitly know their place in society. It would have been as unthinkable for upper-middle-class Lucy to contemplate wedlock with, say, lower-middle-class Harker, as it would have been for school-ma'am Mina to be courted by Holmwood. Dracula proscribes socially vertical liaisons — the bedrock of much literary romance. Indeed, a firm and tacitly acknowledged social hierarchy pervades the book. Long after the Harkers are first introduced to the socially elevated Lucy Admiration Society, they persist — even in the privacy of their journals — in their expressions of respect, usually referring to their 'betters' deferentially as Dr Seward, Mr Morris, and Lord Godalming. Even more noteworthy, all the questers speak respectfully of their aristocratic foe as 'the Count', notwithstanding the utter loathing with which they regard him. (In this instance Stoker may be alluding to the tradition among occultists of never speaking of malign forces by name for fear of summoning them.)

Yet the novel is not totally static in its hierarchical structure. There is one instance of upward social mobility — Jonathan Harker, and with him his wife. They are 'special' in many ways, not just in their shared capacity to survive the attentions of Dracula. Originally a provincial solicitor's clerk, Jonathan Harker graduates as a fully-fledged west-country solicitor at the commencement of the novel. In time he becomes a partner ('Hawkins & Harker') before inheriting his mentor's legal practice. He also sires the child supposed to represent the light of the twentieth century. Harker, in other words, comes to possess a fortune beyond his dreams, a wife who is his fairy princess, and a child of the future — pure fairy tale.

What is curious is that in the expression of his class prejudices Stoker is seen to have been unconsciously influenced by the pseudo-sciences of his time, which themselves contributed greatly to the reinforcement of social divisions. In particular, Dracula reveals an indebtedness to the 'science' of physiognomy, which blossomed in the late eighteenth and nineteenth centuries. Given its respectability by a Swiss clergyman, John Casper Lavater, and later modified by Charles Darwin and many others, physiognomics held that the true character of an individual could be deduced by the structure of the head and body, as well as from facial expressions and physical gestures. Regarded with disdain nowadays, its practitioners once insisted that the shape and angles of the forehead and the nose, together with the size and contours of the eyes and mouth, constituted reliable guides to the bearer's strength of character. Lavater had noted that a pale face was an indication of a natural inclination towards sexual pleasures, [3] and Dracula fully complies. As late as 1873 a Dr Joseph Simms, in a quack work entitled *Nature's Revelations of Character*, propagated a clear distinction between the 'straight' and the 'curly'. Those persons with curly hair, and preferably with rounded features to match, were dismissed as thoughtless and careless, and to be avoided at all costs; whereas those blessed with straight hair and straight features were naturally endowed with 'straight' minds.

In *Dracula*, Van Helsing obviously approves of physiognomy (as does Stoker), for the professor comments favourably on Harker's casual deduction of personality from physical features (*D* 14:226). Perhaps Stoker had read Simms, for Dracula has 'curly hair that seemed to curl in its own profusion', and virtually all that is said of the flaccid aristocrat Godalming's appearance is that he is 'curly-haired'. Similarly, the Count's forehead is 'domed' (i.e. rounded), while the professor's is 'almost straight, then sloping backwards'. Dracula's nose is hooked and curved, 'aquiline', whereas Van Helsing's is 'rather straight'. The Dutchman also has a 'square chin' to match, and his big, wide apart eyes are those, according to Simms, of the turtle dove: they signify the morally chaste.

Further instances of Victorian pseudo-science emerge when Van Helsing gives vent to his 'philosophy of crime' (*D* 25:405-6). Criminals, apparently, are all of a type. They are at one and the same time necessarily insane, childish, and incapable of breaking the habits of a lifetime: 'in all countries and at all times' criminals stick to the one form of crime with which they are most familiar. 'The Count is a criminal and of criminal type', pronounces Mina, and Stoker draws upon the theories of contemporary doctors and criminologists to develop his argument. Max Nordau's controversial book *Degeneration* (1893) had set out to demonstrate the close correlation between genius and moral degeneracy, [4] and Cesare Lombroso, often considered to be the father of modern criminology, was in no doubt about the relevance of physiognomy as regards criminal tendencies. According to Lombroso, those individuals best described as 'born criminals' are physiologically related to their primordial ancestors. Among the personality traits Lombroso attributes in his *Criminal Man* to those of a law-breaking predisposition are sensuality, laziness, impulsiveness, and vanity. Needless to say, these also refer to Dracula; but when it comes to the visible hallmarks of the criminal there can be no doubt about the association. If Stoker had read Simms, he had certainly assimilated Lombroso:

Harker:    '[The Count's] face was . . . aquiline, with high bridge of the thin nose and peculiarly arched nostrils.'

Lombroso: '[The criminal's] nose . . . is often aquiline like the beak of a bird of prey.'

Harker:    'His eyebrows were very massive, almost meeting over the nose.'

Lombroso: 'The eyebrows were bushy and tend to meet across the nose.'

Harker:    'his ears were pale and at the tops extremely pointed'.

Lombroso: 'with a protuberance on the upper part of the posterior margin . . . a relic of the pointed ear'. [5]

It was a popular Victorian view that each society is afflicted by the criminals it deserves. This would imply that as Dracula is the worst possible criminal, England in the 1890s was the worst possible society. This equation of vampirism with criminality serves to indicate where in Stoker's mind virtue and purity reside — in those whose lives have been sorely touched by Dracula. Leaving physiognomy aside, what Stoker seems not to appreciate is that the bulk of criminal activity is performed not by Dracula but by his opponents. Senf expresses this succinctly:

Even if Dracula is responsible for all the Evil of which he is accused, he is tried, convicted, and sentenced by men (including two lawyers) who give him no opportunity to explain his actions and who repeatedly violate the laws which they profess to be defending: they avoid an inquest into Lucy's death, break into her tomb and desecrate her body, break into Dracula's houses, frequently resort to bribery and coercion to avoid legal involvement, and openly admit that they are responsible for the deaths of five alleged vampires. [6]

Further, by happy coincidence, the disposing of Dracula and his three consorts will be accompanied by their rapid dissolution into dust. As Van Helsing cannily explains (*D* 25:398), there is no need to fear prosecution, for without a corpse there is no crime.

None of the foregoing invites a hint of moral questioning in the mind of Bram Stoker. His heroes have stooped to imitate Dracula, and have become primitive, violent, and irrational. They play the game he plays, never stopping to reflect upon the probity of their actions. In short, the ethical standards that Stoker assumes to be laudable are, upon closer examination, far from comforting.

Stoker's attitudes to race are similarly ambivalent, and there is more than a hint of racial prejudice in *Dracula*. Even the sweeter-than-sweet Lucy is not immune from it. When she relates to Mina the 'anguish' of having had three proposals of marriage she recalls *Othello* and sympathizes with Desdemona having been regaled by tales of adventure poured in her ear — 'even by a black man' (D 5:74). Gypsies are shown as despicable hirelings of the Count, taking Harker's gold and then betraying him (D 4:56); and the one Jewish figure encountered is pure stereotype, down to requisite 'sheep's' nose and a reluctance to impart information except through 'a little bargaining' (D 26:415). And of course, to Stoker, no country can be truly civilized if its trains fail to run on time, as Transylvania's notably fail to do.

More fundamental to the racial structure of the novel is the composition of its three major foreign imports, none of whom are allowed to speak standard English, which immediately makes them objects of suspicion. The Count, of course, is so malign as totally to deny him the honour of being British. (In fact, in none of Stoker's fiction is the villain a true Briton.) Furthermore, Dracula smells! — and racism over the centuries has frequently harped on the distinctive and offensive smells supposedly emitted by 'foreigners'.

The introduction of a Dutchman and an American seems on the face of it to possess less racial significance; yet Morris' inferiority is persistently demonstrated. Firstly, he is rejected by Lucy in favour of a true-blooded Englishman; secondly, although the provider of raw, frontier courage (which is itself slightly un-British), the American is dispensed with — cancelled out with the Count — at the climax. Perhaps, too, a trace of nationalism can be detected here: the evil Transylvanian and the vulgar Texan are expunged so that, having made full use of Morris, the superior English are no longer compromised by the presence of someone who typifies America's growing power and potential rivalry with Britain.

In the case of Van Helsing, Stoker may have felt uncomfortable about making an English hero a Catholic, in the same way that a native villain would reflect badly on Britain. The effect of this, by revolving the central conflict of the novel around a Continental vampire pitted against a Continental vampire-sleuth, is to emphasize the foreign, alien quality of this demonic invasion of Britain. Once Van Helsing's knowledge has been utilized and his enlightening functions exhausted, he is despatched to the margins of the action, allowing the Anglo-Saxon race the glory of the final scenes.

Throughout, the hard core of Englishness is represented as true grit. Even the insane Renfield is permitted to die a martyr's death in the cause of saving Mina. Returning for a moment to the Victorian 'wasteland' analogy, all the foreign imports in the novel serve collectively to provide that dynamic element of which insular England stands in need if domestic tranquillity is to be restored. [7] Once that objective has been attained, the foreign intruders can be struck out. Two of them meet their end, while the third is an old man whose time was the nineteenth century, not the twentieth.

The English axis around which the novel pivots is reinforced by the manner of its telling. None of the three foreigners is allowed to keep a diary or supply other written records, save for the odd memorandum of Van Helsing and brief inconsequential letters by Morris. The reader is never made privy to Dracula's thoughts, and is left with his tantalizing statement: 'There is reason that all things are as they are, and did you see with my eyes and know with my knowledge, you would perhaps better understand' (*D* 2:32). Without access to his point of view the Count is never described 'objectively', but always through the impressionable eyes of those he encounters. The same is true of Van Helsing and Morris. This gives rise to a peculiarity in the novel's structure. To give an example: what is told by someone to Harker may be passed on to his wife, who might take Van Helsing into her confidence, before he in turn entrusts Seward to summarize the information on his phonograph. The evidence by then is fifth-hand. It follows that the selective epistolary framework of the novel is bound to refract the testimony of those unable to present their case in their own words. As a result, there is a virtual exclusivity of the English point of view in the provision of primary documentation.

To be more precise, there is a virtual exclusivity of the middle-class English point of view, with which Stoker was most able to identify. The bulk of the testimony in *Dracula* is reserved for Harker, Mina, and Seward — solicitor, teacher, and doctor. Stoker can handle the unfamiliar lady of leisure, Lucy, because she is one-dimensional and killed off early. Lord Godalming is effectively neutered. He is allowed to say nothing of importance: as with the three aliens, the reader derives impressions of his Lordship only through the impressions of others. But the case of Renfield is especially curious, for Stoker allows his lunatic the luxury of keeping his own little notebook (*D* 6:88). (The Count, it seems, has the knack of making everyone with whom he has any dealings take up their pencils.) Stoker never allows Seward to divulge the contents of Renfield's scribblings. Irritatingly, Seward will tell only of masses of figures, added up in batches 'as if he were "focusing" some account, as the auditors put it'. What figures? What account? From that moment Renfield's 'diary' is forgotten and does not feature in the accumulating pile of written evidence that awaits posterity.

*Dracula* has also been described as reflecting a concern with 'alienation', a sociological term that refers to a pathological condition of man in modern industrial society. There is dispute as to what produces alienation, but in its Marxist version it is said to occur as a result of capitalist exploitation and the division of labour, leading to a loss of identity between the worker and what he produces. He feels dehumanized, becomes isolated, withdrawn, purposeless, and may end up 'alienated' not only from his work, but also from his fellow men. This can result in total estrangement from the society in which he lives, and detachment from its prevailing moral values.

This concept can be borrowed and applied in a more general sense to the Count, who is alienated from almost everything around him. As a vampire he casts no reflection: metaphysically he has no identity. He is a pure inversion of man, and as such constitutes the complete alienation of mankind. He is, furthermore, a source of epidemic alienation, reminiscent of the social effects of the early dehumanizing period of industrialization, despoiling the lives and identities of his victims. [8] Yet when Dracula confides to Harker that he longs to walk the streets of mighty London, to be in the midst of the whirl and rush of humanity, and to share its life, change and death, he seems to be alluding to more than just the urge to prey on new victims. In human terms, the Count is supremely lonely. He has no more armies to command, no children to rear; he can no longer 'love', and his castle is surrounded by a wasteland devoid of vitality. His loneliness is in vivid contrast to the excessive, almost cloying, friendship and family sentiment expressed by his pursuers, all of whom would willingly sacrifice themselves (Morris fulfilling his offer) for each other. More than one critic has speculated whether Dracula's quest to England might embrace a forlorn hope that he might be defeated and laid to rest in perpetuity. How else, it is asked, could such a formidable warrior and campaigner allow himself to be outmanoeuvred by such opponents?

Renfield, through his incarceration in his small cell and his occasional stints in a 'strait waistcoat', provides an echo of his patron's alienation.[9] But what would have induced Stoker to incorporate such themes into his novel? Very likely, as with other aspects previously noted, he made unconscious use of autobiography. Perhaps Stoker's development from bed-ridden child to athletics champion is reflected in the Count's progress from tomb to master vampire. Again, Stoker spent the first thirty years of his life in Dublin, remote from the hub of British artistic and cultural life. Along with having his early literary and cultural ambitions frustrated, Stoker also had to contend with the 'alienation' of being a minority Protestant in a Catholic land. Most important of all, Dracula was not alone in coming to teeming London to better himself: Bram Stoker had done exactly the same thing when uprooting from Dublin in 1878. The sense of alienation to be experienced in a vast impersonal city (and having to learn how to mix with Irving's elevated circle), was something which Stoker had lived through and understood intimately. And in organizing Irving's many tours with the Lyceum, and the endless crates of stage equipment involved, Stoker must have gained an insight into the problems involved in organizing the fifty boxes of earth which Dracula must transport by land and by sea.

Stoker, it should be remembered, was no political innocent. His inaugural address to the Trinity Historical Society had been a blueprint for a league of nations of the time. He was a committed supporter of Irish Home Rule and of Gladstonian Liberalism. His fiction, by and large, steers clear of overt political comment, but there is one notable exception. One of his later novels, *The Lady of the Shroud* (1909), opens as another, apparent, vampire yarn. By the climax, the supernatural element has been transformed into pure political allegory relating to the Balkan crisis. Even without any 'actual' vampires, *The Lady of the Shroud* still manages to resemble Dracula in its south-east European setting and in its evocation of Turkish menaces, past or present. In the sense that the Austro-Hungarian Empire (of which Transylvania was a part in the 1890s) was a likely British adversary in any future European war, the Anglo-Dutch-American alliance of Dracula hunters lined up against representatives of the Austro-Hungarian and Ottoman Empires comes close to providing a dress rehearsal for the First World War.[10]

The Dracula myth has been hailed over the years as providing justification for, or illumination of, all manner of political beliefs. In this, Count Dracula has merely emulated Vlad Dracula, who, within a century of his death, had his impaling exploits seized upon by Ivan the Terrible in Russia. Vlad had shown himself to be a 'hero' of the Orthodox faith and a model of the harsh, autocratic ruler. As such he was taken to justify Ivan's supposed divine right to tyranny and sadism. [11]

Recent Marxist critics have alighted on *Dracula* as illustrating what they see as the inherent contradictions in capitalism. Through Marxist spectacles the Count presents a distorted extension of feudal *droit de seigneur*, which, irrespective of his own peasant-like links with the soil, is founded on a life-style of constant exploitation: he starves the populace and feeds upon them. As long ago as 1741 the word 'vampire' was used in English, metaphorically, to refer to a tyrant who 'sucks' the life from the people. [12] Karl Marx himself was familiar with the vampire metaphor: 'Capital is dead labour that, vampire-like, only lives by sucking living labour, and lives the more, the more labour it sucks.' He went on to remark that 'the prolongation of the working day quenches only in a slight degree the vampire thirst for the living blood of labour'. [13]

Seen in this light, the 'vampire' presents a metaphor for capital. Dracula is the archetypal capitalist exploiter, for whom the objective, according to classical Marxist theory, is the total 'possession' of every aspect of his victims' lives. He is not interested in any arrangement by 'contract': he demands his slave labour for eternity. Like the vampire, in other words, the capitalist's driving force is seen to be insatiable and unlimited. Like the vampire, too, the capitalist is unable to break the cycle of exploitation followed by yet more exploitation. Neither is propelled so much by the *desire* for blood/wealth as by the *curse* of blood/wealth. The capitalist is enmeshed in the drive for 'accumulation', and is unable to withdraw from the stark choice confronting him — prosper or 'go to the wall'.

As noted previously, Dracula is not a destroyer. He is an accumulator. Moretti describes him as a saver, an ascetic, an upholder of the Protestant ethic. [14] The Count has hoarded his gold for such a plan as now festers in his brain. Armed with his capital he can embark upon his schemes for economic control of the City of London. In this he acts as a perfectly rational entrepreneur. It is noticeable that for several economic groups there is no conflict of interest with Dracula. The assorted solicitors, gypsies, seamen, porters, and estate agents with whom he conducts business do very nicely from their client. He pays well, and in cash. For both his menial requirements and his property deals he is the perfect employer-client. These accomplices have no need to fear his sucking their blood: he can buy it.

In fact, Dracula, the arch-capitalist, is no mere common entrepreneur. In his vampiric/financial dealings he acts as an ardent monopolist, someone who will brook no competition. 'Like monopoly capital, his ambition is to subjugate the last vestiges of the liberal era and destroy all forms of economic independence.'[15] No wonder he holds such terrors for his complacent, bourgeois competitors. In the name of destroying an agent of the devil, Stoker's heroes are, on a socio-economic reading, ridding themselves of a materializing threat to their bourgeois ideology and prosperity.[16] It is they, representatives of a petty free-trade ethos, whom he is out to subjugate. The vampire/monopolist concedes no possibility of independent survival, personal or economic. Unlike Godalming, the 'tamed' aristocrat who accepts the legitimacy of middle-class hegemony, Dracula is the embodiment of the anachronistic land-owning class, seeking to sequestrate the newly-earned privileges of the *nouveaux riches* and reopen the historic struggle between the aristocracy and the bourgeoisie. Feudal monopoly and the free-competition principles of nineteenth-century capitalism are shown as irreconcilable concepts, historically bound to precipitate an economic struggle to the death.

Actually, during the 1890s monopolistic concentration of capital was even more evident in the economies of some of Britain's advanced, industrial competitors than in her own. All the more reason, then, why 'monopoly' should appear as a foreign, alien threat and why Van Helsing is necessarily on the side of the British, for Holland was a neighbouring sanctuary of free-trade.[17] On the other hand, by the end of the Victorian era many economists saw free-trade as already moribund. The age of the giant, multi-national monopoly was about to be born. From this angle, the narrow-minded *laissez-faire* fanatics opposing Dracula who would seek to stifle this development are themselves no better than reactionary relics of a bygone age, attempting to arrest the course of history.[18]

If only for the sake of parity, as Marxism has been read into *Dracula* so has fascism. Elements of Bram Stoker's novel actually found their way into the philosophical underpinnings of Nazi Germany. The late and unexpected flowering of the Gothic genre at the turn of the century unearthed a receptive audience in the German-speaking world. What may have been no more than a harmless release in Britain appeared frighteningly profound elsewhere. In the depths of her disillusionment following the First World War, Germany was searching for her own Teutonic hero capable of restoring her past glory. Count Dracula offered the perfect model, being of a conquering race and descended from Attila the Hun. Many German authors, among them Hans-Heinz Ewers, were attracted by the potential of the vampire metaphor. The sexual element was frequently exaggerated, and a combination of Nordic myths, Teutonic blood rites, and Wagnerian imagery haunted and thrilled the reading public of defeated Germany, gradually acquiring a political significance of its own. In the same way that Dracula could be depicted as a Darwinian 'superman', vampires in German literature came to represent superhuman *Übermenschen*, whose function was to herald the establishment of a New Order based on blood. [19]

Racist elements of German nationalism were also accommodated by German vampire fiction. In the works of Ewers, [20] the undead were on occasions depicted not as supermen but as squalid, wandering Jewesses, symbolic of a race that was seen to be infecting the Continent, and leading to an upsurge of blood-mania in the common people. Prior to gaining power in 1933, Hitler and the ideologists of the National Socialist Party were happy to utilize any powerful myth for their own ends, and Ewers' depiction of sacrilegious blood-lust, gratuitous cruelty, and his exultation of pre-Christian, Germanic forms of worship made him a celebrated author, until he became too much of an embarrassment. [21] *Dracula* was also ripe for a new medium: the screen. The German director F. W. Mirnau adapted the novel for the silent cinema, and the classic *Nosferatu* (1922) was the result. Stoker's widow, however, successfully sued for breach of copyright, so that the only extant copies of the film are pirate versions. [22]

During the Second World War the equation of the Hun-like Dracula with the Hun-like Nazi produced a happy circumstance for the Allies to manipulate and exploit. The Americans recognized the hate-appeal of Stoker's vampire, and Dracula was presented to encapsulate the image of the traditionally cruel Germany. On American wartime propaganda posters a German soldier would appear. He wore a hellish expression on his face and sported bared canine teeth dripping with blood. Later, the association of the Count with whichever enemy America happened to be fighting was reinforced by the provision of free copies of *Dracula* to U.S. forces serving overseas. [23]

With the passing of the years the immortal Count has confirmed his adaptability. After Germany's second defeat he proved equally adept at symbolizing the perceived Soviet menace in the Cold War. In the era of the McCarthy-ist witch-hunts for alleged communist sympathizers in the United States, Dracula switched from exemplifying the cruelty of the Nazi to personifying the Red threat. Similarly, he was no longer the exemplar of capitalism: he was now its staunchest enemy. These turn-arounds were made all the more plausible in the light of the adjustment of European frontiers. Transylvania was again part of Romania, and conveniently lay behind the Iron Curtain. Dracula was a communist; the bogeyman from the East.

In fact, the novel consistently leans heavily on the distinction between East and West, dark and light, the primitive and the modern. Harker, in the first paragraph of the book, is made aware as he travels beyond 'Buda-Pesth' that he is leaving the West and entering the East — that part of Europe that had been indelibly influenced by the Ottoman Empire (and later by the Soviet Union). Then, as his calèche carries him up the Borgo Pass leading to Dracula's castle, he notes the dark, rolling clouds overhead, and a heavy, oppressive sense of thunder in the air: 'It seemed as though the mountain range had separated two atmospheres, and that now we had got into the thunderous one' (D 1:18). Everything, to the cloistered Harker, that is civilized and enlightened about the West is being left behind. So, in the 1890s no less than today, the upright citizen of the West is alarmed by the concealed terrors presented by the East.

*Dracula* as a Cold War parable equates the demonic Count with the power of Soviet-inspired communism: both present a material threat to the Western world.[24] Neither intends to further its ends by outright invasion, which carries too many risks. Subversion is the chosen instrument. The complacent defences of the West are not attacked by storm but infiltrated by stealth, though the aim in each case is the subjugation of the West into East European colonies/vampires. Furthermore, just as communist subversion has the industrial work-force as its principal focus, so Dracula directs his attack at helpless women, turning them, in effect, into a 'fifth column' to assist his schemes. Dracula is now a Red under the Bed, as well as a vampire hovering above it. His subversive strategy is revealed in his painstaking legal preparations, so as not to arouse suspicion in the British police or legal profession. He ensures he has numerous hideaways once he arrives. He shrewdly does not permit any of his unwitting official collaborators (solicitors, estate agents, etc.) to know the identities, far less anything of the duties, of the others (D 3:43-4). That is why he employs an Exeter solicitor to purchase a house in London, while he himself arrives at Whitby.

The Cold War moral is that constant vigilance must be observed. Otherwise the vampire/communism will achieve its objectives by taking advantage of the built-in vulnerability that has accompanied the West's rapid scientific and technological progress. This smug superiority has contemptuously discounted the probability of successful subversion, and even British laws will assist the Count: the 'innocent until proven guilty' philosophy hands him a ticket to success. Moreover, the Van Helsing clique dare not publicize the danger for fear of ridicule. They are therefore compelled to act as clandestinely on their part as Dracula does on his: they must operate outside the confines not only of conventional medicine and religion, but also of the law.

This hawkishness in the name of defending home values is manifested in Van Helsing's strictures against the naïve liberalism of Seward: 'Do you not think that there are things which you cannot understand, and yet which are; that some people see things that others cannot?' (D 14:229). Van Helsing is referring to hidden knowledge shared only with Dracula, and he is seeking to override 'rational' objection so that he can perform his desecrations without opposition. Dissenters against the McCarthy excesses were swept aside in ways which were uncomfortably comparable.[25] It is significant that the war against Dracula/communist infiltration should be spearheaded by a specialist of the mind, who is well able to manipulate the inarticulate fears of honest citizens for devious ends. One isolated attack on appropriately-named Light-of-the-West Lucy is to be avenged by the full weight of Western revenge.

Intruding into this analysis, and not for the first time, is the strange twist provided by Quincey Morris, the embodiment of the United States. It has been proposed that Stoker is covertly challenging United States reluctance to involve herself in world affairs, and to bring about an end to the isolation behind which she was, in the 1890s, sheltering.[26] The evidence for this emerges when Renfield, in a bubble of sanity, comments upon the Monroe Doctrine (D 18:291) — an axiom of American foreign policy dating back to 1823, but operational for a century thereafter. The Monroe Doctrine, in essence, decreed that Europe should stay out of

American affairs, and the United States would reciprocate. This policy naturally hampered Anglo-American understanding and contributed to the mutual ignorance that prompted Stoker's book *A Glimpse of America*. Renfield probably speaks Stoker's thoughts, looking forward to the day 'when the Pole and the Tropics may hold allegiance to the Stars and Stripes' (*D* 18:291).

Actually, Stoker did not have long to wait. The year of *Dracula's* publication, 1897, also marked Diamond Jubilee Year, celebrating sixty years of Queen Victoria's reign. The year was awash with imperial pageantry and festival. The British Empire, although actually in decline, had never appeared stronger. But across the Atlantic the American giant was beginning to stir. *Dracula*, in fact, becomes in retrospect curiously prophetic of the Spanish-American war of 1898, which is often taken to mark the United States' inaugural appearance in global power-politics. By the time of Stoker's final years the United States was on the brink of superseding the old-established European balance-of-power system and its ageing empires — such as that of Austria-Hungary, which Dracula represented.[27] Moreover, in the novel Morris provides military aid to the effete Europeans in the form of Winchester rifles (*D* 25:396). America thereby becomes the arms supplier of the free world in fiction not long before she does so in fact.

It might be said that the Texan has declared war on a European adversary with the objective of gaining ultimate supremacy over the Old World. America fails in the novel, only to succeed in the real world over the course of the twentieth century. Some might say that America has come to colonize Britain as effectively as Dracula had once aspired to do. Morris' spirit has been recycled through the triumphant 'family' to flourish in economic terms in the succeeding generations.[28] America is the *land* of the future, just as Quincey lends his name to the *child* of the future.

Ideologically, it is the collective resources and talents of the West that must be seen to prevail; the alliance of free men and women. It can be no isolated hero operating alone who will slay Dracula, but a corporate body in which everybody has a part to play in the downfall of the 'solitary' Count. The totalitarian monolith, embarked on a kind of inversed imperialistic quest — 'the primitive trying to colonise the civilised world'[29] — must meet his match against the power of combination; the strength and solidarity which emanate from the democratically organized, committee-style 'Council of War' (*D* 18:285; 26:420). The Western partners would weaken their own security should they withdraw from their alliance. A disorganized group of individuals is easy prey to the concentrated force of the vampire/communism. Only when the alliance is forged in the second half of the novel can Dracula be confronted by an adversary whose combined strength is superior to that of its constituent elements.

The NATO allies in *Dracula* (Britain, the United States, and the Netherlands) possess two other decisive advantages over their Eastern adversary. The first is their freedom of thought and action: the Dracula-hunters perceive themselves as having 'self-devotion in a cause and an end to achieve which is not a selfish one' (*D* 18:285) — that is, they want to save the world (or so they think), not control it. Even Stoker's mode of address — diaries, letters, journals, etc. — emphasizes the plurality of perception and sense of individuality which the vampire threatens to subjugate, until they are collated to present an amalgamated account prior to the trans-continental quest. The second advantage is that of scientific ingenuity and progress. The East, then as now, is described as lacking sophisticated technological hardware. Transylvania is behind the times, run-down, unable to advance from traditional crafts and practices. Britain, however, is portrayed in *Dracula* as a veritable showpiece of efficiency and modern engineering: Mina taps away on her typewriter, Seward goes one better and records his diary on to a phonograph, Harker takes advantage of a telephone, and Morris is an amateur photographer. Throughout, letters and telegrams are delivered with improbable despatch. It is, then, no surprise that armed with these weapons — social, political, psychological, and technological — ultimate victory for the West is assured.

# POSTSCRIPT

'Rubbish Watson, rubbish! What have we to do with walking
corpses who can only be held in their graves by stakes driven through
their hearts? It's pure lunacy.'

'But surely', said I, 'the vampire was not necessarily a dead man?
A living person might have had the habit. I have read, for example,
of the old sucking the blood of the young in order to retain their
youth.'

'You are right, Watson. It mentions the legend in one of these
references. But are we to give serious attention to such things? This
agency stands flat footed upon the ground, and there it must remain.
The world is big enough for us. No ghosts need apply.'

Sherlock Holmes,
in Sir Arthur Conan Doyle, 'The Adventure of the Sussex Vampire'

SHERLOCK HOLMES may not have been impressed by
vampires, but then he had never met Count Dracula.[1] Bram
Stoker's creation has taken hold of the twentieth-century
imagination like almost no other fictional being. Dracula belongs
with a select group of characters — Frankenstein, Sherlock Holmes
himself, Mickey Mouse, Tarzan, James Bond — who have become
part of the popular mythology of our age. No fictional detective
can compare with Holmes: nor can any dark figure from hell claim
to match Dracula in the possession of unbridled wickedness. Yet
he is even more universal than his mythical rivals. He can cross
language and cultural barriers with ease. The cinema has
transported him to all corners of the globe, where he presents a
stark image of darkness, of death, of evil.

The previous chapters have attempted to illuminate the sources
of *Dracula's* power; to explore the numerous competing
interpretations that can be made of the novel; and thereby seek

to substantiate the claim that *Dracula* stands as one of the richest of English novels, measured in cultural terms, to appear within the last hundred years. For the cultural impact of *Dracula* lies all around us. It is possible to buy 'Count Dracula ice lollies' and for young children to watch Count *Duck*ula and *Bunn*icula on television. And what else is Batman but the Count cleansed of his evil and endowed with a social conscience?

How would one summarize the novel's appeal and its pervasive power and imagery? Some critics have suggested that Dracula reminds us of the dark side of ourselves: that in each of us there is a hidden, repressed, ferocious quality that we recognize in him. He panders to man's morbid excitement at the prospect of sadistic pleasures. Even if the reader rejects this view of him/herself, Dracula is still a figure to envy. Many men would like to be able to seduce *like* him: many women would like to be seduced *by* him. His masculinity is also a source of envy: he goes in fear of nobody and is able to command and manipulate people at his imperious whim. In short, he provides a ready model for a society such as ours, eager to exploit corrupt power and sexual titillation, and to celebrate passion at the expense of restraint.

But Dracula does more than this. At a time of increasing secularization in the industrialized world, he serves to unite the world-views of East and West, preaching transmigration, rebirth, and immortality. He also serves to reassure the elderly. In their fantasies they can become young, as he has, and in any case why worry about death if it is as he describes? In death there is no pain, no decay, no hell; rather a world of voluptuous physical excess. More pertinently, *Dracula* fascinates becauses of its irreverence when it comes to clear-cut boundaries. The novel blurs the distinction between the natural and the supernatural, between life and death, good and evil, dream and reality, desire and dread, love and lust. It blurs the Oedipal configuration, together with the question of personal identity — particularly in the case of Lucy. It is a vehicle for Stoker's obsessive ambivalence towards women, and their lighter and darker aspects. Punter adds this assessment:

> It is hard to summarize *Dracula*, for it is such a wide-ranging book, but in general it is fair to say that its power derives from its dealings with taboo . . . [which] Dracula blurs . . . He blurs the line between man and beast . . . he blurs the line between man and God . . . and he blurs the line between man and woman by demonstrating the existence of female passion.[2]

These floutings of taboos have always presented sources of illicit pleasure in literature, but perhaps nowhere quite so outspokenly and unashamedly as in *Dracula*.

# REFERENCES

## Introduction

1   This claim is found in several sources, among them Grigore Nandris, 'The Historical Dracula: The Theme of his Legend in the Western and in the Eastern Literatures of Europe', p. 369. The claim is, of course, impossible to substantiate.
2   Franco Moretti, *Signs Taken for Wonders: Essays in the Sociology of Literary Forms*, pp. 15-16.
3   A. N. Wilson (introduction), *Dracula* (Oxford University Press, 1983), p. x.
4   ibid.

## Chapter One: The Vampire

1   Ernest Jones, 'On the Vampire', in Christopher Frayling (ed.), *The Vampyre: Lord Ruthven to Count Dracula*, p. 315.
2   Ornella Volta, *The Vampire*, p. 10.
3   Leonard Wolf, *A Dream of Dracula*, p. 125.
4   Devendra Varma (introduction), *Varney the Vampire*, (Vol. 1), pp. xiv, xviii.
5   Anthony Masters, *The Natural History of the Vampire*, p. 48.
6   Plato, *Phaedo*, 77E.
7   Varma, op. cit., p. xiii.
8   Homer, *Odyssey*, X-XI.
9   Jones, op. cit., p. 317
10  Varma, op. cit., p. xiv.
11  Montague Summers, *The Vampire: His Kith and Kin*, p. 165.
12  Ghouls and vampires sometimes invite confusion. Generally speaking a ghoul is a corpse that devours other corpses, though having no special delectation for blood. Moreover, ghouls are robotic, under external control, whereas vampires move and direct themselves.
13  Volta, op. cit., p. 80.
14  Summers, op. cit., p. 18.

## Chapter Two: The Vampire in Christian Europe

1 John 6:54-6.
2 Genesis 9: 4; Leviticus 17: 10-14, 19: 28; Deuteronomy 12: 16, 23.
3 Gabriel Ronay, *The Dracula Myth*, p. 10.
4 The searcher after vampire folklore has few reliable sources. The doyen is Montague Summers, building on the work of earlier Catholic scholars like Dom Augustine Calmet. Summers' problems are twofold: he does not know fact from heresay; and he believes passionately in the existence of vampires. Nonetheless, few other investigators are as thorough. Other, secondary, works, such as Masters, Garden, and Wright offer little that cannot be found in Summers.
5 Montague Summers, *The Vampire: His Kith and Kin*, pp. 140-1.
6 Ernest Jones, 'On the Vampire', in Frayling, p. 322.
7 See A. Murgoci, 'The Evil Eye in Roumania, and its Antidotes'.
8 Montague Summers, *The Vampire in Europe*, p. 302.
9 Ronay, p. 10.
10 Felix J. Oinas, 'Heretics as Vampires and Demons in Russia', pp. 437, 40.
11 Summers, *The Vampire: His Kith and Kin*, p. 95
12 ibid., pp. 153-4.
13 Jones, p. 321.
14 Summers, op. cit., pp. 31-3.
15 ibid., pp. 182-3.
16 ibid., p. 179.
17 Ornella Volta, *The Vampire*, pp. 12, 83.
18 Dudley Wright, *Vampires and Vampirism*, p. 13.
19 Summers, op. cit., p. 30.
20 Bernard Davies, 'Mountain Greenery', *The Dracula Journals*, No. 1, p. 10.
21 Anthony Masters, *The Natural History of the Vampire*, p. 180.
22 Davies, pp. 12-13.
23 Summers, op. cit., pp. 165-6.
24 ibid., pp. 194-5.
25 Masters, p. 107.
26 Summers, op. cit., p. 202.
27 ibid., p. 204.
28 Summers, *The Vampire in Europe*, p. 311.
29 Volta, p. 129.
30 Wright, p. 107.
31 *British Medical Journal*, 31 October 1885, p. 841.
32 Summers, *The Vampire in Europe*, p. 284.
33 Lionel Milgrom, 'Vampires, Plants, and Crazy Kings', p. 13.
34 Ronay, p. 16.
35 Summers, *The Vampire: His Kith and Kin*, p. 56.

36   Ronay, p. 24.
37   ibid., p. 27.
38   ibid., p. 11.

## Chapter Three: The Vampire in Literature

1   James Twitchell, *The Living Dead: A Study of the Vampire in Romantic Literature*, p. 33.
2   ibid., pp. 4-5.
3   Christopher Frayling (ed.), *The Vampyre: Lord Ruthven to Count Dracula*, p. 15.
4   M. M. Carlson, 'What Stoker Saw: an Introduction to the History of the Literary Vampire', p. 27.
5   For comparisons with Stoker's description of Dracula, see *D* 4:63.
6   For many years it was accepted that Prest was the author. Some scholars indicate that *Varney* might have had multiple authors (Twitchell, p. 123). Current opinion favours Rymer as the author.
7   Frayling, pp. 42-3.
8   See David Punter, *The Literature of Terror*, p. 239.
9   Frayling, p. 64.
10   Carlson, pp. 30-1.
11   Leonard Wolf, *A Dream of Dracula*, p. 170.

## Chapter Four: The Life and Works of Bram Stoker

1   Bram Stoker, *Personal Reminiscences of Henry Irving* (hereafter: *Reminiscences*).
2   Harry Ludlam, *A Biography of Bram Stoker: Creator of Dracula*. This biography was first published under the confusing title *A Biography of Dracula: The Life Story of Bram Stoker*.
     Daniel Farson, *The Man Who Wrote Dracula: A Biography of Bram Stoker*. Both biographies are deficient in that they do not provide the sources for information presented, hampering further research. Phyllis A. Roth's *Bram Stoker* is a thorough guide to Stoker's literary career: while Richard Dalby's *Bram Stoker: A Bibliography of First Editions* demonstrates that many reprints of Stoker's novels in circulation are abridgements of the originals.
3   Ludlam, p. 14.
4   Farson, p. 19.
5   ibid., p. 39.
6   *The London Society*, Vol. 22, No. 129.
7   Farson, p. 25.
8   *The Shamrock*, Vol. 12, Nos. 446-9.
9   Farson, p. 26.
10   Peter Denman, 'Le Fanu and Stoker: a Probable Connection', p. 153.
11   Ludlam, p. 27.
12   *Reminiscences*, Vol. 2, p. 31.

13    ibid., Vol. 1, p. 31.
14    Ludlam, p. 63.
15    Farson, p. 38.
16    ibid., pp. 26, 42.
17    ibid., p. 45.
18    Douglas Oliver Street, 'Bram Stoker's "Under the Sunset", with Introductory Biographical and Critical Material' (unpublished Ph.D. thesis), pp. xci-xcii.
19    Punch, 3 December 1881.
20    Spectator, 12 November 1881.
21    The Academy, 10 December 1881.
22    Ludlam, p. 72.
23    A Glimpse of America, p. 22.
24    Reminiscences, Vol. 1, p. 51; Vol. 2, p. 6.
25    A Glimpse of America, pp. 14, 23.
26    North American Review, Vol. 190, November 1909.
27    A Glimpse of America, p. 42.
28    Farson, p. 78.
29    A Glimpse of America, p. 23.
30    Reminiscences, Vol. 2, p. 274.
31    ibid., p. 199.
32    ibid., p. 290.
33    ibid., pp. 100-1.
34    ibid., Vol. 1, pp. 200, 350, 355, 359.
35    ibid., Vol. 2, p. 29; Ludlam, p. 88.
36    Ludlam p. 169.
37    Slains Castle ceased to be inhabited in the 1920s.
38    See The Athenaeum, 23 February 1895.
39    ibid., 16 November 1895.
40    See Ludlam, pp. 120-1.
41    The Bookman, August 1897.
42    Punch, 26 June 1897.
43    The Athenaeum, 26 June 1897.
44    Ludlam, p. 122.
45    Farson, p. 192.
46    Laurence Irving, Henry Irving: The Actor and his World, p. 453.
47    Ludlam, pp. 143-4; Dalby, p. 43.
48    The Times, 22 April 1912.
49    Farson, p. 233.
50    ibid., pp. 212, 214.

## Chapter Five: The Origins of Dracula

1    See, for example, Sir William Wilde, Irish Popular Superstitions (1853), and Lady Wilde, Ancient Legends of Ireland (1888).
2    Reproduced in Ludlam, pp. 27-34.

3    In Street, pp. 36-54.
4    ibid., pp. 97-117.
5    Peter Haining, *The Leprechaun's Kingdom*, pp. 91, 99.
6    Sean O'Sullivan, *Legends from Ireland*, p. 72.
7    ibid., pp. 21, 23.
8    Haining, pp. 21, 25, 39. Consider Harker's experience with Dracula's coach (*D* 1:19-20).
9    ibid., p. 107.
10   O'Sullivan, pp. 114-15.
11   Phyllis A. Roth, *Bram Stoker*, p. 96; Raymond T. McNally and Radu Florescu, *The Essential Dracula*, p. 21.
12   See James B. Twitchell, *The Living Dead: A Study of the Vampire in Romantic Literature*, pp. 166-7; David Punter, *The Literature of Terror*, p. 248.
13   Edouard Roditi, *Oscar Wilde*, p. 115.
14   Nuel Pharr Davis, *The Life of Wilkie Collins*, p. 211.
15   For example, the names Harkwright, Marian, and Laura in *The Woman in White* are only slightly modified into Harker, Mina, and Lucy in *Dracula*. Similarly, both books feature a grotesque/lunatic.
16   See Mark M. Hennelly Jr, 'Twice Told Tales of Two Counts', pp. 26-7, also pp. 15-18.
17   Reprinted in Raymond T. McNally and Radu Florescu, *In Search of Dracula*, pp. 177-8.
18   R. A. Gilbert, *The Golden Dawn: Twilight of the Magicians*, p. 81.
19   Personal correspondence from R. A. Gilbert.
20   *Reminiscences*, Vol. 1, pp. 350-6.
21   Oswald Doughty, *A Victorian Romantic: Dante Gabriel Rosetti*, pp. 416-17.
22   Ludlam, p. 112 (see also p. 107). Ludlam's date, 1895, for the commencement of Stoker's writing of *Dracula* has passed into many other secondary sources.
23   ibid., p. 123.
24   *Reminiscences*, Vol. 1, pp. 107-8.
25   I am grateful to James Drummond for his insights into the many similarities between *Macbeth* and *Dracula*, which extend even to the cast. There is a Siward in *Macbeth* and a Seward in *Dracula*.
26   James Drummond, 'The Scottish Play', p. 46.
27   Personal correspondence from James Drummond.
28   The Rosenbach Museum and Library.
29   Whitby Glossary, 1876, F. K. Robinson. Curiously, this dialect has many similarities to that of Cruden Bay (James Drummond, 'Bram Stoker's Cruden Bay', p. 28).
30   F. C. and J. Rivington, *Theory of Dreams*, 2 vols. (1803).
31   *Nineteeth Century*, Vol. 28, July 1885. This journal was edited by a friend of Stoker's, Sir James Knowles.

32 Stoker's notes list his sources as: Sabine Baring-Gould, *Curious Myths of the Middle Ages; Germany Past and Present; The Book of Were-Wolves;* Fletcher S. Bassett, *Legends and Superstitions of the Sea and of Sailors in All Lands at All Times;* Rushton M. Dorman, *The Origin of Primitive Superstitions;* John Jones, *The Natural and the Supernatural;* W. Jones, *Credulities Past and Present; History and Mystery of Precious Stones;* Revd W. H. Jones, *Magyar Folk Tales;* Henry Charles Lea, *Superstition and Force;* Sarah Lee, *Anecdotes of Habits and Instincts of Birds;* Frederick G. Lea, *The Other World, Sea Monsters Unmasked; Sea Fables Explained;* Maury (in French); Herbert Mayo, *Letters on the Truths Contained in Popular Superstition;* T. J. Pettigrew, *Superstitions Connected with History and Medicine;* Reville, *History of the Devil;* Sir T. Browner, *Necromacy — divination by the dead.*

Other works from which Stoker took copious notes are: *Magyarland,* by a Fellow of the Carpathian Society; *Golden Chersonese,* by Miss Bird; *Round About the Carpathians,* by A. F. Crosse; *On the Track of the Crescent,* by Major C. Johnson; and *Transylvania,* by Charles Bonner.

33 There is further internal evidence in support of 1893. In a diary extract of 26 September Van Helsing speaks of the pioneer of hypnotism, Charcot, and adds 'alas that he is no more' (*D* 14:230). Charcot had died on 16 August 1893. Clearly, then, the book cannot be set earlier than 1893, and Van Helsing's expression of sadness suggests Charcot died very recently. Furthermore, a little cross-checking confirms that 21 September must have fallen on a Thursday (*D* 13:206; 14:221). This could only happen in 1893. Stoker's careless references to the moon previously threw researchers off the scent. He pays scant regard to the lunar cycle in *Dracula,* having the moon shine on the nights of 5 May, 15 May, 24 June, 11-13 August (when the moon is full), 17 September, 29 September, 1 October, and 3 October. Not only is this combination not possible, but on the nights of 11-13 August 1893, instead of there being a full moon, there was in fact no moon at all.

34 *Reminiscences,* Vol. 1, pp. 371-2.

35 The decorator was Joseph Harker. Stoker kept his initials for his character Jonathan Harker.

36 Paul Dukes, 'Dracula: Fact, Legend and Fiction', p. 45.

37 Joseph S. Bierman reaches the same conclusion in 'The Genesis and Dating of "Dracula" from Bram Stoker's Working Notes', p. 41.

38 Radu Florescu and Raymond T. McNally, *Dracula, A Biography,* p. 7.

39 See Grigore Nandris, 'The Historical Dracula: The Theme of his Legend in the Western and in the Eastern Literatures of Europe', p. 370.

40 Gabriel Ronay, *The Dracula Myth,* p. 57.

41  One view is that the brothers had been handed over to the Turks by their father as a sign of his goodwill (Florescu and McNally, op. cit., p. 36).

42  Grigore Nandris, 'A Philological Analysis of Dracula and Rumanian Place-names and Masculine Personal Names in -a/-ea', pp. 371-2. See also Nandris, 'The Historical Dracula' pp. 369, 94. The name 'Dracula' has a peculiarly feminine feel about it.

43  For a list of Tepes' tortures and cruelties, see Nicolai Stoicescu, *Vlad Tepes: Prince of Walachia*, p. 157.

44  Even today many Romanian towns are known by a German/Saxon equivalent: Sibiu was, and is, also known as Hermannstadt; Brasov is Kronstadt; and Sighisoara is Schassburg.

45  Stoicescu, p. 77.

46  Florescu and McNally, op. cit., p. 114. This claim is vigorously denied by Stoicescu, p. 43.

47  Florescu and NcNally, op. cit., p. 121.

48  McNally and Florescu, *In Search of Dracula*, p. 115.

49  Ronay, p. 74.

50  Andrew MacKenzie, *Romanian Journey*, p. 110.

51  The Renaissance era produced many cruel statesmen: Richard III, Cesare Borgia, Ivan the Terrible, to name some. See Nandris, 'The Historical Dracula', pp. 370-1.

52  William Wilkinson, *Account of the Principalities of Wallachia and Moldavia*, p. 19.

53  Nandris, 'The Historical Dracula', p. 377.

54  This has not prevented conjecture, especially before the discovery of Stoker's notes. His cavalier attitude to central European history encouraged confusion. For example, Dracula calls himself a 'boyar' (*D* 2:31) and a 'Szekely' (*D* 3:41), neither of which was applicable to Vlad Tepes. See Ronay, pp. 58-9; Nandris, 'The Historical Dracula' pp. 371 ff. Stoker's contradictory clues suggested several contempories of the Impaler as possible sources for Count Dracula.

55  McNally and Florescu, *In Search of Dracula*, p. 180.

56  Montague Summers, *The Vampire in Europe*, p. 132.

57  See Raymond T. McNally, *Dracula Was a Woman*.

58  See Richard Dalby, *Bram Stoker: A Bibliography of First Editions*, p. 26.

## Chapter Six: From Vlad Dracula to Count Dracula

1  Stoker's final decision to have Dracula 'on view' as little as possible appears, from his notes, to have been reached in a late draft. Earlier ones show Dracula onstage more frequently.

2  Nicholas Modrussa, in Radu Florescu and Raymond T. McNally, *Dracula: A Biography*, p. 50.

3  Newspaper report from *New York Tribune*, November 1883, reprinted in Austin Brereton, *The Life of Henry Irving*, Vol. 2, p. 14.

4    Franco Moretti, *Signs Taken For Wonders: Essays in the Sociology of Literary Forms*, pp. 90-1.

5    Stoker's working notes interestingly intend that Dracula will only register fear at relics more ancient than himself.

6    Leonard Wolf, *A Dream of Dracula*, p. 264.

7    Most of Stoker's information on the Scholomance came from Emily Gerard's 'Transylvanian Superstitions'.

8    Gerard, op. cit.

9    Here again, Stoker relies heavily on the works of Emily Gerard, *The Land Beyond the Forest*, and *The Waters of Hercules*.

10   The only possible exception to this principle is Dracula's 'attacks' on the crew of the *Demeter*. Whether he merely kills them, or kills them for their blood, or they throw themselves overboard in terror, is not made clear.

11   See Thomas P. Walsh, '*Dracula*: Logos and Myth', p. 230.

## Chapter Seven: 'Thank God for Good Brave Men'

1    Franco Moretti, *Signs Taken for Wonders: Essays in the Sociology of Literary Forms*, p. 84.

2    For example, Dracula recruits the services of a wolf named 'Bersicker'. Stoker had noted from *The Book of Were-Wolves* that Berserkers were particularly fierce Norse warriors who fought with seemingly preternatural strength and ferocity.

3    Harry Ludlam, *A Biography of Bram Stoker: Creator of Dracula*, p. 110.

4    Mark M. Hennelly Jr, 'Dracula: the Gnostic Quest and the Victorian Wasteland', p. 20.

5    Thomas P. Walsh, '*Dracula*: Logos and Myth, p. 233.

6    See Leonard Wolf, *The Annotated Dracula*, p. 24.

7    Hennelly, op. cit., p. 22.

8    The expression is from Leonard Wolf, *A Dream of Dracula*, p. 215.

9    See E. Randolph Johnson, 'The Victorian Vampire', p. 210.

10   Stephanie Demetrakopoulos, 'Feminism, Sex Role Changes, and Other Subliminal Fantasies in Bram Stoker's *Dracula*', p. 104.

11   Ronald Schleifer, 'The Trap of the Imagination: the Gothic Tradition, Fiction and the "Turn of the Screw"', p. 299.

12   He may even have caused her death more directly. See Chapter Nine, note 16.

13   Robert Dowse and David Palmer, ' "Dracula": the Book of Blood' p. 428.

14   See Royce MacGillivray, ' "Dracula": Bram Stoker's Spoiled Masterpiece', p. 525.

15   Walsh, p. 234.

16   This view is not universally held. MacGillivray, for example, thinks that the portrayal of Renfield is unsuccessful, p. 525.

17    Johnson, op. cit., p. 209.
18    *Punch*, 26 June 1897.
19    See Walsh, p. 233.
20    Philip Temple, 'The Origins of Dracula'.
21    Hennelly, op. cit., p. 19.
22    Walsh, p. 233. The present writer is not generally impressed by much
      of the linguistic speculation employed on characters' names. The
      striking nature of 'Lord Godalming', however, does present a
      powerful exception.
23    In 'The Squaw', Elias P. Hutcheson hails from Nebraska. He is a
      'cheery stranger, full of racy remarks and a wonderful stock of
      adventures'. He has fought grizzlies and Injuns and carries a pistol
      illegally. The middle initial 'P' is transferred to Morris, and the only
      perceptible difference from Morris is the State of origin.
24    Walter Lord, *A Time to Stand*, p. 26.
25    ibid.
26    L. W. Newton and H. P. Gambrell, *A Social and Political History
      of Texas*, p. 224. As for the word 'Quincey', this is similar to the
      name for a throat disease, quinsy — a Victorian description for
      bronchitis (Walsh, p. 234). Dracula could also be said to bring about
      a disease of the throat.
27    The floods of immigrants from the 1830s into Texas came from as
      far as Britain, Germany, and France. There was an indigenous
      Mexican population, but they were soon submerged by waves of
      Americans moving west. Among them were farmers, artisans, and
      professional men, cultivated and educated southern gentlemen. The
      harshness of life on the frontier, however, soon encouraged a tough,
      independent, empire-building spirit that is still encapsulated in the
      name 'Texan' today. Interestingly, Texas was one of the few States
      with which Stoker was hardly acquainted, and it is not even known
      if he went there. Not until early 1896, on the Lyceum's fifth tour
      of North America, were performances given in the Deep South,
      and even then New Orleans was the nearest venue to Texas (Austin
      Brereton, *The Life of Henry Irving*, Vol. 2, p. 226). Farson, in
      contrast, asserts that the Lyceum performed for the first time in New
      Orleans in 1884 (Daniel Farson, *The Man Who Wrote Dracula: A
      Biography of Bram Stoker*, p. 74).
28    Newton and Gambrell, p. 224.
29    Bram Stoker, *A Glimpse of America*, p. 28.
30    Moretti, pp. 94-6.
31    For example, Brutus M. Moris and Quincey P. Adams (which comes
      rather too close to being John Quincy Adams, the sixth President
      of the United States).

## Chapter Eight: 'Sweet, Sweet, Good, Good Women'

1    Jeffrey B. Russell, *A History of Witchcraft: Sorcerers, Heretics, and Pagans*, pp. 113-15.

2    Penelope Shuttle and Peter Redgrove, *The Wise Wound: Menstruation and Everywoman*, p. 225.

3    Though venerated by the early Church, from the twelfth century onwards the cult of the Blessed Virgin proliferated all over Europe.

4    Charlotte Brontë, *Jane Eyre*, Chapter 25.

5    Leonard Wolf, *A Dream of Dracula*, pp. 208-9.

6    Stephanie Demetrakopoulos, 'Feminism, Sex Role Changes, and Other Subliminal Fantasies in Bram Stoker's *Dracula*', p. 104.

7    In Stoker's notes Dracula reactivates Lucy's sleepwalking by means of a magic brooch which he has deposited, and she discovers, on Whitby beach.

8    Carol A. Senf, ' "Dracula": Stoker's Response to the New Woman', p. 42.

9    Stoker was fond of using the same initials in his fictional works. Lucy Westenra re-emerges as Lilla Watford, and Mina as Mimi, in *The Lair of the White Worm*. Stoker seemed particularly fond of the initial 'M'; other heroines of his being Margaret and Marjorie.

10   At least she has dark hair as a vampire (*D* 16:252). Beforehand, things may have been different. The very first edition of the novel and some modern reprints refer to her 'sunny' ripples. The second, and subsequent, editions were published under copyright: they speak, instead, of 'shiny' ripples (*D* 12:194). (See Roger Johnson, 'The Bloofer Ladies', in *The Dracula Journals*, Vol. 1, No. 4, p. 133.) Stoker's use of the dark-haired Lucy demonstrates his conformity to the traditional 'light-dark' equation with 'good-bad' — a common technique of Victorian fiction.

11   Dracula etymologists have suggested that the name 'Wilhelmina' implies a wish for protection, and 'Murray' derives from the name for a plague, dead flesh, or the infliction of death (Thomas P. Walsh, '*Dracula*: Logos and Myth', p. 234). Matthew Lewis, author of *The Monk*, had also known of a vampire tale called 'Mina': (Christopher Frayling (introduction), *The Vampyre: Lord Ruthven to Count Dracula*, p. 70).

12   Judith Weissman, 'Women and Vampires: *Dracula* as a Victorian Novel', p. 399.

13   See Carrol L. Fry, 'Fictional Conventions and Sexuality in Dracula', p. 21.

14   Senf, op. cit., p. 48.

15   Weissman, p. 398.

16   Demetrakopoulos, p. 104.

17   Phyllis A. Roth, 'Suddenly Sexual Women in Bram Stoker's *Dracula*', p. 113.

18 Weissman, p. 405.
19 See Senf, op. cit., p. 34.
20 In Brian Murphy, 'The Nightmare of the Dark: the Gothic Legacy of Count Dracula', pp. 10-11.
21 Gail Cunningham, *The New Women and the Victorian Novel*, p. 2.
22 Senf, op. cit., p. 46.
23 A. R. Cunningham, *The New Women in Fiction of the 1890s*, p. 178.
24 See, for example, the attitudes of Herminia Barton in Grant Allen's *The Women Who Did*.
25 Demetrakopoulos, p. 110.
26 ibid., p. 104.
27 Weissman, p. 399. This point is stronger in principle than in practice. Mina would not know when the time had come: she would have to leave that decision to others.
28 See Senf, op. cit., p. 39.
29 Peter T. Cominos, in Demetrakopoulos, p. 107.
30 See Phyllis A. Roth, *Bram Stoker*, p. 102. Stoker's notes lend support to this contention, for Lucy and Mina were originally scheduled to perform acts eventually undertaken by the other.
31 Demetrakopoulos, p. 107.
32 ibid.
33 Roth suggests that such an ending would disconcert the reader because the destruction of Lucy hints at matricide, and this anxiety must be assuaged (Roth, 'Suddenly Sexual Women', p. 117).
34 Although Stoker dedicated *Dracula* to a man (Hall Caine), almost all his other novels are dedicated to women.

## Chapter Nine: Sexual Symbolism

1 C. F. Bentley, 'The Monster in the Bedroom', p. 27.
2 Maurice Richardson, 'The Psychoanalysis of Ghost Stories', p. 427.
3 Bentley, p. 27.
4 David Pirie, *The Vampire Cinema*, p. 26.
5 James Twitchell, 'The Vampire Myth', p. 88.
6 See Raymond T. McNally, *Dracula Was a Woman*, p. 93.
7 James Twitchell, *The Living Dead: A Study of the Vampire in Romantic Literature*, p. 136.
8 See Bentley, p. 28.
9 Judith Weissman, 'Women and Vampires: *Dracula* as a Victorian Novel', p. 404.
10 Dante Gabriel Rosetti, in 'Eden Bower', had written of Lilith's vengeance on Adam and Eve. Lilith also appears, fleetingly, on Walpurgis Nacht in Goethe's *Faust*.
11 This Oedipal configuration will be taken up in the following chapter.
12 Ornella Volta, *The Vampire*, p. 33.
13 Many nineteenth-century poets and writers exploited the erotic

symbolism entailed in the colour red. See, for example, Keats' 'The Eve of St Agnes'.

14    C. S. Blinderman, 'Vampurella: Darwin and Count Dracula', p. 422.

15    Ernest Jones, in Christopher Frayling (ed.), *The Vampyre: Lord Ruthven to Count Dracula*, pp. 323-4.

16    See Volta, p. 23. In fact, the practice of performing blood transfusions was extremely dangerous in the 1890s. Not until 1901, with Landsteiner's discovery of different blood groups, could it be made safer. Van Helsing's transfusions were likely to (did?) kill Lucy.

17    See Brian Murphy, 'The Nightmare of the Dark: the Gothic Legacy of Count Dracula', p. 10.

18    Penelope Shuttle and Peter Redgrove, *The Wise Wound: Menstruation and Everywomen*, p. 267.

19    Twitchell, *The Living Dead*, p. 138.

20    See Bentley, p. 30. Stoker may have known of the belief held in parts of Italy that a young girl could secure the attentions of her lover by his drinking some of her menstrual blood (Volta pp. 26,92).

21    Sigmund Freud, 'Contributions to the Psychology of Love: The Taboo of Virginity', in *Collected Papers* IV, pp. 221-2.

22    Daniel Farson, *The Man Who Wrote Dracula: A Biography of Bram Stoker*, p. 214.

23    Shuttle and Redgrove, p. 266.

24    See Burton Hatlen, 'The Return of the Repressed/Oppressed in Bram Stoker's *Dracula*', pp. 86-7.

25    Sigmund Freud, 'A Connection between a Symbol and a Symptom', in *Collected Papers* II, pp. 162-3. In the Marquis de Sade's *Justine* a sexual embrace often involved the decapitation of the partner.

26    Bentley, p. 31.

27    ibid., p. 32.

28    Leonard Wolf dissents from this view, interpreting Lucy's three suitors as linked by 'dimly homosexual bonds' (*A Dream of Dracula*, p. 210).

29    Bentley, p. 32.

30    Carrol L. Fry, 'Fictional Conventions and Sexuality in *Dracula*', p. 21.

31    See Blinderman, p. 422, and Chapter Eleven.

32    See Hatlen, pp. 93, 95.

33    Thomas P. Walsh, '*Dracula*: Logos and Myth', p. 231.

34    Phyllis A. Roth, 'Suddenly Sexual Women in Bram Stoker's *Dracula*', p. 119.

35    Jill Conway, in Stephanie Demetrakopoulos, 'Feminism, Sex Role Changes, and Other Subliminal Fantasies in Bram Stoker's *Dracula*', p. 106.

36    See Demetrakopoulos, pp. 106, 108.

37    See Bentley, p. 32.

38    See Murphy, p. 10.

39    Thomas Ray Thornburg, 'The Quester and the Castle: the Gothic Novel as Myth, with Special Reference to Bram Stoker's Dracula' (unpublished Ph.D. thesis) p. 146.

40    Bram Stoker, 'The Censorship of Fiction', pp. 483-5.

## Chapter Ten: Psychoanalytical Approaches

1     Maurice Richardson, 'The Psychoanalysis of Ghost Stories', p. 427.

2     Grigore Nandris, 'The Historical Dracula: The Theme of his Legend in the Western and in the Eastern Literatures of Europe', p. 370.

3     Technically, 'castration' refers to the removal of the testicles. Psychoanalytically its meaning is somewhat more flexible, referring to the loss of testicles, or penis, or both. Sometimes, too, it is used completely metaphorically, meaning male loss of control over females.

4     Richardson, p. 427.

5     Royce MacGillivray, ' "Dracula": Bram Stoker's Spoiled Masterpiece', p. 522.

6     Richard Astle, 'Dracula as Totemic Monster: Lacan, Freud, Oedipus and History', p. 102.

7     Sigmund Freud, Totem and Taboo.

8     Astle, p. 100.

9     MacGillivray, p. 522-3.

10    Phyllis A. Roth, 'Suddenly Sexual Women in Bram Stoker's Dracula', p. 118.

11    Ornella Volta, The Vampire, pp. 30, 94.

12    Astle, p. 103.

13    Richardson, p. 427.

14    Roth, op. cit., p. 119.

15    Franco Moretti, Signs Taken for Wonders: Essays in the Sociology of Literary Forms, p. 104.

16    ibid.

17    Ernest Jones, in Christophyer Frayling (ed.), The Vampyre: Lord Ruthven to Count Dracula, p. 317.

18    ibid., p. 314.

19    Penelope Shuttle and Peter Redgrove, The Wise Wound: Menstruation and Everywoman, p. 262.

20    Marie Bonaparte, The Life and Works of Edgar Allan Poe: A Psychoanalytic Interpretation, pp. 209-10.

21    Ernest Jones, in Richardson, p. 425.

22    Moretti, p. 104.

23    David Punter, The Literature of Terror, p. 263.

24    Ronald Schleifer, 'The Trap of the Imagination: The Gothic Tradition, Fiction and "The Turn of the Screw" ', p. 306.

25    Stoker, it will be remembered, had taken rough notes on a theory of dreams. The dreams manifested in Dracula, moreover, are

psychoanalytically classifiable into certain recognizable types: 'dental' and 'anticipatory' dreams on the part of Harker; 'flying' dreams on the part of Lucy. See Thomas Ray Thornburg, 'The Quester and the Castle: the Gothic Novel as Myth, with Special Reference to Bram Stoker's *Dracula*' (unpublished Ph.D. thesis) pp. 145-54.

26 Moretti, p. 102.

27 See Jean Gattengo, 'Folie, Croyance, et Fantastique dans "Dracula". In an earlier draft Stoker had Dracula himself restore sanity to Renfield, thereby hoping to secure his release from the asylum, where he might be of greater use to him.

28 Joseph S. Bierman, 'Dracula: Prolonged Childhood Illness and the Oral Triad', and Seymour Shuster, 'Dracula and Surgically Induced Trauma in Children'.

29 Bierman, op. cit., pp. 186-7.

30 In Shuster, p. 259.

31 K. A. Menninger, 'Polysurgery and Polysurgical Addiction', in *Psychoanalysis* Q 3 (1934), p. 173.

32 Shuster, p. 259.

33 ibid., p. 264. Shuster makes the important qualification that his hypothesis collapses if Stoker's infant disorders were treated at home. Occasional hospitalization is an essential prerequisite for Shuster's argument. Farson insists that the primitive conditions of Irish hospitals at that time would have made them a last resort for a respectable middle-class family (Daniel Farson, *The Man Who Wrote Dracula: A Biography of Bram Stoker*, p. 160).

34 Shuster, pp. 266-7. Shuster's train of thought, while perceptive, is speculative to say the least. Moreover, his attempts to link the name 'Dracula' with the abbreviation for 'Doctor', in that both begin with the letters 'Dr', is best not pursued too far.

35 Bierman, op. cit., p. 189.

36 ibid., p. 193. This argument is raised for the reader to ponder: not because the present writer is convinced. The number 'seven' is regarded as 'special' throughout Western symbolism, and features prominently in the Bible and classical astrology. Stoker would use the number in connection with Egyptology in *The Jewel of Seven Stars*.

37 See Bertram Lewin, *The Psychoanalysis of Elation*, p. 118.

38 Bierman, op. cit., p. 195.

39 ibid., p. 196. Bierman makes a number of other observations. Regrettably they are dependent on the long-held presumption that *Dracula* was conceived in 1895, rather than in 1890, as is now known to be the case.

40 ibid., p. 197.

41 Nandris, op. cit., pp. 392-3.

## Chapter Eleven: Dracula as Christian Parody

1   Leonard Wolf, *The Annotated Dracula*, p. 14.
2   ibid., p. 215.
3   Paul Johnson, *A History of Christianity*, p. 20.
4   The 'blood' of Christ is mentioned in the New Testament nearly three times as frequently as the 'Cross' of Christ, and five times as frequently as the 'death' of Christ. There is theological dispute as to whether the biblical use of 'blood' refers to 'life' or 'death'.
5   Wolf, op. cit., p. 100. Wolf also propounds further possible explanations.
6   Raymond T. McNally and Radu Florescu, *The Essential Dracula*, p. 111.
7   Wolf, op. cit., p. 248.
8   See Wolf, op. cit., pp. 188-9.
9   Wolf, op. cit., p. 194.
10  This is not explicit, but presumed from her marriage to non-Catholic Harker by an Anglican chaplain.
11  Wolf, op. cit., p. 104.
12  Wolf, op. cit., pp. 301,319.
13  Carmilla was also known as Mircalla and Millarca.
14  See McNally and Florescu, op. cit., p. 227.
15  This apology for Dracula requires giving him the benefit of many doubts. It is not clear whether he is responsbile for the disappearance of the crew of the *Demeter*, while the death of old Mr Swales at Whitby could be attributable to his blocking access to the grave of a suicide, where Dracula must sleep (*D* 7:109).
16  C. S. Blinderman, 'Vampurella: Darwin and Count Dracula', p. 418. Much of the remainder of this chapter draws heavily on Blinderman's excellent and original article.
17  G. J. Allman, in Blinderman, p. 418.
18  Blinderman, pp. 420-1.
19  Stuart P. Sherman, in Blinderman, p. 421.
20  E. Ray Lankester, *Degeneration: A Chapter in Darwinism*, pp. 18-19, 32.
21  Blinderman, p. 426.
22  ibid., p. 413.
23  ibid., pp. 427-8.

## Chapter Twelve: The Tarot and the Grail

1   Thomas Ray Thornburg, 'The Quester and the Castle: the Gothic Novel as Myth, with Special Reference to Bram Stoker's *Dracula*' (unpublished Ph.D. thesis) p. 3.
2   See Thornburg, pp. 108-36.

3   Robert Dowse and David Palmer, ' "Dracula": the Book of Blood', p. 428.
4   Thornburg, p. 125.
5   ibid.
6   ibid., p. 129.
7   ibid., p. 132.
8   Thomas P. Walsh, 'Dracula: Logos and Myth', p. 233. Dracula returns to Transylvania on board the Czarina Catherine, a vessel named after a woman of legendary sexual appetites.
9   ibid., p. 232.
10  Mark M. Hennelly Jr, 'Dracula: the Gnostic Quest and the Victorian Wasteland'.
11  ibid., pp. 16-17.
12  Dracula was not Stoker's first fictional expression of the 'wasteland'. A threatening wilderness surrounds the kingdom Under the Sunset.
13  Hennelly, op. cit., pp. 17-18.
14  Brian Murphy, 'The Nightmare of the Dark: the Gothic Legacy of Count Dracula', p. 13.
15  Intriguingly, in Stokers manuscript Dracula's castle disappears from sight following a volcanic 'convulsion of the earth'. In the published edition the castle is left standing. It is not clear why Stoker made this late change. Perhaps he was conscious of the excessive similarity with the fate of Poe's Fall of the House of Usher.

## Chapter Thirteen: Dracula as Social and Political Commentary

1   Rosemary Jackson, Fantasy: the Literature of Subversion, p. 121.
2   Burton Hatlen, 'The Return of the Repressed/Oppressed in Bram Stoker's Dracula', p. 83.
3   Ornella Volta, The Vampire, p. 145.
4   See the discussion on evolutionary degeneration, page 190.
5   Reproduced in Leonard Wolf, The Annotated Dracula, p. 300.
6   Carol A. Senf, 'Dracula: the Unseen Face in the Mirror', p. 163.
7   Mark M. Hennelly Jr, 'Dracula: the Gnostic Quest and the Victorian Wasteland', p. 22.
8   R. W. Johnson, 'The Myth of the Twentieth Century', p. 433.
9   Royce MacGillivray, ' "Dracula": Bram Stoker's Spoiled Masterpiece', pp. 525-6.
10  Richard Astle, 'Dracula as Totemic Monster: Lacan, Freud, Oedipus and History', p. 103.
11  See Gabriel Ronay, The Dracula Myth, pp. 149-55.
12  Ernest Jones, in Christopher Frayling (ed.), The Vampyre: Lord Ruthven to Count Dracula, p. 327.
13  Karl Marx, Das Kapital, Chapter X.
14  Franco Moretti, Signs Taken for Wonders: Essays in the Sociology of Literary Forms, p. 91.

15 ibid., p. 92.
16 Jackson, p. 122.
17 See Moretti, p. 93.
18 ibid., p. 94.
19 Ronay, pp. 157-9.
20 For example: *The Sorcerer's Apprentice* (1910), *The Vampire* (1921), *Nightmare* (1922).
21 Ronay, pp. 159-60.
22 Harry Ludlam, *A Biography of Bram Stoker: Creator of Dracula*, p. 190.
23 Ronay, p. 166.
24 See Richard Wasson, 'The Politics of Dracula'.
25 See Ronay, p. 169.
26 Wasson, p. 26.
27 See Astle, p. 103.
28 Moretti, pp. 251-2.
29 Senf, op. cit., p. 164.

## Postscript

1 This deficiency has been remedied in two recent novels: Fred Saberhagen, *The Holmes-Dracula File* (1978), Loren D. Estleman, *Sherlock Holmes Vs Dracula* (1979).
2 David Punter, *The Literature of Terror*, pp. 262-3.

# SELECT BIBLIOGRAPHY

## Articles

Norman Adams, 'Bram Stoker', *Leopard*, 2:8 22, June 1976.

Richard Astle, 'Dracula as Totemic Monster: Lacan, Freud, Oedipus and History', *Sub-Stance* 25, 1980.

C. F. Bentley, 'The Monster in the Bedroom: Sexual Symbolism in Bram Stoker's *Dracula*', *Literature and Psychology* 22, 1972.

Joseph S. Bierman, 'Dracula: Prolonged Childhood Illness, and the Oral Triad', *American Imago* 29, 1972.

_____, 'The Genesis and Dating of "Dracula" from Bram Stoker's Working Notes', *Notes and Queries* 24, Jan-Feb 1977.

Charles S. Blinderman, 'Vampurella: Darwin and Count Dracula', *Massachusetts Review* 21, Summer 1980.

Wanda Bonewits, 'Dracula, the Black Christ', *Gnostica* 4:7, March-May 1975.

M. M. Carlson, 'What Stoker Saw: An Introduction to the History of the Literary Vampire', *Folklore Forum*, 10:2, 1977.

Bernard Davies, 'Mountain Greenery', *The Dracula Journals*, 1:1, Winter 1976-7.

Stephanie Demetrakopoulos, 'Feminism, Sex Role Exchanges, and Other Subliminal Fantasies in Bram Stoker's *Dracula*', *Frontiers: A Journal of Women Studies*, 2:3, 1977.

Peter Denman, 'Le Fanu and Stoker: A Probable Connection', *Eire-Ireland (Irish American Cultural Institute)* 9, Autumn 1974.

Robert E. Dowse and David Palmer, ' "Dracula": the Book of Blood', *The Listener*, 7 March 1963.

James Drummond, 'Bram Stoker's Cruden Bay', *Scots Magazine*, April 1976.

_____, 'Dracula's Castle', *The Scotsman*, 26 June 1976.

_____, 'The Mistletoe and the Oak' *Scots Magazine*, October 1977.

_____, 'The Scottish Play', *The Scottish Review*, 23 August 1981.

Paul Dukes, 'Dracula: Fact, Legend and Fiction', *History Today* 32, July 1982.

Christopher Frayling, 'Vampyres', *London Magazine* 14:2, June-July 1974.

Carrol L. Fry, 'Fictional Conventions and Sexuality in *Dracula*', *Victorian Newsletter* 42, 1972.

Jean Gattegno, 'Folie, Croyance et Fantastique dans "Dracula" ', *Littérature* 8, December 1972.

Burton Hatlen, 'The Return of the Repressed/Oppressed in Bram Stoker's *Dracula*', *The Minnesota Review* 15, 1980.

Mark M. Hennelly Jr, '*Dracula*: the Gnostic Quest and the Victorian Wasteland', *English Literature in Transition* 20:1, 1977.

_____, 'Twice Told Tales of Two Counts', *Wilkie Collins Society Journal* 2, 1982.

E. Randolph Johnson, 'The Victorian Vampire', *Baker St Journal* 18, December 1968.

Roger Johnson, 'The Bloofer Ladies', *The Dracula Journals* 1:4, Summer 1982.

R. W. Johnson, 'The Myth of the Twentieth Century', *New Society*, 9 December 1982.

Bacil F. Kirtley, '*Dracula*, the Monastic Chronicles and Slavic Folklore', *Midwest Folklore* 6:3, 1956.

Royce MacGillivray, ' "Dracula": Bram Stoker's Spoiled Masterpiece', *Queen's Quarterly* 79, 1972.

Lionel Milgrom, 'Vampires, Plants, and Crazy Kings', *New Scientist*, 26 April 1984.

Agnes Murgoci, 'The Evil Eye in Roumania, and its Antidotes', *Folklore* 34, 1923.

_____, 'The Vampire in Roumania', *Folklore* 37, 1926.

Brian Murphy, 'The Nightmare of the Dark: the Gothic Legacy of Count Dracula', *Odyssey* 1, 1976.

Grigore Nandris, 'A Philological Analysis of *Dracula* and Rumanian Place-names and Masculine Personal Names in -a/-ea', *Slavonic and East European Review* 37, 1959.

_____, 'The Historical Dracula: The Theme of His Legend in the Western and in the Eastern Literatures of Europe', *Comparative Literature Studies* 3:4, 1966.

Felix J. Oinas, 'Heretics as Vampires and Demons in Russia', *Slavic and East European Journal* 22, Winter 1978.

Christopher Gist Raible, 'Dracula: Christian Heretic', *The Christian Century* 96, 31 January 1979.

Maurice Richardson, 'The Psychoanalysis of Ghost Stories', *Twentieth Century* 166, December 1956.

Phyllis A. Roth, 'Suddenly Sexual Women in Bram Stoker's *Dracula*', *Literature and Psychology* 27, 1977.

Ronald Schleifer, 'The Trap of the Imagination; The Gothic Tradition, Fiction, and "The Turn of the Screw" ', *Criticism* 22, Autumn 1980.

Carol A. Senf, '*Dracula*: the Unseen Face in the Mirror', *Journal of Narrative Technique*, 1979.

_____, ' "Dracula": Stoker's Response to the New Woman', *Victorian Studies* 26:1, Autumn 1982.

Seymour Shuster, 'Dracula and Surgically Induced Trauma in Children', *British Journal of Medical Psychology* 46, 1973.

Gerard Stein, ' "Dracula" ou la Circulation du "Sans" ', *Littérature* 8, December 1972.

Bram Stoker, 'The Censorship of Fiction', *Nineteenth Century* 64, September 1908.

Philip Temple, 'The Origins of Dracula', *The Times Literary Supplement*, 4 November 1983.

James Twitchell, 'The Vampire Myth', *American Imago* 37, 1980.

Thomas P. Walsh, '*Dracula:* Logos and Myth', *Research Studies* 47:4, December 1979.

Richard Wasson, 'The Politics of Dracula', *English Language in Transition* 9:1, 1966.

Judith Weissman, 'Women and Vampires: *Dracula* as a Victorian Novel', *Midwest Quarterly* 18:4, 1977.

### Books

Lory Alder and Richard Dalby, *The Dervish of Windsor Castle: The Life of Arminius Vambery*, Bachman and Turner (London, 1979).

Glen St John Barclay, *Anatomy of Horror: Masters of Occult Fiction*, Weidenfeld & Nicolson (London, 1978).

Austin Brereton, *The Life of Henry Irving*, 2 vols., Longmans, Green and Co. (London, 1908).

Basil Copper, *The Vampire: In Legend, Fact and Art*, Hale (London, 1973).

Richard Dalby, *Bram Stoker: A Bibliography of First Editions*, Dracula Press (London, 1983).

Hamilton Deane and John Balderston, *Dracula: the Vampire Play in Three Acts*, Samuel French Inc. (New York, 1960).

Daniel Farson, *The Man Who Wrote Dracula: A Biography of Bram Stoker*, Michael Joseph (London, 1975).

Leslie Fielder, *Freaks: Myths and Images of the Secret Self*, Simon and Schuster (New York, 1978).

Radu Florescu and Raymond T. McNally, *Dracula: A Biography*, Hale (London, 1973).

Christopher Frayling (ed.), *The Vampyre: Lord Ruthven to Count Dracula*, Gollancz (London, 1978).

Nancy Garden, *Vampires*, Lippincott (London, 1973).

Michael Geare and Michael Corby, *Dracula's Diary*, Buchan and Enright (London, 1982).

Donald F. Glut, *The Dracula Book*, Scarecrow Press (New York, 1975).

Peter Haining (ed.), *The Dracula Scrapbook*, New English Library (London, 1976).

_____, *The Leprechaun's Kingdom*, Pictorial Presentations/Souvenir Press (London, 1979).

_____, *Shades of Dracula: The Uncollected Stories of Bram Stoker*, Kimber (London, 1982).

Bernhardt J. Hurwood, *Vampires*, Omnibus Press (London, 1981).

Laurence Irving, *Henry Irving: The Actor and his World*, Faber and Faber (London, 1951).

Rosemary Jackson, *Fantasy: The Literature of Subversion*, Methuen (London, 1981).

Harry Ludlam, *A Biography of Bram Stoker: Creator of Dracula*, New English Library (London, 1977).

Elizabeth MacAndrew, *The Gothic Tradition in Fiction*, Columbia University Press (New York, 1979).

Andrew MacKenzie, *Dracula Country: Travels and Folk Beliefs in Romania*, Arthur Barker (London, 1977).

_____, *Romanian Journey*, Hale (London, 1983).

Raymond T. McNally and Radu Florescu, *In Search of Dracula*, New York Graphic Society (Connecticut, 1972).

_____, *The Essential Dracula*, Mayflower Books (New York, 1979).

Raymond T. McNally, *Dracula was a Woman*, Hale (London, 1984).

Anthony Masters, *The Natural History of the Vampire*, Hart-Davis (London, 1972).

Franco Moretti, *Signs Taken for Wonders: Essays in the Sociology of Literary Forms*, New Left Books/Verso (London, 1983).

Charles Osborne (ed.), *The Bram Stoker Bedside Companion*, Quartet (London, 1974).

Sean O'Sullivan, *The Folklore of Ireland*, Batsford (London, 1974).

_____, *Legends from Ireland*, Batsford (London, 1977).

Barrie Pattison, *The Seal of Dracula*, Lorimer Publishing (London, 1975).

David Pirie, *The Vampire Cinema*, Hamlyn (London, 1977).

John Polidori, *The Vampyre*, Gubblecote Press (Tring, Herts, 1973).

Mario Praz, *The Romantic Agony*, Oxford University Press (London, 1933).

David Punter, *The Literature of Terror*, Longman (London, 1980).

John R. Reed, *Victorian Conventions*, Ohio University Press (Ohio, 1975).

Martin V. Riccardo, *Vampires Unearthed: the Complete Multi-Media Vampire and Dracula Bibliography*, Garland Publishing (New York, 1983).

Gabriel Ronay, *The Dracula Myth*, W. H. Allen (London, 1972).

Phyllis A. Roth, *Bram Stoker*, Twayne Publishers, G. K. Hall (Boston, 1982).

Raymond Rudorff, *The Dracula Archives*, Sphere (London, 1973).

Penelope Shuttle and Peter Redgrove, *The Wise Wound: Menstruation and Everywoman*, Gollancz (London, 1978).

Jacob Sprenger and Heinrich Kramer, *Malleus Maleficarum* (translated by Montague Summers), Pushkin Press (London, 1948).

Nicolai Stoicescu, *Vlad Tepes: Prince of Walachia*, Academy of the Socialist Republic of Romania (Bucharest, 1978).

Bram Stoker,* *The Duties of Clerks of Petty Sessions in Ireland*, Published by Authority (Dublin, 1879).

_____, *Under the Sunset*, Sampson Low, Marston, Searle, and Rivington (London, 1881).

_____, *A Glimpse of America*, Sampson Low, Marston & Co. (London, 1886).

_____, *The Snake's Pass*, Sampson Low, Marston, Searle and Rivington (London, 1890).

_____, *The Watter's Mou'*, Constable (Westminster, 1895).

_____, *The Shoulder of Shasta*, Constable (Westminster, 1895).

_____, *Dracula*, Constable (Westminster, 1897).

_____, *Miss Betty*, Pearson (London, 1898).

_____, *The Mystery of the Sea*, Heinemann (London, 1902).

_____, *The Jewel of Seven Stars*, Heinemann (London, 1903).

_____, *The Man*, Heinemann (London, 1905).

_____, *Personal Reminiscences of Henry Irving*, 2 vols., Heinemann (London, 1906).

_____, *Lady Athlyne*, Heinemann (London, 1908).

_____, *Snowbound: The Record of a Theatrical Touring Party*, Collier (London, 1908).

_____, *The Lady of the Shroud*, Heinemann (London, 1909).

_____, *Famous Impostors*, Sidgwick and Jackson (London, 1910).

_____, *The Lair of the White Worm*, Rider (London, 1911).

_____, *Dracula's Guest — And Other Weird Stories*, Routledge (London, 1914).

Douglas Oliver Street, 'Bram Stoker's "Under the Sunset" with Introductory Biographical and Critical Material (unpublished Ph.D. thesis), University of Nebraska-Lincoln (1977).

Montague Summers, *The Gothic Quest*, The Fortune Press (London, no date).

_____, *The Vampire: His Kith and Kin*, Kegan Paul (London, 1928).

_____, *The Vampire in Europe*, Kegan Paul (London, 1929).

Thomas Ray Thornburg, 'The Quester and the Castle: the Gothic Novel as Myth, with Special Reference to Bram Stoker's Dracula' (unpublished Ph.D. thesis), Ball State University (1970).

James B. Twitchell, *The Living Dead: A Study of the Vampire in Romantic Literature*, Duke University Press (North Carolina, 1981).

Devendra P. Varma, *The Gothic Flame*, Arthur Barker (London, 1957).

_____, Introduction to *Varney the Vampire; or, the Feast of Blood*, Arno Press (New York, 1970).

Ornella Volta, *The Vampire*, Tandem Books (London, 1965).

Leonard Wolf, *The Annotated Dracula*, New English Library (London, 1975).

_____, *A Dream of Dracula*, Little, Brown and Co. (Boston, 1972).

Dudley Wright, *Vampires and Vampirism*, Rider (London, 1924).

* Publisher given relates to the first standard British edition for all Bram Stoker's works.

# INDEX